A DRAMA INTIME

First published in 2019 by
Profile Editions, an imprint of
PROFILE BOOKS LTD
29 Cloth Fair
London EC1A 7NN
www.profileeditions.com

10 9 8 7 6 5 4 3 2 1

Design: Justine Bannwart
Managing Editor: Catherine Thomas

Printed and bound in Italy by LEGO

ISBN 978 1 78816 285 2

A DRAMA IN TIME

THE NEW SCHOOL CENTURY

JOHN REED

PROFILE
EDITIONS

NEW SCHOOL BULLETIN

Fall 1962 / Vol. 20, No. 3 / September 4, 1962

VOL

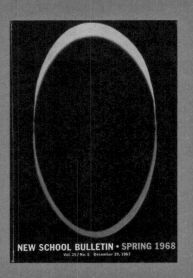

NEW SCHOOL BULLETIN · SPRING 1968

Vol. 25/No. 5 December 20, 1967

NEW SCHOOL BULLETIN

SUMMER 1963
VOL. 20, NO. 17
APRIL 5, 1963

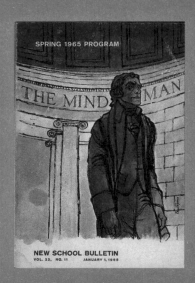

SPRING 1965 PROGRAM

THE MIND OF MAN

NEW SCHOOL BULLETIN
VOL. 22, NO. 11, JANUARY 1, 1965

LYF

SUMMER-'64

NEW SCHOOL
BULLETIN

VOL. 21, NO. 17 / APRIL 5, 1964

NEW SCHOOL BULLETIN SPRING 69

The New School at the half century

NEW SCHOOL BULLETIN

ART CLASSES
1950   1951

66 WEST TWELFTH STREET   NEW YORK 11, N. Y.

VOL. 8, No. 2   OREGON 5.2700   SEPTEMBER 11, 1950

NEW
SCHOOL
BULLETIN

SUMMER 1966

VOL. 23, NO. 17
APRIL 14, 1966

/NO. 1   SEPTEMBER 1, 1967

New
school
Bulle-
tin

FALL 1967

NEW SCHOOL BULLETIN · FALL 197

Volume 28 Number 11 · July 30, 19

RUSSO

Summer 69 New School Bulletin

VOL. 26, NO. 11, JUNE 2, 1969

Spring 1962
Vol. 19, No. 1/
January 15, 1962

NEW SCHOOL BULLETIN

ONE MILLION STORIES, UNTOLD

The bus stop at the Farm & Garden nursery was freezing cold. My coat would billow with the wind. I'd ride the bus up Sixth Avenue to PS 41. It was something like 1977, and I was in something like second grade. I'd see the digital clock above the Nedick's hotdog place at Bleecker Street, and know whether or not I was late to school, and wonder if there'd ever be a time I'd remember that moment — if there'd ever be a day I'd stand on a street corner and look past the spire of the Jefferson Library, look all the way down the avenue to the Twin Towers, and think about how time had changed me, and changed the world.

What is new, what is now? The question is personal and historical, and perhaps equivalent to the question of consciousness. We check into self-awareness — recalibrating, correcting, cross-examining — and just as quickly check out, to do, to hurry, to leap. It is always a wonder, the suddenness of who we are, of where we are — so inevitable, and so precarious.

The generation that founded The New School endured World War I, fighting in it and losing loved ones and ways of life. With peace came the flu epidemic, which killed as many as 50 million people — the total death count of the war was only 19 million. Then, the 1920s; in the United States, that meant Prohibition, which frenzied the decade with temperance fanaticism, intemperate extravagance, speakeasies, and cabarets. Then, global economic depression, fascism in Europe, and another world war. And for that turn-of-the-century generation, this war took the lives of their children. Next, the Cold War, McCarthyism, and the puzzling, displeasing arrival of the beatniks and hippies, who did not, apparently, value civilization.

The proposal set forth in The New School — egalitarian, lifelong, progressive education that changed with the times — is indicative of a generational balance of intellectual foresight, strength, and startling naivety. After only seven semesters, The New School's notion of administrative absence had to be re-examined, and if it hadn't been understood before, it must have become clear then that The New School's model was intrinsically aspirational. The utopic vision inspirited by the Russian Revolution did not look quite so imminent after all.

A 100-year history of The New School, to be written and published within a year, is consistent with The New School's tradition of impossible undertakings. When I was first brought to the discussion of the project, I couldn't envision how the goals might be met — on any timetable. There was no lack of subject matter, with so many remarkable chapters in the history, but a single narrative seemed unwieldy, and preoccupied with the past, and not particularly indicative of what the school is now.

The précis of the school's origin goes something like this: a group of Columbia University professors, with the beginning of the nineteenth century, were increasingly at odds with their academic administration. Some professors were pacifists, and some defended the right to be pacifists, and all were progressive in their vision of higher education and the world. With the onset of the war, advocating a united national front, Columbia University fired several of the professors, and several resigned, and in the back room of The New Republic magazine, the dissident academics looked to contemporaneous endeavors in education, and conceived of a new academic model. The New School offered its first classes in 1919.

It's a powerful origin story, but it doesn't speak to The New School's weighty presence throughout the century — in philosophy and the arts and subjects far afield from the inceptional course list of 1919. There were defining moments for The New School; during the era of the University in Exile, for example, scholars fleeing European fascism came to the United States — several hundred passed through The New School in temporary positions, and a handful stayed to form The New School's first degree tracks, which were not to be undergraduate degrees, but graduate degrees, doctorates. But the early years of The New School and the University in Exile are well-explored terrains, and, for example, give no cartography of Atelier 17, or John Cage, or Clara Mayer, or Sekou Sundiata.

The story we wanted to tell was an epic — a weave of extraordinary people who thread by thread made a single cloth. That sounded like an old-fashioned narrative history: page after page of blocky text. How would readers pluck out what interested them? And would that mean hundreds of pages before the present tense? And wasn't the narrative unattainable anyway? In 2019, there are just over 10,000 students at The New School, with maybe 3,000 more non-matriculated students. Academic staff is about 2,200. Adding in administrative staff and event attendees and participants, the number of people at The New School each year rises considerably, but just to make an estimate, let's say there are about 15,000 people at The New School right now. That's 15,000 stories to tell. If we track back to the large lecture classes of The New School, and the history of people who passed through Mannes College of Music and Parsons School of Design, I'd rough that number to 10,000 stories to tell, per year, for a century. That gives us one million stories.

Previous pages: Opposite:

Covers of The New School Bulletin through the ages   Artist's rendering of exterior of the 66 West 12th Street building, 1930

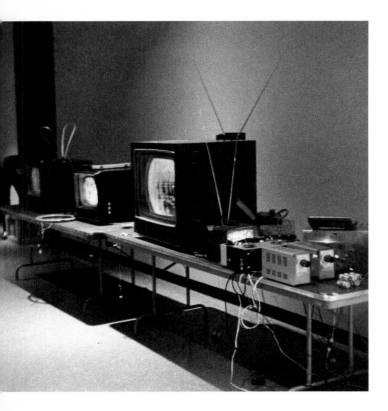

The book couldn't be comprehensive. All I could hope to do is assemble histories and people who, in gestural, made for a portrait of The New School. That realization led me to the structure of *A Drama in Time*. With the stories I tell here, I've sought a characterization of The New School. The internal journey of the school is what most concerned me, and for that reason, and the sake of keeping the present foremost, the stories are not told chronologically. My design is biographical, to stage a now-and-then tableau that renders The New School.

I confess my biases. I've been teaching at The New School since 2003, and I revel in the academic freedom and 'let's try it' attitude of the community. One might view this project as a collaged kind of brag book, where numerous stories about the school are offered individually. Working with the history has been an amazing and humbling process; I've encountered so many heroes, and enjoyed the opportunity to explore the twentieth century. Since we locked the text, not a day has gone by that I haven't discovered another incredible person or moment that I wish I'd included. I would be thrilled if these pages sparked more investigation. Quite a few people have been involved in this project — researchers, photo researchers, fact checkers, designers — and even in the course of this writing a large quotient of new material has been discovered and digitized. My sincerest hope is that I've provided a few footholds, and that new routes scale to uncharted elevations.

In the more beleaguering stretches of the project, I would sleep fitfully, and dream about the research and writing. One particularly blatant dream had me bagging each story, a large hunk of raw meat, in a Ziploc bag. My son assisted. In another dream, I was called before an academic committee to explain how my position differed from that of a Nazi sympathizer. The committee members were stern University in Exile types, something like contemporary incarnations of The New School's erstwhile Graduate Faculty. I had evidently prepared my statement thoroughly, and I put forth an eloquent explanation as to how my position was inherently different from that of

This page:

▬▬▬ Nam June Paik's first solo exhibition in the United States, *NJ Paik: Electronic TV, Color TV Experiments. 3 Robots, 2 Zen Boxes & 1 Zen Can.* The New School for Social Research, Peter Moore, 1965

a Nazi sympathizer. When I was finished, the committee chair opened with her first question: 'But how can we take anything you've said seriously, when you don't speak a word of German?'

The original plan called for 35–40,000-words of text; what you see here will be more like 85,000 words of text. I had input from numerous readers and consultors; they had new areas to explore, and the suggestions were terrific. To the very last, we've been stuffing one more inclusion into place. The courses, quotes, and events that accompany the stories are meant to somewhat alleviate the task, to provide a fallback, to point in exciting directions, and to broadly contextualize whatever the historical marker. The project became Zenonian-reverse, with every next step twice as hard, twice as far, as the step that preceded it. The end was farther and farther away, and lost from even imagination.

Eventually, we had to reconcile the exemptions. For example, listing all the members of the original founding committee of The New School was accompanied by a bittersweet compromise. Of the nineteen 'founders', nine were men and ten were women; seeing the compiled née names of the women, listed in one place for I believe the first time, was electric, and I owe a huge debt of thanks to Samantha Kirby, who helped me sort it all out. (The change of name due to marriage was a significant obstacle not only in this circumstance, but throughout our research.) Still, there was a chapter left behind; the spouses of the original committee members were also compelling historical figures and, given what I did learn about them, I expect quite influential to the early envisioning of the school, and its founding in relation to its benefactors and acceptance by society in New York City.

To give an accounting of a few other areas I would love to have written more about, and would love to learn more about in the future;

— The history of media and film at The New School spans different departments of the school, and new technologies and directions, such as 'experimental television,' would variously take hold. Tracking film and media throughout the history of The New School would be a great curiosity. Maya Deren's time at the school in the late 1930s would be an appropriate place to begin such a survey; the period is post the 1931 adoption of workshop-style courses at The New School, and Deren exemplifies the creative and divisional separation of writing and filmmaking that was newly underway. (And there are of course other divisional puzzles, notably printmaking, that would benefit from such an approach.)

— I didn't talk enough about the history of food studies at The New School; this field of study is robust today and tracks through the century. Writing about food and the Zero Waste Food Conference were the entryways I was considering — before I ran out of time.

— I missed innumerable writers; I was sorry to not feature, for example, Lorraine Hansberry. Nor did I take a careful look at Tennessee Williams. I certainly could have written more about Sekou Sundiata. Sara Ruddick was another compelling figure. (The list here is inexhaustible.)

— The historical relationship of The New School and Parsons to the New York Women's House of Detention, which was torn down in 1974: an investigation would cover prison reform in design as well as intention and institutionally. About the time of the prison closing, circa 1970, Parsons was mounting proposals for prison redesign, and The New School was investigating the possible acquisition of the prison—the only art-deco prison known to exist—as a property. The prison as a holding area for women radicals and protesters—through the century, but with an emphasis on the 1960s and 1970s—would make for a large, captivating chronicle.

— Parsons' Master of Fine Arts in Transdisciplinary Design exemplifies an evolution in academics, with increasing cooperation interdepartmentally; subjects and fields of disciplines will simultaneously become more specialized and more generalized, and the Transdisciplinary Design MFA is at the vanguard of the challenge. The program, not quite ten years old, already has an impressive cohort of alumni.

— The international stories required the most in the way of research, and I only hinted at The New School's increasingly worldly outlook on education, which jibes with The New School's 1919 mission (wide-eyed in retrospect, but nevertheless prescient) of global political change.

— Individuals championed departments and ideas throughout the history of the school; that's at the very core of this project, and yet the project as a whole can't be regarded as a judgement of 'what's best' or 'what's most important'. Ira Katznelson would have been, for example, an ideal candidate to lead into a more complete discussion of the Institute for Retired Professionals; for the arts, I might have looked to Horace Kallen or Camilo Egas. And I almost certainly should have written more about the devout benefactors, who literally built and, time and again, reinvested in The New School's philosophy.

Even the subjects I put to paper are no more than sketches; just about every story herein warrants a book of its own. The images, as well, have been chosen to spur what I hope will be significant advancements. A wish list of 'more abouts':

— Spouses, husbands, and wives of the founders (by which I mean those nineteen individuals named in the 1918 pamphlet announcing The New School, although other founder tallies abound).

— The connection of David and Clara Mannes to settlement schools; the settlement schools are fascinating in the context of the suffragette movement and the formation of The New School and what was to become Parsons. A more complete picture of Hull House, I expect, would yield a wealth of associations.

— The various deans: Chuck Kaufman, for example, of Mannes, would make for a strong profile. In 1979, in the words of *The New York Times*, he 'led a faculty coup that spared the century-old Mannes College of Music in Manhattan from a troublesome merger'. This chapter in the Mannes history parallels the formation of The New School, as well as Alvin Johnson's 1962 return from retirement to rescue The New School from a merger with NYU, and the intrigues of 1970 that led to The New School's acquisition of Parsons.

— The McCarthy era and the influence and presence of the Central Intelligence Agency on The New School's campus (and other U.S. campuses), especially in the context of the Congress for Cultural Freedom.

— James Reese Europe, and his friendship with David and Clara Mannes.

— Clara Mayer. (What I would really like is a new library dedicated to her.)

— Fluxus and The New School.

— Black Mountain College and The New School.

— Isamu Noguchi's affiliation with The New School.

— Agnes and Sigrid de Lima.

— The Human Relations Center (the precursor to the Vera List Center, which for decades functioned as a way to draw women together to think about career options).

— Mentorship at The New School; the generational exchanges of artists to artists, thinkers to thinkers. Examples: Henry Cowell to Johanna Beyer and John Cage, or Sekou Sundiata to Ani DiFranco.

I expect some criticism for my flybys of The New School standards: the University in Exile, John Dewey, etc. But these were measured quantities and, in many cases, recently measured. If I have a larger criticism of The New School narratives to date it is in the overemphasis of the expected; the school has a sprawling history, replete with iconoclasts and false starts and promising failures. To me, the mythology of The New School is more honest in pantheism than monotheism.

As an undertaking, The New School was never intended to be monotheistic or monolithic, or any kind of singular, eternal thing. In New York City itself, there can be no cherished street corner, and everything you cling to will eventually be gone, or changed. There's a kind of brutal beauty to New York City, which is not a small town, which will not guard your cherished childhood memories. For The New School, this principle of change is further complicated by institutional growth. Stature, size, political currents, myriad conditions and influences force all organizations to reinvent continually. It's a lesson of life, as well: there is no staying the same; to remain true to oneself, one must become different.

The New School, as I would break it down, was founded on five major precepts:

1. There would be no need for academic degrees when class society came to an end (in 1919, the Russian Revolution is still a cry of optimism).

2. Academic learning had to become more contemporary, proactive, and responsive.

3. Higher education was not merely for the young; rather, learning was a lifelong endeavor.

4. An interdisciplinary approach was critical to practical, contemporary learning.

5. Experiential learning was preferable to passive learning. (This idea was active as of the 1930s.)

Of those five ideals, The New School has remained constant to four. The end of class society, alas, did not arrive on schedule, and the institution has adopted a more traditional degree structure. It is another lesson of The New School century, and a sad one, that radical innovation is often subsumed by mainstay infrastructure.

That tension, with multiple contributors—I would not hesitate to say dozens—arises in this project. Archivists, academic deans, two fact-checkers, a photo researcher, a designer, and more designers and researchers and contributors affiliated with the administration: in all, I believe we made our own little tornado of historical revision. We researched, talked, wrote, adjusted, and the archive digitized new information, and new information was published, and facts that looked right in October looked wrong in February. Frustrating, but also a delight; to be a part of historical revision as it happened. We had to be continually wary of our intoxication, exerting pressure on ourselves not to be overly celebratory, and to enforce a personal determination to find fault in our assertions. The only thing as dangerous as being wrong is being right: that's a century-long truism of The New School in practice, and in educational philosophy. The confidence of 'being right', or of 'dogma', as Alvin Johnson would call it, is the great risk of historical or political or social postulations. If Hannah Arendt is over-attributed in the reminiscences of The New School, it is because her simultaneous mistrust of top-down authority and bottom-up revolutionary zeal is perfectly indicative of the promise of 'the new' in The New School.

A cautionary tale: from the outset, I would encounter tantalizing clues about Warhol's Factory and The New School. I was enthusiastic about a story that knotted some tie, in part because I had taught a class at The New School, 'Being Andy Warhol', which carefully reconstructed a corner of the Factory; the fairly accurate reconstruction served as a set for a fictionalized 'doc'. But, however tantalizing, the leads would ultimately source back to Internet chatter. Still, I'd indulge, and, one morning, I clicked through a series of links to find a YouTube channel that had posted lost footage from the Warhol Factory. Here was the origin of the vaporous leads! Since I taught the Warhol course which produced the web series 'Andy Presents Nothing Special', I'd completely forgotten that we, as a class, tossed our B-Roll onto a YouTube channel. The Internet fugue state that connected Warhol and The New School, at least as I had been encountering it, was generated by a mockumentary produced in my own course.

All of 'history' is to some degree anachronistic. Even to tell a story a second time—the exact same story—is to change its meaning. The issue is more than abstract; how do we address the students who attended The New School in the decades prior to the institution of academic degrees? Is it fair to call them alumni? What about the students who attended many courses? Did the school have no alumni until the middle of the twentieth century? And if so, isn't that an argument against the progressive ideals of a school without degrees? There are no answers to these quandaries, and such unanswerables, macro and micro, are bountiful in these pages. What about Yoko Ono? With her soon-to-be husband, Toshi Ichiyanagi, she attended a course taught by John Cage. Later, she and Cage and Ichiyanagi collaborated. What do we say about her participation in the course? Was she an 'audit' student? Do we have the attendance records?

Hmm, and another historical miasma: the quotations paired with the entries cite people who were somehow associated with The New School—and it seemed a very good idea to provide attributions. That, unfortunately, only sounds easy. People who attended The New School later visited and lectured at The New School; some of them taught at The New School; some of them worked at The New School. With 400-plus citations, and undefined, unorganized, inconsistent, and often nonexistent documentation, that's a research assignment that has no finish. If anything, we vastly undersold the cited associations, and I'll look forward to the found facts and proofs our hesitations inspire.

In my inclusions and pairing of quotes, I reveal my own subjectivity, as I do in all my selections; I confess to making some corrections in the course descriptions—copy editing things, mostly. There were a few courses that were so riddled with errors that we left them as is: 'Filmmakers on Filmmaking' with Richard Brown (1994), for example. If you look closely at that course description, you'll see the actors hardly match the films, etc. Some courses ran for years, and I chose a representative description and semester for whatever balance of: a) what description sounded the best; b) what semester/year seemed most relevant.

The presumption would be that the archive is progressively more complete, that the more recent the history, the more comprehensive the record. But that isn't the case, for two reasons: first, the beginning of the era of digital administration and course offerings, let's say the late 1990s through the mid-2000s, is utterly lost to antiquated technologies. The related problem of decentralized academic departments was the second major obstacle: graduate departments and specialized departments, steadily more important to The New School as of the

mid-century, quite frequently offered curriculums only to their own students, and courses were not listed to the general campus. This remains true today; many of the higher-level courses, i.e. graduate courses, etc., which bring eminent people to teach and visit students, have limited presence to the larger school, or its memory. The charge of *A Drama in Time* is to contend with this imperfect internal memory, which is often little better than the external memory of The New School.

In 2003, when I first began teaching at The New School, my grandfather approved. He was a slender World War II flyboy from San Diego, and not very political. I was surprised he knew anything about The New School, and really, in the specifics, he didn't know much more than its location, the West Village. But he regarded it as the locus of a quintessentially American narrative — perhaps in the auspice of the John Dewey discussion, or the University in Exile discussion, or the veterans pursuing degrees discussion, or an amorphous jumble of all three.

Until 2010, my relationship to The New School was peripheral; I taught a few classes a year. David Van Zandt was named President of The New School in 2011; he's the president I associate with The New School, and I've felt the school become more unified in that time. Parsons moved downtown, from the garment district to the new University Center on 13th Street and Fifth Avenue. The Mannes School of Music, likewise, came downtown, to Arnhold Hall on 13th Street. Another building, adjacent to Arnhold Hall, acquired recently by Van Zandt's administration, is in the design stage. Interdepartmentally, I've seen the academic campus gain a sense of self-awareness and community. Mary Watson and Tim Marshall (Mary is the Executive Dean of the Schools of Public Engagement and Tim is The New School Provost) have gradually come to the forefront of my university awareness; they are seemingly everywhere, with a no less galactic vision of learning and change.

The New School, today, sums 134 degree and diploma programs and thirty-five centers, institutes, and labs. Events and visitors are far too spanning and fabulous for me to contemplate summarizing. I have an impression of The New School and Parsons that recalls Anatole Broyard's The New School, post-World War II: 'Education was chic and sexy in those days. The people in the lobby of The New School were excited, expectant, dressed to the teeth. They struck poses, examined one another with approval. They had a blind date with culture, and anything could happen.'

Broyard's is a personal story of The New School, as is mine; the collectivization, the making of history, is a gathering of the subjective, the felt. Frank Salomon, in a touching email of thanks sent in January 2019, recalled Eva H. Simons, wife of New School President Hans Simons, who hired him to assist in ticket sales for a series of concerts by Rudolf Serkin in 1959 (the duty was the beginning of Salomon's professional life), as well as New School President Alvin Johnson's intervention in assisting the Salomon family when they were halted by the immigration bureaucracy of Ellis Island:

My father Albert Salomon was saved from Hitler by Alvin Johnson in 1935 when he was invited to join the Graduate Faculty of The New School as a sociologist. In 1932, he had contracted polio shortly after marrying Anna Lobbenberg, a medical doctor, and he was told that he would never walk again. With the support of his wife and his personal determination, he regained his mobility, although only with the use of a cane, for the rest of his life. When he came to the American Embassy in Cologne for his physical exam to obtain his visa, the doctor (suspected of anti-Semitic leanings) stamped his visa — 'physically unable to earn his living', even though my father had showed him his contract with The New School. As a result, the Salomon family, which included their eighteen-month-old daughter Hannah, were detained overnight at Ellis Island with the prostitutes and criminals. Word was gotten to Alvin Johnson and the next day he came to Ellis Island and, reportedly, was furious, pounding on the desk of one of the officials saying, 'I didn't hire this man to teach gymnastics, I hired him to teach sociology. Now, you let him go.' That was the start of a thirty-one-year relationship with The New School.

In thinking about The New School, Thelma Armstrong, who works in my Dean's office, remembers Wally Osterholz; as I prepared to make the final push on this project, Thelma mentioned to me that I had surely written about Wally. I admitted guiltily that I hadn't, that Wally's was one of the many stories I had not told. I myself had met Wally only once, when, a cigarette dangling from her lips, she sorted out some intractable registration problem with a throaty phone call. Wally, a mentor to Thelma and many others, was a phenom of an administrator, who joined the administrative staff in 1962 and served the school variously until her retirement in 2007. (Her husband, Tom Pollack, was an artist and faculty at Parsons and The New School.) A solver of all problems, Wally, as poetically encapsulated in Thelma's five-word tribute, was The New School's: 'Altruistic. Unpretentious. Institutional memory keeper'. Nicholas Birns, faculty at The New School, and a child of members of the faculty at The New School, shared a similar impression of Wally in his memorial remarks:

This page:

John Reed and
'Being Andy Warhol' students,
2011

Often, one or the other of my parents would leave me in the fishbowl room to read while they taught. Wally was there to ultimately watch over me but never interfered, just letting me read and adventure amid real and imagined worlds, Meanwhile, I would hear Wally typing — one still typed back then — and talking on the phone, laughing, improvising, reacting, arranging, and above all receiving the Hogarthian parade of humanity that passed through the third floor. To me she was The New School. I was not far off.

I've taught at other schools in New York City, and I haven't experienced this campus closeness anywhere else. The sudden passing away of campus security officer Will Gary crushed The New School community. There would be no more crowds of laughing fans at the front desk. There would never be a warmer, safer smile.

There is a bond between staff and academics at The New School, and the security force provides a good example; the guards on campus know more or less who people are and what they're up to — and to stop at a security desk of any of The New School buildings and chat with a guard is to spend time with someone extraordinary. Tony De Nonno, for example, is an artist, filmmaker, and master puppeteer. As President Van Zandt explained in a 2018 interview that was part of the discovery process for this book:

Whether it's people working on urban sustainability projects that could help New York withstand another Hurricane Sandy, seeking ways to remedy the fragility of the U.S. retirement systems, or advocating for prison reform, we have people who are working to improve lives, communities, and cities. Students from all over the university collaborate to understand complex problems and find innovative ways of solving them. The proposed solutions might be based on better communication, products, policies, organizational structures, or systems, but they're always oriented to people: responding to needs, respecting experience, and listening to feedback. This is the work that propels The New School. And it is evident throughout university culture, as true among the staff as it is among the students and faculty. People take on amazing challenges at work, and then, outside of work, they take on other extraordinary challenges. People who choose to work at The New School are drawn to its special character. I'm inspired by the creativity and commitment I see around the university, and the collective drive to make the world a better place.

The New School is ideological. Ideological in its bones, and ideological in origin; it is the first secular institution to be that, an educational enterprise founded upon ideals that in 1919 were termed 'progressive'. This claim of primacy is fuzzy enough for debate, but given the research materials available at present, I'll stand by 'first secular institution of higher education founded upon an ideology'. Here are the caveats:

— Prior to 1919, there were many secular 'professional' schools, offering trade educations.

— There were secular European institutions of higher education before The New School; France went secular with education in 1905. That said, higher education, as re-envisioned by the French State, was not particularly ideological.

— Historically, there have been secular institutions of higher education that were formed in opposition to the Church; these were state or monarchic, not independent from existing power structures, and fundamentally authoritative.

— There were secular outreach and education institutions in the United States in the nineteenth century, but these were not dedicated to higher education, nor were they exclusively educational, nor were they all that secular. The 'machine age' and an 'age of science', along with the progressive idealism at the end of the nineteenth century, inspired much in the way of secular lip service. But 'secular' seems to have presumptively meant that an institution was Christian — and more often than not Christian in infrastructure — but non-denominational. U.S. state schools are the obvious categorical examples; in 1779, Thomas Jefferson failed to mandate that the University of Virginia be strictly secular. [1]

There has been an ebb and flow of secularization in U.S. universities, and The New School was very much a response to half steps toward non-religious education. In establishment, the school was to be a high-concept rejoinder to an educational system that was flawed in genesis, and halting in evolution. As was trumpeted in the 1918 pamphlet that announced The New School's formation: 'Nothing like it has ever been attempted; this is the hour for the experiment; and New York is the place, because it is the greatest social science laboratory in the world and of its own force attracts scholars and leaders.'

When I was a kid at PS 41, just a block away from where I sit in my office now, I'd have lunch at Ray's Pizza, and I'd tiptoe past Café Loup, which was too fancy for my likes, and I'd get thrown out of the corner Blimpie for splitting sandwiches. Today, all those places are gone, and Blimpie is La Contenta Oeste, where I sometimes sip an artful cup of coffee, well beyond the menu of Blimpie, amazed that I'm still there, amazed that the 200-year-old Portuguese-Jewish cemetery, just a few dozen steps east, is still there, amazed that, just a bit farther down 11th Street, The New School, despite all of its unlikelihoods, despite all the contraventions of the city and the world, is still there.

JOHN REED, MAY, 2019

In 1864, Matthew Vassar, the founder of Vassar College, reminded his trustees of his 'secular' views regarding religion in the education of young women: 'I would rather be remembered as one who earnestly sought to fuse the Christian element of the world into one grand Catholic body. Let our pupils see and know that beyond every difference there is, after all, but one God, one gospel; and that spires of whatsoever church forever point toward one heaven. And upon this point again, without disparagement to any other religious source, permit me to add that the strongest incentives to goodness, and the most valuable religious tendencies, will be found to flow most of all, like an emanation, from the presence of gifted, cultivated Christian women'. The *Reed College Bulletin*, in 1920, explained: 'Reed College is undenominational. No Sectarian considerations enter into the election of trustees or faculty or the admission of students. There are religious meetings — daily chapel and Sunday vespers services, Bible-study classes and Christian association activities — in which all may take part without compulsion'.

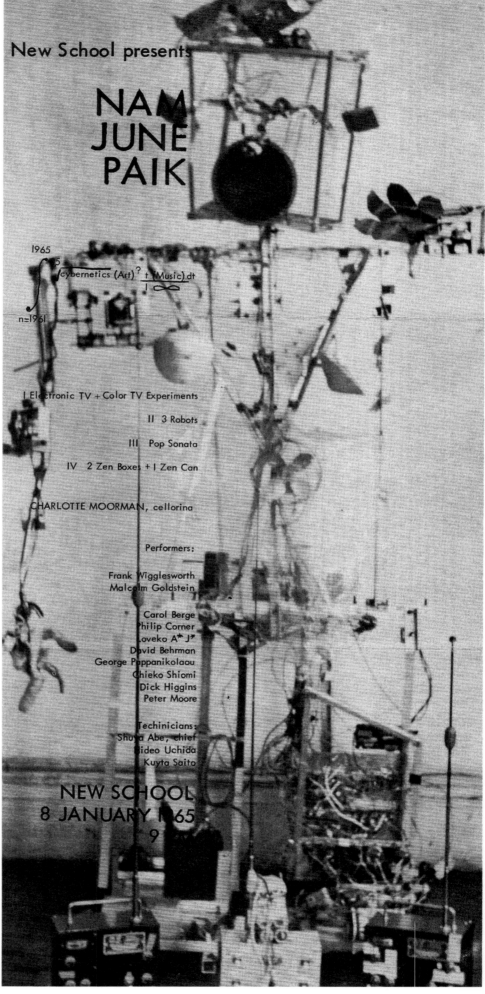

This page:

Announcement for a four-part performance and installation at The New School by the artist Nam June Paik and featuring 'cellorina' Charlotte Moorman, 1965

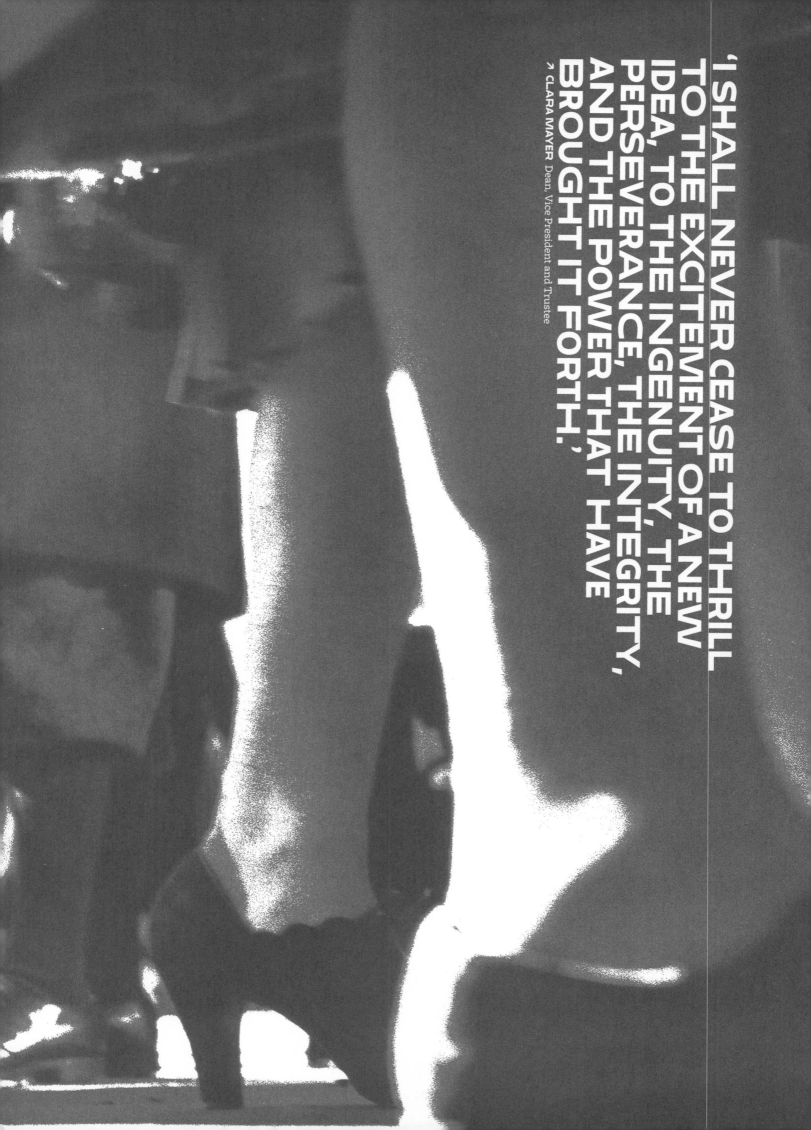

'I SHALL NEVER CEASE TO THRILL
TO THE EXCITEMENT OF A NEW
IDEA, TO THE INGENUITY, THE
PERSEVERANCE, THE INTEGRITY,
AND THE POWER THAT HAVE
BROUGHT IT FORTH.'

↗ CLARA MAYER Dean, Vice President and Trustee

THE VILLAGE FINDS ITS VOICE

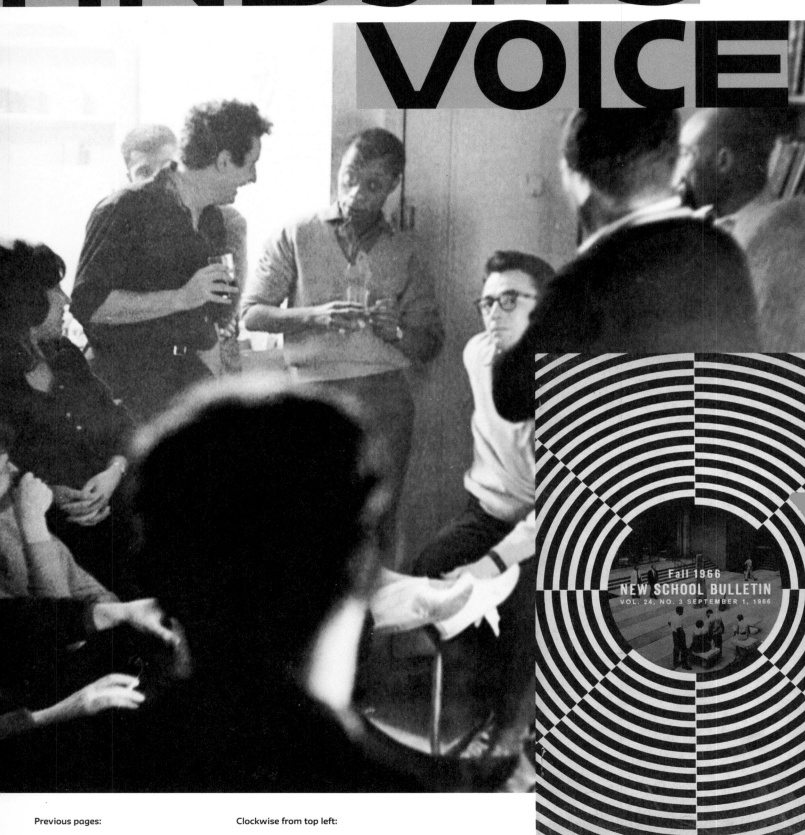

Previous pages:

Clockwise from top left:

Lisette Model, *Running Legs, NYC.* 1940

Guests including Shel Silverstein, Gloria Schoffel, James Baldwin, Howard Hart, Norman Mailer, and Ted Joans gather in a Greenwich Village apartment to discuss *The Funeral of the Beat Generation*, 1961

The New School Bulletin, 1966

In her opening remarks at The New School's 1952 commencement, university Vice President Clara Mayer speaks to a decade of inexorable change:

> Less than a hundred years have elapsed since we were embattled that government of, by and for the people might not perish. The outlook today is often discouraging. And it may never turn on battle. Yet we face a loss of freedom just as dire, perhaps more serious. The way to win it back is the way we lost it — through ourselves.

Commencement speaker Supreme Court Justice William O. Douglas urges graduates toward global thinking, 'to make common cause with the revolutionary struggles for independence and for equality that are now sweeping the world'.

In 1955, Edwin Fancher and Dan Wolf, graduates from New School programs directed to veterans (the university's first undergraduate degree offerings), answer the challenge. Dissatisfied with the local downtown paper, *The Villager*, which is stuffy and old hat, Fancher and Wolf put out their own newspaper, *The Village Voice*. With support from Norman Mailer — who was introduced to the *Voice* founders through New School associations and courses — as Wolf will write in 1962, the *Voice* seeks to counter 'the vulgarities of McCarthyism', which had 'withered the possibilities of a true dialogue between people'.

PHILOSOPHY AND MUSIC, 1932
CHARLES SEEGER

Musicians and laymen meet upon equal terms on at least one common ground — both think they can talk intelligently about music. The premises for this talk, the viewpoints, methods, scope, and aim involved are seldom investigated by either and are least understood by musicians. The problem envisaged by this course is the definition of these elements and the interrelation of music and deliberately methodical language.

PLASTIC ARTS AND THE WAR, 1943
CAMILO EGAS

This course is given in response to government request and carries no tuition fee. A preliminary survey, both practical and theoretical, of the function of the various arts in the war effort, given in cooperation by members of the art department: Berenice Abbott, Alexey Brodovitch, Stuart Davis, José de Creeft, Camilo Egas, Stanley Wiliam Hayter, Yasuo Kuniyoshi, and Paul Zucker.

Photos by Gerhard Heese

STUDENT COUNCIL ELECTED FOR SPRING TERM. Left to right, clockwise, Louis Nathanson, president; Jerry Zeitlin, executive director; Herbert Levine and Charles Villency, council members; Ben Ames, treasurer; Ed Fancher, council member; Bert Elgot, alternate; Rose Schoen, vice president. Dorothy Dover, also a council member, and Marilyn Berman, alternate, are not in photo.

'EVERYTHING IN THE DREAM IS THE DREAMER.'

↗ SEKOU SUNDIATA Faculty

Clockwise from top left:

New School Poetry Readings poster, 1962

The New School News, 1949

OUTDOORS IN THE NEW SCHOOL COURTYARD

NEW SCHOOL POETRY READINGS

SUNDAY EVENINGS AT 8:30

JUNE 17
MARIANNE MOORE

JUNE 24
STANLEY KUNITZ

JULY 1
ALAN DUGAN

JULY 8
LEONIE ADAMS

JULY 15
KENNETH KOCH

JULY 22
FRANK O'HARA

The first annual summer series of New School Poetry Readings honors the memory of William Troy faculty member and literary critic

Poet Robert Lowell is chairman of the 1962 series

For these events use West 11th Street New School Entrance between 5th and 6th Avenues

For ticket orders, contact:
OFFICE OF PUBLIC INFORMATION
New School for Social Research
66 West 12th Street, New York 11, N. Y., ORegon 5-2700

SERIES SUBSCRIPTION: $10.00
TICKETS TO SINGLE READINGS: $2.00

'I feel the hints, the clues, the whisper of a new time coming', writes Mailer in 1956, when Greenwich Village and The New School are the embodiment of change. Anatole Broyard, in his 1993 memoir, *Kafka Was the Rage*, will recount arrival in Greenwich Village in the late 1940s:

I opened a bookstore, went to The New School under the G.I. Bill. I began to think about becoming a writer. I thought about the relation between men and women as it was in 1947, when they were still locked in what Aldous Huxley called a hostile symbiosis. In the background, like landscape, like weather, was what we read and talked about. In the foreground were our love affairs and friendships and our immersion, like swimmers or divers, in American life and art.

Broyard, a writer and revered literary critic, will go on to teach at The New School. When Mailer lectured at the school in 1953, his novels had already been called out in several course descriptions; like many New School faculty members, he would soon be an ongoing subject in course offerings. Mailer will frequent lectures and events at The New School until his death in 2007.

'Intellectually and creatively, the center of the postwar Village was The New School. When the Servicemen's Readjustment Act of 1944 — the G.I. Bill — was passed, The New School's Adult Education Division added a B.A. program in order to take advantage of the act's education benefits, and enrollment more than tripled.'
↗ LOUIS MENAND Faculty

EXPLORE GREENWICH VILLAGE

Clockwise from top left:

The New School Bulletin, 1955

Anatole Broyard, undated

Greenwich Village. Bob Adelman, circa 1970

'THE ONLY RECOGNIZABLE FEATURE OF HOPE IS ACTION.'
↗ GRACE PALEY Student

'The mumbo-jumbo of city madness generates excitement which drives through to us. Reflections are mirrored in a manner acutely visual and selective without being 'impressionistic'. These reflections, whether double or triple, are indeed amusing, jog our ribs, and suggest many related images. To dramatize a subject, to emphasize, or to verify, even to distort — these are all the photographer's tools. Here, too, is the strong time-sense, so vital and so tangible, which this medium can best suggest. The old, the new, fused into the now, side by side, nicely blended. Then the tempo of today. Hurry — hurry — hurrying to death.'
↗ **BERENICE ABBOTT** Faculty

This page:

Anti-Vietnam War demonstrators, New York City. Bob Adelman, 1968

NEW PLAYS IN WORK, 1947
THE DRAMATIC WORKSHOP
MARIA LEY-PISCATOR, CHAIRMAN
JOHN F. MATTHEWS, INSTRUCTOR
EDWARD MABLEY, LECTURER

The mid-century lectures and highly selective workshops of The New School attract students who go on to extraordinary success; among the many are James Baldwin, Marlon Brando, Enrico Donati, Red Grooms, Grace Paley, Lorraine Hansberry, Jack Kerouac, Madeleine L'Engle, Sigrid de Lima, Judith Malina, Sidney Poitier, Mario Puzo, Julio Rosado del Valle, William Styron, and Tennessee Williams. In lectures, workshops, and degree courses, students are mentored at the forefront of academic and creative fields. Sampling the curriculum: students take classes in psychoanalysis with Karen Horney and Eric Fromm; gestalt psychology with Rudolf Arnheim; economics with Adolphe Lowe; philosophy with Hannah Arendt and Hans Jonas; art criticism with Meyer Schapiro; musicology with Charles Seeger, Henry Cowell, and Cowell's protégé, John Cage; photography with Berenice Abbott, Joseph Breitenbach, and Lisette Model; literature with W.H. Auden, Alfred Kazin, Robert Lowell, and Jean Malaquais; writing with Kay Boyle and Frank O'Hara; printmaking with Stanley Hayter and Clare Romano; studio art with Robert Gwathmey, Robert De Niro Sr., Seymour Lipton, José de Creeft, and Lorrie Goulet; and theater in the Dramatic Workshop with Stella Adler, Erwin and Maria Ley-Piscator, and Lee Strasberg.

A production laboratory for the discovery, development and presentation of original plays with auditors and selected active author-participants. ... Scripts are criticized at various stages of production level. The outstanding new play of the year will be presented in the March of Drama Repertory. The Dramatic Workshop's playwriting courses under John Gassner have included such playwrights as Tennessee Williams (*Glass Menagerie*), Edwin Bronner (*A Young American*), Robert Anderson (*Come Marching Home*). New plays originally produced in the Dramatic Workshop include Philip Yordan's ... *Any Day Now*, Frank Gabrielson's *Days of Our Youth*, Dan James' *Winter Soldiers*, Jay Bennett's *No Hiding Place*, Joseph Shore's *The Soldier Who Became a Great Dane* ... and the musical revue *Middle Man, What Now?*

FACTS / ALTERNATIVE FACTS, 2019
LIESL SCHILLINGER

What is 'fake news'? How does it differ from 'real' news, and how can you ensure your own writing is accurate? This hybrid course blends lessons in political philosophy, history, and communications with practical journalistic instruction to prepare the next generation of journalists to safeguard the truth—and their own careers—at a time when press freedom is under unprecedented attack. Students will read excerpts and articles that address the importance of freedom of speech and of the press, and explore past and present threats to those freedoms, interpolating the readings with current headline news. The texts range from the origins of our democracy and Constitution to the rise of broadcast media, digital media, and the alt-right; from the First Amendment and Tocqueville's vision of America to Watergate and the social-media-assisted Russian hack of the 2016 election.

Clockwise from left:

Eleanor Roosevelt with Edith Sommerich, *circa 1949*

Berenice Abbott, *Young Painter In Her Greenwich Village Studio, circa 1949*

Following her term as one of the longest-serving first ladies of the United States, Eleanor Roosevelt is a frequent contributor to the intellectual psyche of The New School. She refers to the school often in her 'My Day' column — a national syndicated newspaper column — and is a frequent guest at The New School. In 1954, she delivers a seemingly prophetic speech that warns of the dangers of 'America First' policy proponents in the country.

In 2013, under the directorship of program founder Heather Chaplin, The New School's Eugene Lang College offers the first undergraduate program in Journalism and Design. The program simultaneously draws on the history of writing at The New School, the history of design at Parsons, and The New School's engagement with contemporary writers, artists, organizations, enterprises, and cultural issues and currents.

'THE WHOLE UNIVERSE INTERESTS ME.'

↗ GEORGE BRECHT Faculty

PARSONS IN PARIS, & THE PARSONS TABLE

'BEAUTY IS THE QUALITY OF HARMONIOUS RELATIONSHIPS. A FORMULA TO PRODUCE IT DOES NOT EXIST.'

FRANK ALVAH PARSONS Director of the New York School of Fine and Applied Art and Parsons

1921

Clockwise from top left:

Parsons School of Design student, 1987

Parsons, Midtown & Greenwich Village Catalog, 1988

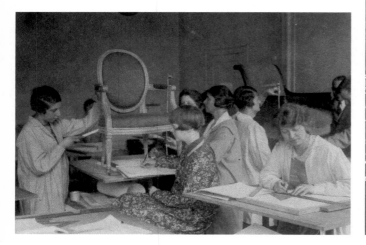

Jean-Michel Frank is a brilliant but restless designer. Through the 1920s, basing himself out of New York City, where he teaches at the School of Fine and Applied Art — later to be known as Parsons School of Design — Frank travels the world, developing an ethos of elegance and strength in minimalism. The clarity of his creative purpose belies personal tragedy; in 1915, he lost his two older brothers to World War I, and his father to a resultant suicide — a decade later, his mother will die in a Swiss asylum. Frank (uncle of Anne Frank) becomes a figure of fascination through the evolution of Modernism to the emergence of Pop, inspiring obsessive collecting, for example, on the part of Andy Warhol.

 Circa 1927, Frank returns to his hometown of Paris from New York City. In 1921, the School of Fine and Applied Art, then known as The Chase School, had opened the Paris Ateliers. The satellite campus, the first international program in U.S. higher education, was announced in the School of Fine and Applied Art catalogue: 'The Paris School has become a reality. ... Its courses of study duplicate and supplement those in New York, so that students may now transfer from one school to the other at the end of each semester without loss of time or instruction'. Frank, already lauded for his homeware designs for Hermès, works with his Ateliers students on examples of drafting. Circa 1929, they render the Parsons Table; without flourishes, of economic allure, the table exemplifies twentieth-century design.

 Until the onset of World War II, the Paris Ateliers conducts courses in architecture, interior design, theatrical design, graphic design, and fashion; an additional research program in Italy is also interrupted by the onset of fascism and global conflict. After the war — redesignated the Parsons School of Design in 1936 — Parsons returns to France, as well as to Italy, and introduces a United Kingdom outpost in 1955. Through the 1970s, Parsons offers summer sessions in Paris, and in 1980 adopts a full-year calendar, building toward what will become 'Parsons Paris'. In 2013, The New School draws the New York and Paris campuses closer together, with a 'one degree–two cities' ideology.

 'We set about to design a design school,' explains current provost Tim Marshall, 'that could operate more deftly and strongly in The New School context, and — more broadly — that would have the agility to respond to, anticipate, and lead.'

THE NEW SCHOOL, 1941 ABSTRACT COMPOSITION IN PAINTING AND DRAWING STUART DAVIS

Emphasis is laid on working from nature in abstract terms. Maximum use of color, the spatial identity of color and form, the relation of abstract art to the American environment are principal subjects of study. The direct approach to structure in art is useful in fields of art other than easel and mural painting, such as illustration, advertising, and applied design.

THE NEW SCHOOL, 1961 WOODCUT, COLOR AND BLACK AND WHITE WORDEN DAY

Creative woodcut, in black, white, and color, is explored in all of the experimental aspects, combining new means to new ends. ... The classic approach of the occident and orient in carving, printing, registering, selecting papers and inks is presented. The student is oriented to that creative freedom achieved through mastery of the craft.

Clockwise from top left:

A group of New York School of Fine and Applied Art students in the Paris Ateliers, 9 Place des Vosges, 1920s

Class in the Paris Ateliers, 1920s

Painters of the Village, a group show by artists associated with Greenwich Village. The New School for Social Research, 1955

Parsons School of Design students in the studio, 2019

Parsons Paris Fashion Design students carry out a collaborative performance at the Centre National de la Danse, Paris, 2019

Student watercolor of L'Institut de France. Paris Ateliers, NY School of Fine and Applied Art, 1934

In November, 1934, as part of her lecture tour of American schools, museums, and other institutions of art and learning, Gertrude Stein stops at The New School for Social Research. The celebrity author, who hasn't been stateside for almost three decades, limits her audiences to 500 people; the restriction proves unenforceable at The New School, where eager New Yorkers argue for admittance to an auditorium that seats nearly one thousand.

Paintings by

Milton Avery
Peggy Bacon
Ben-Zion
Isabel Bishop
Louis Bouché
Louise Bourgeois
Paul Cadmus
Glenn Coleman
Ralston Crawford
Stuart Davis

José de Creeft
Willem de Kooning
Camilo Egas
Perle Fine
William Glackens
Arshile Gorky
Philip Guston
Samuel Halpert
Grace Hartigan
Morris Kantor
Yasuo Kuniyoshi
Julian Levi
Loren MacIver
Reginald Marsh

George L. K. Morris
Mercedes Matter
Walter Pach
Abraham Rattner
Jeanne Reynal
Manfred Schwartz
Charles Sheeler
Thomas Sills
John Sloan
Moses Soyer
Raphael Soyer
Tomayo
Marguerite Zorach
William Zorach

Arrangements Committee: Holger Cahill, Camilo Egas, Lloyd Goodrich, Edith Halpert, Julian Levi, Dorothy Miller. An exhibit presented in conjunction with five Sunday evenings on Greenwich Village at 8:30 P.M. Oct. 23: Music; Oct. 30: Off Broadway Theater; Nov. 6: Fine Arts; Nov. 13: Literature; Nov. 20: The Greenwich Village Community.

NEW SCHOOL FOR SOCIAL RESEARCH · 66 West Twelfth St., New York 11, N.Y. · Tel.: ORegon 5-2700

PAINTERS OF THE VILLAGE

October 23 - November 14, 1955
Hours: Monday-Friday: 9 a.m.-9:30 p.m.
Saturday, 9 a.m.-noon. Sunday, 7 p.m.-10 p.m.

In 1927, a year after his arrival in Paris, Stanley William Hayter establishes an experimental workshop in graphic arts. Upon its move to a studio space at 17 Rue Campagne-Première, the workshop takes the name Atelier 17. In 1940, with the Nazi occupation of Paris, Hayter brings the Atelier to The New School in New York City, where the workshop remains until 1955. For five years, 1950 to 1955, the workshop has studios in New York and Paris. The Atelier spans Modernism, Surrealism, and Abstract Expressionism, with an early cohort of Alexander Calder, Salvador Dalí, José Guerrero, Jacques Lipchitz, Roberto Matta, Joan Miró, Pablo Picasso, David Smith, and many others. The New School cohort includes William Baziotes, Louise Bourgeois, Minna Citron, Worden Day, Dorothy Dehner, Sue Fuller, Adolph Gottlieb, Willem De Kooning, Robert Motherwell, Louise Nevelson, Jackson Pollock, Mark Rothko, Anne Ryan, and Alice Trumbull Mason. A 1942 portrait at The New School Atelier captures Berenice Abbott, André Breton, Leonora Carrington, Marcel Duchamp, Jimmy Ernst, Max Ernst, John Ferren, Peggy Guggenheim, Stanley William Hayter, Frederick Kiesler, Fernand Léger, Piet Mondrian, Amédée Ozenfant, and Kurt Seligmann.

'I NEED AN APARTMENT. BUT IT HAS TO BE ONE WITH A VIEW.'

↗ VINNETTE CARROLL Student

'I also occupy myself somewhat with art that, in a sense, is not definable as art as such. For example, the lanterns or playgrounds or parks. ... I thought it a more honorable way of making a living, and I needed money also. It's part of the same kind of motivation. You know the American idea – every American is an inventor, in a sense. After all, that's how America was made, by invention – a screwdriver, a gear, or what-have-you. I recently did a nozzle for the fountain I'm doing in Detroit. It's a real invention. That sort of thing pleases me a lot. We Americans admire people like Alexander Graham Bell. They are the real artists of America.'

↗ ISAMU NOGUCHI Site-Specific Artist

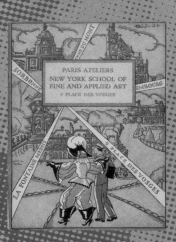

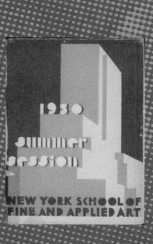

Previous pages:

▬▬▬▬ The Parsons Table

Clockwise from top left:

▬▬▬▬ *New York School of Fine and Applied Art,* 1928

▬▬▬▬ Covers for *The New School of Fine and Applied Art* course catalogs, 1920-1930s

▬▬▬▬ Paris Ateliers fashion illustration class, 1920s

'Consider that something you take for granted today may be the one thing you might pine for someday, and there might not be any more of it left, but you'll remember its sweetness. Remember the curve of the sun in your bedroom window late in the day, the way your little brother's hair smelled after his bath, and the sound of your mother and father talking in the kitchen.'
↗ **PAM CONRAD** Student

'A CITY IS MORE THAN A PLACE IN SPACE, IT IS A DRAMA IN TIME.'
↗ **PATRICK GEDDES** Faculty

COMRADES & LOVERS

Neon signs glow with a pressurized infusion of gas. Glenn Ligon, the celebrated American artist, was to be one of three new site-specific works of art installed in the near-completed University Center at 63 Fifth Avenue. His work, *Comrades and Lovers*, would quote from Walt Whitman, and summon, in neon, the American spirit, while Rita McBride's *Bells and Whistles* would coil through the architecture of the new building, breathing life into its substructures, and Alfredo Jaar's *Searching for Africa in LIFE* would take up permanent residence in the library, a visual survey of the popular magazine and a reminder of historical inequality cast to all researchers, and all subjects.

There is a challenge for the Ligon: the gas that constitutes neon isn't eco enough for the environmental building status of the University Center. Ligon, who has worked with neon for ten years, confers with artisans of the material, and arrives at an original solution: pure argon gas in clear glass rods. Circling the entrance stairwell and reception of the University Center, the neon scripts read:

> *Dead poets, philosophs, priests,*
> *Martyrs, artists, inventors, governments*
> *   long since,*
> *Language-shapers, on other shores,*
> *Nations once powerful, now reduced,*
> *   withdrawn, or desolate,*
> *I dare not proceed till I respectfully credit*
> *   what you have left wafted hither,*
> *I have perused it, own it is admirable,*
> *   (moving awhile among it),*
> *Think nothing can ever be greater, nothing*
> *   can ever deserve more than it deserves;*
> *Regarding it all intently a long while, then*
> *   dismissing it,*
> *I stand in my place with my own day here*

Ligon carves a quiet but forceful palette for the quotation, which inspires students, faculty, and visitors. The electric glow is as if perennial, emanating from the glass tubes which themselves are ever-flowing, ever-liquid.

At the 2018 Commencement Ceremony, Ligon is conferred an honorary degree.

THE LANGUAGE & TECHNIQUE OF POETRY, 1940
W.H. AUDEN

There is some reason to believe that many people, even among lovers of poetry, experience considerable difficulty in grasping poetic uses of language, and hence in forming a reliable critical judgement for themselves. Must one, for example, share the beliefs of a poet to appreciate his work? What is the real difference between poetry and prose? How does the form of a poem contribute to its meaning? What are the ways in which a poem can be bad? What is the relation between the experiences of a poet and the poem he writes about them? What goes on in the mind while one is reading a poem?

POLITICS IN THE TIME OF MALARIA, 2009
JEFFERY RENARD ALLEN

This course looks at contemporary novels and short stories from around the world that deal with health issues. Key is the question of how such issues frame or shape matters of democratic process and the struggle for social equality. ...

'Eventually, I ran away to Greenwich Village, where no one had been born of a mother and father, where the people I met had sprung from their own brows, or from the pages of a bad novel.'
↗ **ANATOLE BROYARD** Student and Faculty

2015

Clockwise from top left:

Glenn Ligon, *For Comrades and Lovers* (detail), 2015. Neon, 193.8 ft. New York, The New School Art Collection

Glenn Ligon, *For Comrades and Lovers*, 2015. Neon, 193.8 ft. New York, The New School Art Collection

Sekou Sundiata's final major project, *The 51st (dream) State*, which is described by *The New York Times* as 'a hyperactive mosaic of poetry, music, dance, and videotaped interviews', premieres in 2006, first at the Melbourne Festival, and then at the Brooklyn Academy of Music. *The 51st (dream) State* remembers and considers 9/11, America, and the world. The poet tells the *Times*: 'I discovered an active discourse in academic circles about the 51st state. Maybe the 51st state is a state of war. Rumsfeld has said the twenty-first century will be a time of constant war. You need dream language to get at it.' Sundiata passes away, at fifty-eight years old, in 2007.

In 2015, in cooperation with the Healthy Affordable Materials Project, the Healthy Materials Lab, through collaborative, educational investigation, seeks practical design and material solutions in building that are nontoxic. Toxic materials in construction disproportionately impact lower-income residents; the Healthy Materials Lab, the first academic program of its kind, seeks a material, economic, and cultural understanding of the subject, and proposes, samples, and evaluates practical solutions.

'I WANT TO GO BACK TO A TIME BEFORE HARD LINES AND DIVISIONS, WHEN ART AND SCIENCE WERE JOINED IN ALCHEMY.'

↗ RITA MCBRIDE Site-Specific Artist

'It was at The New School that I really learned the art of political engagement. I learned that with any heart, and with a solid basis of mutual respect, you can go toe to toe in fierce debate with someone and then shift gears when the meeting or class is over and relate once again as friends. I came to relish this new exercise of social tension and release, of engaging in difficult and troublesome realities without breaking connections or forfeiting one another. Speaking up and being true to oneself, meeting and challenging one another, and then ultimately accepting differences and forgiving trespasses felt ... so much better than the alternative.'

↗ ANI DIFRANCO Student

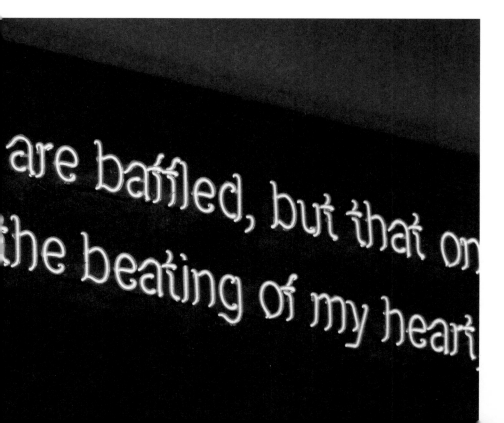

'I THINK THE MOST BEAUTIFUL INVENTIONS ARE THE ONES YOU DON'T THINK OF.'

↗ DIANE ARBUS Student

CAPITAL IS HUMAN DIGNITY & CREATIVITY

Frank Alvah Parsons joins The Chase School as faculty. William Merritt Chase, dubbed by *Life* magazine 'the ruler of the art world', founded the school in 1896. Alumni include Kate Freeman Clark, Edith Dimock Glackens, Marsden Hartley, Edward Hopper, Rockwell Kent, Guy Pène du Bois, Martha Walter, and Georgia O'Keefe, who in 1905 is appointed 'class monitor'. The programs initiated by Parsons — dedicated to fashion, interior design, and advertising — are firsts in the United States. Parsons' emphasis on material and practical design is simultaneously trade-oriented and correspondent to politically egalitarian trends of the moment, such as printmaking.

'One of the things that fascinated me about modeling was that you had the freedom to look any way you wanted.'
↗ **VERONICA WEBB** Student

In 1969, Charles Harbutt, writer turned photographer, publishes his first book, *America in Crisis*. Harbutt had gained his reputation as a photographer in 1959, when he documented the Cuban revolution from the inside; his photographs of Cuba were subsequently published in Modern Photography. In Travelog (1974), Progreso (1986), and Departures and Arrivals (2012), he furthers an aesthetic which reconciles social conscience, odyssey, and immediacy. He is faculty at Parsons from 1999 until his death in 2015.

Joseph Beuys, of renown in Europe, makes his first visit to the United States in 1974. Having refused to visit the United States during the Vietnam conflict, the German artist agrees to a series of performances — political discussion, lecture, and live diagraming. He chooses not to exhibit object-based art. The tour begins in January at The New School with 'The Energy Plan for the Western Man', a three-hour performance / talk / conference. Beuys advocates for an expansive cultural and political definition of art. 'Creativity,' he tells the audience, 'is national income.' In 1995, The New School hosts 'Considering Joseph Beuys', a one-week schedule of panels, discussions, events, and screenings.

'Design is a series of creative choices — it's a collaborative effort, an evolutionary process. You choose your fabrics depending upon what you want to say, then you work with mills to get those fabrics. Through the process, you realize what you want it to be.'
↗ **MARC JACOBS** Student and Visiting Critic

Clockwise from top left:

▬▬▬ Parsons School of Design alumnus Marc Jacobs, after 1984

▬▬▬ Solange Knowles at Parsons Spring Benefit, 2018

▬▬▬ Charles Harbutt. *Empire State Building, New York*, 1970

▬▬▬ Class of William Merritt Chase, 1903

In 2018, Parsons celebrates its seventieth anniversary of the Parsons Benefit, an annual fashion show where current fashion design students showcase their work to New York City fashion designers and influencers. The seventieth anniversary honors singer, songwriter, and actress Solange Knowles; Marco Bizzarri, President and CEO of Gucci; and José Neves, founder and CEO of Farfetch.

'SEWING IS THE FIRST STEP TO DESIGNING, FOR YOU GET IDEAS OF WHAT TO MAKE.'
↗ **MILDRED ORRICK** Student

In 2000, the Fusion Fashion Show kicks off the first of seventeen seasons at the Parsons School of Design; the show brings bright young designers to compete for their schools, and foretells Bravo's Project Runway, which kicks off in 2004. Project Runway is shot on campus for fourteen seasons; Tim Gunn, Chair of Fashion Design at Parsons, presides.

'You can make clothing as art, but I like the idea of my clothes actually being worn and being useful to women.'
↗ **TRACY REESE** Student

'MONEY AND CAPITAL CANNOT BE AN ECONOMIC VALUE, CAPITAL IS HUMAN DIGNITY AND CREATIVITY.'
↗ **JOSEPH BEUYS** Guest Speaker

'THE MAIN QUESTION ... SHOULD NOT BE "IS IT GOOD MUSIC?" BUT "WHAT IS THE MUSIC GOOD FOR?"'
↗ **CHARLES SEEGER** Faculty

1904

PUSH

'COASTING TO THE BOTTOM IS THE ONLY DISGRACE.'

↗ **JOHN POPPER** Student

DANGER, EDUCATION & NEW YORK

'Look down at your feet. And look at your neighbor's feet. Here's what I know about your feet: they've worked hard. Here's what I know about this New School education. It was weird and amazing. That's why I'd like to hire you. Here's another thing I know. Outside of those doors, it's also weird and amazing. You were born with these two feet and they've brought you here. Today you have an education that no one can take away from you. My request is to stay weird and be amazing.'

↗ **NANCY LUBLIN** Honorary Degree Recipient

Bob Kerrey, the former Nebraska governor, is appointed to the Presidency of The New School in 2001.

'I like danger,' Kerrey explains to *The New York Times*. 'I like education. I like New York.'

From the beginning, Kerrey's celebrity presidency is beset by protest, student and labor unrest; in 2002, while ACT-UAW organizes toward a part-time faculty union at The New School, students, joining a citywide action, criticize Kerrey's participation in the White House-approved Committee for the Liberation of Iraq.

A decorated veteran of the Vietnam War, Kerrey, undeterred, embarks on the largest building project in the school's history; the University Center will serve to bring together a campus that's fractured academically and geographically. Despite the obvious need for more space, Kerrey is unable to present a convincing argument to students and faculty, many of whom see the project as a massive assault on the endowment, and an unnecessary, extreme fiscal stress for the university. An initial proposal for the signature building features a 'distributed library', which would have no single location, but as is argued by Paul Goldberger—architecture critic for *The New York Times*, *Vanity Fair* and *The New Yorker*, former Dean of the Parsons School of Design, and The New School University's Joseph Urban Professor of Design—a library that is everywhere is nowhere:

> While the library may appear to be primarily a storehouse of past treasures, and seemed for a while to be a relic of a pre-digital age ... university libraries are becoming more and more central to academic life ... almost like the town square or the village commons of a university. To be without a central library would not only dishonor the university's past, it would compromise its future.

In 2008, faculty deliver Kerrey a resounding vote of no confidence, and students, days later, take over the cafeteria. With slapstick glee, a national and international press reports that students chase Kerrey down Fifth Avenue (Kerrey wears a prosthetic on a portion of his leg due to an injury he sustained in Vietnam) and throw a tomato at him.

In 2009, Kerrey meets several student demands, which students have scaled back. Protests and tensions continue on campus, but the new building, as wide as a city block and a third the length of the avenue, breaks ground in August, 2010. In 2011, just shy of the completion of his contract, Kerrey steps down from the presidency.

Previous pages:

This page:

Occupied office of the Graduate Center, The New School for Social Research, *circa* 1970

"A student expresses her support for the protesters." *The New York Times*, April 10, 2009

'IDEAS ARE ONE THING AND WHAT HAPPENS IS ANOTHER.'
↗ JOHN CAGE Student and Faculty

'Often we are asked what is the fundamental doctrine of The New School? Are we seeking to indoctrinate our students with radicalism, conservatism or what? We are not seeking to indoctrinate our students at all. We leave indoctrination to Stalin and the Devil. We love liberalism; we love democracy. These are infinite values; we should feel infinitely happy if we could feel that they are shared by all mankind. But they will not spread by any scheme of indoctrination. They can lodge firmly in a mind if it is an open mind.'
↗ **ALVIN JOHNSON** First President and Founder

Fifth Avenue, the building, and 13th Street are flooded during the final stage of construction, but the University Center, delayed, opens in 2014.

The University Center adds 370,000 square feet to the campus, featuring a 600-bed dormitory, with views, nineteen fashion studios, seventeen drawing studios, fifteen faculty offices, twelve classrooms, seven science labs, three lounges, three new site-specific art installations, an auditorium, a library, and a cafe. The integration of academic disciplines through shared and interlaced spaces recalls the collaborative ideology of the Joseph Urban design at The New School's first dedicated site at 66 West 12th Street. As an example of green architecture, the building, christened Kerrey Hall, is conferred multiple awards and distinctions. In 2013, Kerrey announces that fresh academic ventures require him to resign his President Emeritus status at The New School. Kerrey's term of office sees the faculty-to-student ratio improve by twofold: in 2001, there are 50.4 students to one professor; in 2012, there are twenty-six students to one professor. Tenure, additionally, becomes available to full-time faculty in all colleges in the university; until 2007, tenure had only been available to faculty in The New School for Social Research. As of 2019, The New School endowment, at 300 million dollars, triples the endowment of 2001.

'They say I don't understand higher education,' Kerrey told *The New York Observer*, in 2008. 'To a certain extent it's true I don't understand. It's baffling at times.'

'I CAN ONLY WORK AGAINST BOURGEOIS SOCIETY, I CAN NEVER WORK WITH IT OR THROUGH IT.'
↗ **ERWIN PISCATOR** Faculty and Founder of the Dramatic Workshop

Maya Wiley, newly appointed as The New School's inaugural Senior Vice President for Social Justice, and the Henry Cohen Professor of Urban Policy and Management at The New School's Milano School of Policy, Management, and Environment, holds a campus-wide town hall in the wake of the 2016 U.S. presidential election. 'I hope to help create more pathways for students and faculty and staff to be able to work together across those boundaries,' Wiley tells *The New School Free Press*. 'The New School really has the ability to be seen as the leader that it is in social innovation.'

Mexican poet and diplomat Octavio Paz delivers a lecture at The New School in 1994. His name and influence permeates New School catalogs from the 1960s to the 2000s, his affiliation with the school dating back to the 1940s with his involvement in The New School's École Libre des Hautes Études.

Occupy Wall Street (OWS) arrives at The New School in October, 2011. While protestors remain camped out in lower Manhattan, where they've been for a month, students and faculty at The New School stage a teach-in, which debates and imagines the future of the movement. The administration takes a nonconfrontational position. OWS engages multiple student organizations and academic programs, which, in many cases, act cooperatively for the first time. The protestors vacate campus areas, which are significantly damaged, after approximately one month.

During the month of March in 1985, Eugene Lang College hosts a panel discussion with members from the U.S. Army War College on the role of the United States military in Latin America and the Caribbean. The event, highly contentious, attracts such outspoken protest of Reagan administration policy that few members of the Army College get a chance to speak. The event draws questions about free speech in the role of the academics, and The New School amends its own bylaws.

'DOUBT TEMPERS BELIEF WITH SANITY.'
↗ BARBARA KRUGER Student

Clockwise from left:

▬▬▬ The New School University Center

▬▬▬ Maya Wiley, Senior Vice President for Social Justice at The New School and the Henry Cohen Professor of Urban Policy and Management at The New School's Milano School of Management, Policy, and Environment, 2018

MUSIC IS MY FAITH

The Music School Settlement for Colored People is founded in Harlem. The school offers the first community music education in the neighborhood, and is intended to make formal music lessons accessible to black children. David Mannes, wishing to honor his childhood violin instructor, John Thomas Douglass, a musician and composer of prominence in African-American popular ensembles of the late nineteenth century, garners supporters and patrons for the school, which is a counterpart to the Third Street Music School Settlement, established in 1894, of which Mannes is then director. The Third Street Music School, at the time, is oriented to poor white communities of New York City's Lower East Side.

The Music School Settlement for Colored People follows in the 'settlement movement' of U.S. education, with precedents such as the Henry Street Settlement in New York City, which was founded by Lillian Wald in 1893, and Hull House in Chicago, which was founded by Jane Addams and Ellen Gates Starr in 1889. Henry Street was one of the few settlements to accept people of color, but it also had a separate unit specified for people of color; Hull House had its first black resident in 1893.

In his 1938 memoir, *Music Is My Faith*, Mannes, in his seventies, recalls his thirteenth year, and the impression that John Douglass made on him:

> He composed much music, of which piles of manuscript in his home were ample evidence. He occasionally played at entertainments by people of his race, but outside of his friends few knew of his existence. He tried to enter a symphony orchestra in this country, but those doors were closed to a colored man. Being of a modest and retiring nature he was not able to insist on being heard. Douglass was like a fish out of water, ahead of his time by thirty or forty years.

In addition to violin, Douglass played guitar. He toured with several popular 'All-Negro' entertainment companies. In 1868, his opera *Virginia's Ball* was performed at the Stuyvesant Institute on Broadway. *Virginia's Ball*, a lost work, is believed to be the first opera by an African-American.

As of this writing, a twentieth-century history of the Mannes School of Music and students of faculty of color is not established. Joining The New School in 1989, Mannes redoubles efforts toward a more diverse and contemporaneous community and curriculum. In 2015, just in time for its centennial, Mannes moves from the Upper West Side to The New School's Greenwich Village campus, and the university's Arnhold Hall, on 13th Street off Sixth Avenue. The nine-story building, after a $25 million renovation, unifies the College of Performing Arts, which encompasses Mannes, the School of Jazz and the School of Drama. The New School's 2019 *Almanac*, which gathers statistical data about the university, breaks down the domestic student body as: 51% White, 16% Hispanic, 13% Asian, 9% Black/African-American, 5% two or more races, <1% Native American, and 6% unreported. A breakdown of international students, who make up 34% of the student body, is not available. In U.S. News rankings, 2017/18, The New School, at 32%, is tied for first in the category of Most International Students.

'O, the things that we have learned in this unkind house that we have to tell the world about! Despair? Did someone say despair was a question in the world? Well then, listen to the sons of those who have known little else if you wish to know the resiliency of this thing you would so quickly resign to mythhood — this thing called the human spirit! Life? Ask those who have tasted of it in pieces rationed out by enemies. Love? Ah, ask the troubadours who come from those who have loved when all reason pointed to the uselessness and foolhardiness of love ... Out of the depth of pain we have thought to be our sole heritage in this world — O, we know about Love! Perhaps we shall be the teachers when it is done. And that is why I now say to you that, though it be a thrilling and marvelous thing to be merely young and gifted in such times, it is doubly so — doubly dynamic — to be young, gifted and black'.

↗ LORRAINE HANSBERRY Student

'I was discovering what some American blacks must discover: that the people who destroyed my history had also destroyed their own.'
↗ JAMES BALDWIN Student and Guest Speaker

ARTISTS AS ACTIVISTS, 2019
MANNES SCHOOL OF MUSIC
EMILY BERRY, DANIEL ROUMAIN

The role of the artist has always varied from performer, composer, author, and scholar, to administrator, community [...] entrepreneur, and activist. [...] to Nina Simone to Jawole W[...] Kendrick Lamar, artists and [...] inform and reflect the joys, dre[...] and horrors of our ever dense [...] world. This course will offer c[...] alternate to the word 'student'[...] another as 'contributors', all of [...] equally — to a classroom of ide[...] analysis of selected works by [...] activists, and the complex art [...] cultural impact of the artist as ac[...] will have the opportunity to [...] the work of world-class activi[...] in discussions and an intervi[...] them; learn how to contextuali[...] within a personal, appropriate, [...] and present an in-class perfo[...] peers, based on their current w[...]

Clockwise from top left:

■ *The New School Bulletin,* 1961

■ Mannes Prep student performance, 2018

■ David Mannes leads a concert at the Metropolitan Museum of Art, 1940

■ *Camera Study (David Mannes holding a violin).* Editta Sherman, 1940–59

In May, 1912, a 'Concert of Negro Music' is held at Carnegie Hall. The program, overseen by David Mannes and showcasing James Reese Europe, raises funds, awareness, and enthusiasm for Mannes' recently established Harlem-based organization, the Music School Settlement for Colored People.

The May 29, 1915 issue of *Musical America* notes that 'Mr. and Mrs. David Mannes gave a piano and violin recital at Sing Sing prison on May 11. The convicts showed their appreciation of classical music by crowding the chapel to the doors. Some of them even went without part of their supper in order to be sure of their seats'.

For forty years, David Mannes conducts free concerts at the Museum of Art. *Museum Bulletin* claims the conc 'America's larg audiences'. By Mannes' retirem Met events in 1 cumulative aud the millions. Ac Mannes advise on the acquisit and historical i He returns to th for a final conc the program ce ninetieth birth

In 'Old Weird America: Music as Democratic Speech—from the Commonplace Song to Bob Dylan', Visiting Professor Greil Marcus curates a survey of music and culture which welcomes, among its celebrated guests, Hilton Als, Carrie Brownstein, Stanley Crouch, Samuel Delaney, Mary Gaitskill, Marybeth Hamilton, Todd Haynes, Michael Lesy, Walter Mosley, Ann Powers, Luc Sante, A.O. Scott, Dana Spiotta, Lee Smith, David Thomas (of Pere Ubu), David Thomson, John Rockwell, and Sean Wilentz. The course, which runs from 2007 to 2013 as part of the Riggio Honors Program, actively integrates writing and democracy: 'Throughout American history people excluded from or ignored by that narrative have seized on music as a means of both affirming and questioning individual and cultural existence and of making symbolic statements about the nature of their country and of life itself. This course examines 'commonplace' or authorless songs as elemental, founding documents of American identity—as a form of speech that is always in flux.'

In April 2017, as part of the Mannes Centennial program at Carnegie Hall, the Mannes Prep Chorus (members aged between four and eighteen) takes the stage to perform 'What the World Needs Now Is Love' by Mannes alumnus Burt Bacharach. The chorus is applauded and, when leaving the stage, high-fived by Mannes luminaries that include Ricky Ian Gordon, Frederica von Stade, and Diana Krall and Elvis Costello.

1911

NEW SCHOOL BULLETIN
66 WEST 12th STREET, NEW YORK 11, N.Y. • VOL. 19, NO. 8, OCT. 23, 1961

In This Issue
ROGER SESSIONS LEADS A REHEARSAL
WRITING COURSES MARK 30th YEAR
100 EDUCATORS TO ATTEND CONFERENCE
HAYDN • SCHOENBERG • KOUSSEVITZKY
November Calendar, pages 5–8

'THE DOOR IS OPEN AND THE WAY IS BROAD.'
↖ **CHARLES BEARD** Founder

'MY BIGGEST DREAM WAS TO GET OUT OF MICHIGAN — TO DISCOVER LIFE BEYOND THE SACRED HEART CONVENT.'
↗ **ELAINE STRITCH** Student

'MY ICONS DO NOT RAISE UP THE BLESSED SAVIOR IN ELABORATE CATHEDRALS. THEY ARE CONSTRUCTED CONCENTRATIONS CELEBRATING BARREN ROOMS. THEY BRING A LIMITED LIGHT.'

↗ DAN FLAVIN Student

LAST OF THE GRADUATE FACULTY

The headline: 'The New School, a Maverick, Gets Ready to Rebuild.'

The New York Times makes a quick rundown of the situation: The New School, with its radical origin, is looking to rebuild the Graduate Faculty, which was the institutional outcome of the University in Exile. A storied chapter of The New School, the University in Exile offered refuge to scholars fleeing Europe in the 1930s. Approximately twenty permanent faculty positions were initiated for the Europeans, and, through temporary positions, the school ushered 181 scholars into faculty postings in higher education nationwide. As the best, most independent, and most original thinkers in Europe were forced overseas, the University in Exile marked a new beginning in the American academy; the Western mantle of history and scholarship had been annexed by the new world. At The New School, the influx of the Europeans elevated the prominence and on-campus presence of faculty, and led to the university's first degrees, Master's and Doctorates in economics, philosophy, political science, psychology, and sociology.

'Leo Strauss used to say that he liked to sit in a corner in the cafeteria to watch the approach of his enemies. But there were no enemies. Everybody was committed to the same purpose.'
↗ MARY HENLE Faculty

Reporting on the retirement of The New School's President, John R. Everett, the *Times* names Mary Henle, of the Psychology Department, as the only active member of the original University in Exile. In fact, Henle had joined the New School in 1946, thirteen years after the Graduate Faculty was introduced. A graduate of Smith College with a PhD from Bryn Mawr and a formidable roster of mentors, Henle had already served as faculty at the University of Delaware, Swarthmore, Sarah Lawrence, and Bryn Mawr, when she was recruited to join The New School's Graduate Faculty. At thirty-three, while highly regarded, she was considerably younger than her peers.

If the *Times* is wrong to call out Henle as original to the Graduate Faculty, it is right to single her out as the school's last best hope. Henle, with the aging of the Graduate Faculty, has taken on much of the departmental weight, and pushed to update the program; she has been a dogged proponent of student scholarships, fellowships, and teaching positions that will advance diversity on campus. Nonetheless, the Graduate Faculty is in real trouble; from 1976 to 1978, primarily due to the retirement and absentia of professors, New York State has threatened to withdraw the accreditation of three departments core to the Graduate Faculty: Philosophy, Political Science, and Sociology.

1982

Previous pages:

Clockwise from top left:

Graduate Faculty, 1974–5, Vol. 31, No. 12

Corner of Fifth Avenue and 12th Street, New York City

Meeting of the Graduate Faculty, *circa* 1950

Mary Henle's talk given to the Psychology Department, February 1, 1979

Graduate Faculty
of Political and Social Science

1974/1975 NEW SCHOOL BULLETIN   VOLUME 31 NUMBER 12 JULY 15, 1974

'The institution of a leisure class has emerged gradually during the transition from primitive savagery to barbarism; or more precisely, during the transition from a peaceable to a consistently warlike habit of life.'
↗ **THORSTEIN VEBLEN** Founder

'Known as the "University in Exile", The New School had taken in a lot of professors — Jewish and non-Jewish — who had fled from Hitler ... We admired the German professors. We had won the fight against fascism and now, with their help, we would defeat all the dark forces in the culture and the psyche.'
↗ **ANATOLE BROYARD** Student and Faculty

'I felt that I had a debt to pay as a survivor. Writing moral philosophy and philosophy of history for me then became a way to pay my debt as a survivor to the people who could not survive. So in this respect my philosophy became a sacrifice but a sacrifice which I enjoyed. And this is not contradictory, I can sincerely say that my whole life became a sacrifice to pay my debt and simultaneously I enjoyed writing philosophy.'
↗ **AGNES HELLER** Faculty

MARY HENLE - TALK TO PSYCH
DEPT - 1979 · @ FEBRUARY

I accepted the assignment to talk about the history of your psychology department because I feel enormously fortunate and proud to be part of the New School, its Graduate Faculty, ~~and its Psychology Departments.~~ I don't know, of course, why each of you chose this graduate school, but I feel sure that when you know more about it you will be as proud of it as I am and feel as fortunate as I do.

I cannot discuss the history of this department without tal[king] about its setting, the New School for Social Research, and the Gr[aduate] Faculty.

The New School was born out of the need for an educationa[l] institution that, as Alvin Johnson later wrote, would be "honest [and] free." It never forgot its origins. The time was after World War [I, a] period of reaction and of academic repression not unlike the McCa[rthy] era that followed World War II. The founding of a new kind of sch[ool] was discussed by a group of liberal scholars: Alvin Johnson, Ja[mes] Harvey Robinson, one of the most distinguished historians of his [day,] Charles A. Beard, a major figure in history and political science, [John] Dewey, whose influence on American philosophy and education y[ou] know, Wesley Mitchell, an economist well known for his theory o[f] business cycles, Thorstein Veblen, best known for his book, <u>The [Theory]</u> of the 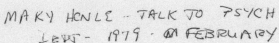 Leisure Class, a scholar once described as "the last m[an] who knew everything." Beard and Robinson had resigned from Co[lumbia] in protest over an issue of academic freedom; Dewey and Mitchell [...]

In 1926, The New School offers the first academic course in psychoanalysis. The course is taught by Freud's associate, Sándor Ferenczi. In 2008, the Department of Psychology establishes the Sándor Ferenczi Center, which is committed to innovation, progressivism, and vitality in the discipline, and an ongoing conversation between psychoanalysis, the social sciences, the humanities, and the arts.

Stanley Diamond, a prominent anthropologist, initiates an anthropology program. The program's 1970 beginnings are fraught with inter-departmental tension. Diamond continues as the Chair of Anthropology for fourteen years.

New School Bulletin | for Spring 1972

Volume 29 / Number 5 / December 31, 1971

SELECTED CHAPTERS IN THE THEORY AND PRACTICE OF PSYCHOANALYSIS, 1926 SÁNDOR FERENCZI

This course is designed primarily to meet the requirements of the intelligent layman, although it will present much material of value to the special student and psychoanalysis practitioner. Among the topics to be discussed are: suggestion and psychoanalysis; the development of the ego and the instincts; the ego and personality; the Freudian metapsychology; the technique of psychoanalysis (transference and resistance); the main forms of neurosis and psychosis; character and its possible changes through psychoanalysis.

MASTER WORKSHOP: PSYCHOLOGICAL PORTRAITURE, 1974 PHILIPPE HALSMAN

The emphasis of the course will be on thinking before any aspect of portrait photography and on the use of every photographic step as a means of reinforcing emotional values. Demonstrations will involve students in all dimensions of portrait lightings and photographic angles. ... The course is aimed at developing the student's awareness of the photographic medium as a means of communication and self-expression.

The *Times*, with its 1982 coverage, is late to the story, and The New School has already added new professors, and sought to reawaken the departments. Henle, in 1983, is conferred an honorary doctorate, in addition to the doctorate and degrees she already has, and on June 3, as she prepares to follow her colleagues into retirement, she addresses her department:

> I did not, of course, belong to what Adolphe Lowe calls the old gang. But I have had the great privilege of witnessing and participating in a large part of the history of the Graduate Faculty. Thinking back on the University in Exile ... It consisted of a handful of immigrant scholars, some of whom knew the English language so little that their courses had at first to be given in German. They found themselves not only in a new country, but in an alien intellectual atmosphere, and they were unfamiliar with the American university.

Henle warns that the rebuilding of the Graduate Faculty will be a challenge, and may even require a miracle, but 'a miracle of good will and dedication ... is nevertheless possible'. She praises her colleagues as 'the most decent and idealistic and devoted faculty I have known', and her students as the best she's had, and as dazzling as the Graduate Faculty itself.

Henle, in emeritus, is listed as faculty until her death in 2007; she's granted emeritus status in multiple organizations, including presidencies for two divisions of the American Psychological Agency, and the presidency of the Eastern Psychological Association. The Guggenheim fellow leaves a voluminous legacy of research and publication (eight books).

'Changing the structure and rules of the global economy will require a mass movement based on messages of compassion, justice, and equality, as well as collaborative and democratic processes ... If we stay positive, inclusive, and democratic, we have a truly historic opportunity to build a global movement for social justice.'
↗ MEDEA BENJAMIN Student

'The peculiar distinction of this faculty was in its European émigré origin and in its dedication to the canon of European, predominantly German, scholarship and deportment. But there is a contradiction latent in all such émigré groups … This paradox is most sharply felt by those scholars who, rightly or wrongly, interpret the Western academic tradition as being necessarily nonpolitical. The academy is their fortress of principled neutrality: as individuals they may choose to take a political position but, as scholars, it is unthinkable and dangerous. This, after all, is the bitter lesson they have learned at home.'
↗ **STANLEY DIAMOND AND EDWARD J. NELL** Faculty

HIGHER EDUCATION FOR MEN & WOMEN

As part of a fundraising campaign to bankroll a progressive experiment in higher education, an organization committee of nineteen members outlines a plan to meet 'the need for an independent school of social science for men and women'. In part a manifesto, in part a diagnosis of society's ills, the committee asserts an educational model that emphasizes women's suffrage, faculty over administration, and learning over hierarchy. The New School is conceived as:

> An institution free from the ancient embarrassments, where well-qualified investigators and thinkers can enjoy the advantage of one another's thought and discoveries, and where they can talk freely upon any theme they judge fit to such grown up and responsible men and women as may wish to seek their instruction. Such a group of teachers and investigators ... would become the center of the best thought in America, would lead in emancipating learning from the narrow trammels of lay boards and trustees, and would be a spirited adventure of the utmost significance. Nothing like it has ever been attempted; this is the hour for the experiment; and New York is the place, because it is the greatest social science laboratory in the world and of its own force attracts scholars and leaders.

SEX IN ETHNOLOGY, 1919
ELSIE CLEWS PARSONS

The course will consist of surveys of a number of societies presenting a distinctive distribution of functions between the sexes, and of topical analyses of the division of labor between men and women; of the divisions in handicrafts, arts and games; of the division in religion and government; of differentiation in dress, speech, and manners; of types of sexual relationship; of the methods of reckoning kinship, and of family organizations.

Clockwise from top left:

▬▬▬ *American Values in Transition: A Reader,* proof of book cover designed by Jeremiah B. Lighter, *circa 1972*

▬▬▬ Mrs. Charles Lewis Tiffany carrying a flag in a suffrage parade, New York City, 1917

▬▬▬ *A Proposal for an Independent School of Social Science for Men and Women, circa 1918*

Of the nineteen members of the original committee, nine are men and ten are women. In order of appearance:

Mrs. George W. Bacon (Caroline Tilden), New School Board Member and a pivotal player in transitioning the school to a financially sustainable model; Mrs. Ruth Standish Baldwin (Bowles), co-founder of the National Urban League and the National League for the Protection of Colored Women; Dr. Charles A. Beard, lauded historian and prolific author espousing a new approach to education and history; Mrs. Henry Bruère (Cornelia Solomea Schoeneich), suffragette, progressive, anti-war organizer, and philanthropist; Mr. Emory R. Buckner, a prominent New York prosecutor and Wall Street lawyer who had been part of a New York City clean-up of the Police Department; Mr. Charles C. Burlingham, President of the New York Bar Association; Mr. Thomas L. Chadbourne, a prominent corporate lawyer who worked toward stabilizing consumer markets during the Depression; Mr. Winston Churchill, British statesman; Mr. Joseph P. Cotton, U.S. Secretary of State; Mr. Herbert Croly, co-founder of *The New Republic*; Mr. Felix Frankfurter, Associate Justice of the Supreme Court; Mrs. Learned Hand (Frances Amelia Fincke), an advocate and patron of education for women; Mr. Alvin Johnson, the first and longtime President of The New School; Mrs. George Haven Putnam (Emily James Smith Putnam), author, classical scholar, and advocate for women's education; Mrs. Raymond Robins (Margaret Dreier Robins), labor leader, progressive activist and organizer, and women's rights advocate; Mrs. Charles C. Rumsey (Mary Harriman), progressive organizer and patron, consumer advocate, and the founder, in 1907, of the Junior League for the Promotion of Settlement Movements, which in 1912 was renamed the Junior League and organized divisionally; Mrs. Willard Straight (Dorothy Whitney), a passionate philanthropist and social reformer, co-founder of *The New Republic*, first President of the Junior League for the Promotion of Settlement Movements, and founding President of the Association of Junior Leagues International; Mrs. Charles L. Tiffany (Katrina Brandes Ely), a suffragette activist; Mrs. Victor Sorchan (Charlotte), the Secretary of the Organization Committee, and a translator, editor, and interior decorator.

'Perhaps my life is nothing but an image of this kind; perhaps I am doomed to retrace my steps under the illusion that I am exploring, doomed to try and learn what I simply should recognize, learning a mere fraction of what I have forgotten.'
↗ **ANDRÉ BRETON** Faculty

MY IDEA OF FEMINISM IS SELF-DETERMINA
IT'S VERY OPEN-ENDED: EVERY WOMAN H
TO BECOME HERSELF, AND DO WHATEVER
↗ **ANI DIFRANCO** Student

MRS. LOUIS C. TIFFANY   4.381-11

'It still holds true that in Germany the fundamental principle is that woman is meant for marriage, while in the United States woman's life is regarded as an end in itself which may find completion without marriage.'
↗ **FRIEDA WUNDERLICH** Faculty

ORGANIZATION COMMITTEE

Mrs. George W. Bacon	Mr. Herbert Croly
Mrs. Ruth Standish Baldwin	Mr. Felix Frankfurter
Dr. Charles A. Beard	Mrs. Learned Hand
Mrs. Henry Bruère	Mr. Alvin Johnson
Mr. Emory R. Buckner	Mrs. George Haven Putnam
Mr. Charles C. Burlingham	Mrs. Raymond Robins
Mr. Thomas L. Chadbourne	Mrs. Charles C. Rumsey
Mr. Winston Churchill	Mrs. Willard Straight
Mr. Joseph P. Cotton	Mrs. Charles L. Tiffany

Mrs. Victor Sorchan, *Secretary*
267 Madison Avenue
New York

'When marriage became frankly proprietary, women were bullied by both economic and religious sanctions into the observance of premarital chastity and conjugal fidelity.'
↗ **ELSIE CLEWS PARSONS (WRITING AS 'JOHN MAIN')** Faculty

1918

'Perhaps the greatest challenge to thinking women is the challenge to move from the desire for safety and approval to the most "unfeminine" quality of all—that of intellectual arrogance, the supreme hubris which asserts to itself the right to reorder the world. The hubris of the god makers, the hubris of the male-system builders.'
↗ **GERDA LERNER** Student and Faculty

VOYEUR TO 'AGENT PROVOCATEUR'

The New Museum initiates its window series at The New School. Over the next two years, window displays by such artists as Mary Lemley, John Ahearn, Laurie Hawkinson, Jeff Koons, David Hammons, and Richard Prince will challenge the passersby on 14th Street.

Two years before, with the assistance of arts executive and prominent New School trustee and benefactor Vera List (presented the inaugural New School President's Medal in 1971), the museum had moved into its first exhibition space at the Social Research Graduate Center, a location that hearkened to the school's historical emergence in the University in Exile. The museum's opening exhibition, *Early Works by Five Contemporary Artists*, featured Ron Gorchov, Elizabeth Murray, Dennis Oppenheim, Dorothea Rockburne, and Joel Shapiro. Marcia Tucker, the founder of the museum, penned the catalogue essay:

> *The artists have no stylistic bonds; rather, their concerns are disparate, their ages varied, their origins diverse. The only unifying characteristic is that their work was, even in its earliest manifestations, idiosyncratic, and remains so today. ... What the five artists have in common, then, is not a shared set of stylistic conventions, but an eschewing of polemic in their work; they are concerned with the clarification of ideas and emotional states, with the support of other artists and ideas which may be different from their own, and with the growth of their own work and ideas in a personal rather than ideological idiom.*

May, 1980, The New Museum's window series at The New School mounts the 'first solo presentation' of works by Jeff Koons. The installation, titled, *The New* displays coarsely lit vacuum cleaners in the series' former storefront windows that are not too different than the actual storefront windows of neighboring businesses.

‘I ALWAYS LIKE TO THINK I'M HAVING A DINNER PARTY, AND I'M THE HOST, AND THE AUDIENCE ARE MY GUESTS.'

↗ CAROLINE RHEA Student

These lectures will deal with painting since 1870. The content of various types of painting will be analyzed in relation to a corresponding content in everyday life. The relations of modern content, form, and society will be verified experimentally in constant comparisons with parallel relations in past arts. It will be shown how the content of art, which appears to have no content or to be indepenent of a necessary content, embodies values, interests, and attitudes which determine also the formal esthetic character; how the value placed on pure seeing, on the enjoyment of abstracted colors and shapes, is related to activities and conditions of modern bourgeois society; how the idealizing of the artist's freedom and his professional world as norms and adequate contexts of individuality is manifested in the content and form of modern painting; and finally, how the artistic character of so-called objective art and of realistic art is conditioned by the practical attitudes and experiences revealed through the content.

HELLO.

We would like to introduce ourselves to those of you we haven't already met. We're THE NEW MUSEUM, located in what was formerly The New School Graduate Art Center.

THE NEW MUSEUM is an independent, not-for-profit organization, formed in January, 1977. It is an exhibition, documentation and information center for new and provocative art. Our first exhibition will open early in November; four exhibitions will follow throughout the year, accompanied by a lecture series and performance events.

Clockwise from top left:

▬ Memoranda introducing New Museum staff, August 25, 1977

▬ Installation view of works by Jeff Koons, *The New*, The New Museum, New York, 1980

▬ Entrance to the New Museum, New York, 1980

▬ Gina Wendkos. *Four Blondes*, 1981. Performance: 14th Street window, The New Museum, New York

▬ Marcia Tucker introducing the panel discussion 'What is the Impact of Homosexual Sensibility on Contemporary Culture?', New School Auditorium, 1982

Founded upon Tucker's dismissal from the Whitney Museum of American Art, The New Museum will become New York City's only museum pledged to contemporary art. Tucker is dedicated to a hands-on, friendships-OK curatorial involvement; her approach is uncomfortable to an historically systemized, hierarchical museum model. Tucker's originating motto for the museum, according to *The New York Times*, is 'Act first, think later—that way you have something to think about.'

For the length of The New Museum's incubation at The New School, Tucker leads an active schedule of events, lecture series, and symposia. With The New Museum's 1983 move to an autonomous space, the window series expands and progresses, and for two decades engages the city and the world. In 1987, ACT UP installs *Let the Record Show*, an up-to-the-moment historical assessment of the AIDS crisis. During its tenure in the window, Erika Rothenberg's installation, *Have You Attacked America Today?*, which offers flag-burning kits and satirical lyrics to the national anthem, is twice defaced by unknown vandals.

'We all have our own personality, unique and distinctive, and at the same time, I think that our own unique and distinctive personality blends with the wind, with the footsteps in the street, with the noises around the corner, and with the silence of memory, which is the great producer of ghosts.'
↗ **OCTAVIO PAZ** Guest Speaker

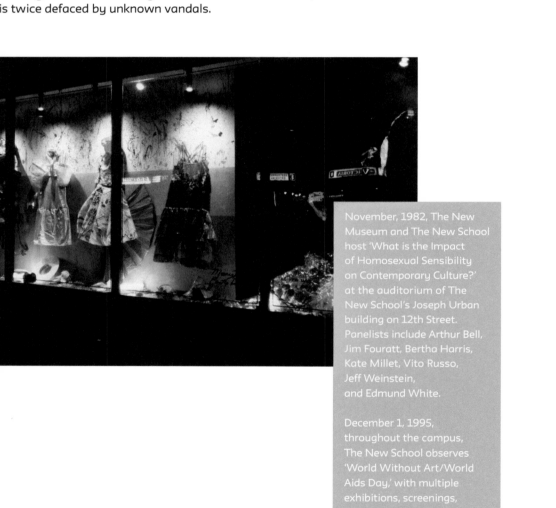

November, 1982, The New Museum and The New School host 'What is the Impact of Homosexual Sensibility on Contemporary Culture?' at the auditorium of The New School's Joseph Urban building on 12th Street. Panelists include Arthur Bell, Jim Fouratt, Bertha Harris, Kate Millet, Vito Russo, Jeff Weinstein, and Edmund White.

December 1, 1995, throughout the campus, The New School observes 'World Without Art/World Aids Day,' with multiple exhibitions, screenings, and performances hosted and sponsored by different organizations, programs, divisions, and administrative arms of the school.

'IT'S GOOD NOT TO HAVE MUCH WHEN YOU ARE YOUNG. IT MAKES YOU INGENIOUS.'
↗ JOSET WALKER Student

Clockwise from top left:

▬▬ Installation view of Mary Lemley's *Party Dresses*. The New Museum, New York, 1979

▬▬ Bonwit Teller window display featuring Women's Ensemble by B.H. Wragge and stuffed lion, 1954

▬▬ Jacob Lawrence, *Dreams # 1*. 1965. *Art Workshops, New School Bulletin, 1967–1968, Vol. 25 No. 1*

LAWRENCE

PAINTING, DRAWING, AND COMPOSITION

ADVANCED CLASS IN PAINTING DRAWING COMPOSITION

**PAINTING, DRAWING, AND COMPOSITION, 1967
JACOB LAWRENCE**

Esthetic problems of the picture plane such as color, line, space, form, and texture. Periodic criticism and demonstrations. ... Students work mostly from the model in various media. Individual instruction and criticism in terms of students' needs, with special emphasis on color and pictorial construction.

**ADVANCED RESEARCH SEMINAR:
ART, MEDIA & TECHNOLOGY
PARSONS PARIS, 2018
CLAIRE MARIETTE
MICHELINE RICHARD**

Research and persuasive argumentation are essential skills for artists and designers who seek to fully develop the imaginative and critical powers. ... Students will enrich their creative practice by embarking on a research project that engages with visual analysis, history, and critical theory. Through the careful analysis of readings, objects, artworks, and films relevant to art, media, and technology, students will gain exposure to key debates in their field as they explore diverse methodologies and formulate individual research questions.

'I see art history, and museums in particular, as a process, an interface, a tool, an "agent provocateur" whose role, rather than being didactic, is to get people to see and think for themselves.'
↗ **MARCIA TUCKER** Curator, Guest Speaker and Lecture Series Coordinator

THE PROGRESSIVE ENCYCLOPEDIA

1930

ECONOMICS OF CAPITALISM, 1932
ALVIN JOHNSON

The nature of capitalism. Contrast with precapitalistic organization. Survivals and supercapitalism. Origin and evolution of capitalism. Effects of increase in stocks of the precious metals; of extension of foreign trade. The destruction of handicraft and domestic production. The problem of markets. Capitalism and colonial policy; capitalism and war. Rise of the industrial working classes. The evolution of credit. The development of the capital market; investment and speculation. Extension of the range of capitalistic conceptions; all property, even intangible, as capital. Tendency toward concentration, industrial and financial. Crises. The labor movement. Government control of capitalistic control of government. The survival power of capitalism.

GESTALT PSYCHOLOGY, 1934
MAX WERTHEIMER

Demonstrations, experiments, discussions. Throughout the course the principal psychological theories, especially the Gestalt theory, will be considered. Introduction: the essential task of psychology.
1. Sensing, perceiving, grasping, understanding. Environment and consciousness. Problems of physiognomy and behavior. Gestalt problems, criteria, and laws. The pathology of perception and understanding.
2. Imagination and memory.
3. Thinking. Facts and theories in the

Five years in the works, compiling over 600 pages of writings by eminent thinkers of the day, the *Encyclopaedia of the Social Sciences* sees the publication of the first of fifteen volumes. (The final volume will be published five years later; the work will remain in print until 1967.)

The *Encyclopaedia* is edited by Edwin Robert Anderson Seligman, an esteemed professor of Political Economy, and Alvin Johnson, the first Director, and later the first President of The New School. Running contrary to conservative currents, the *Encyclopaedia* espouses radical ideas: public responsibility, progressive economics, the primacy of contemporary arts, racial and religious tolerance, gender equality, and international governance. Johnson establishes relationships that will help him to build New School faculty for the next fifteen years. With the University in Exile and the École Libre des Hautes Études, Johnson will not only provide a professional welcome for European scholars fleeing fascist Europe, he will reconvene twentieth-century scholarship—disrupted by totalitarianism—in the upstart city of New York, in the upstart nation of the United States.

The influential volume will be succeeded in 1968 by the *International Encyclopedia of the Social Sciences*.

The New School Art Center Committee requests the pleasure of your company at the preview of the German poster exhibition
Weimar — Nuremberg — Bonn
Art as a Political Weapon
Tuesday, May 7   8 p.m. sharp

at the New School Auditorium • 66 West 12th Street, New York City

Weimar - Nürnberg - Bonn

With the university presidency of Bob Kerrey, The New School increasingly hosts political and political celebrity-guests. In 2004, Al Gore is keynote speaker as part of The New School's Center for Public Scholarship conference, 'Fear, Its Political Uses and Abuses'. Gore emphasizes the necessity for courage in the face of weaponized fear. He also discusses the state of American politics and the use of fear in international policy. In 2005, following his breakout 2004 Democratic National Convention keynote address, future President Barack Obama speaks at an event at The New School's Eugene Lang College. Three years before, Hillary Clinton and New School President Bob Kerrey held a public discourse in the auditorium of The New School's Joseph Urban building; Clinton had visited the school on previous occasions during the office of New School President Jonathan F. Fanton; she would return in 2015 with her run for the U.S. presidency. Other guests include future Vice President Joe Biden, New York City Mayor Michael Bloomberg, and Governor of Pennsylvania Ed Rendell (protestors put a halt to the conversation in the Lang Center). In 2018, Al Gore returns to speak at the Teen Vogue Summit co-hosted by The New School.

AMERICAN PROTEST IN POETRY AND PROSE, 2016
HETTIE JONES

This course will address four categories in which literary response to U.S. political and social positions will be considered: Labor, War, Civil Rights, and Environmentalism. ... There will be relevant video presentations where those can be secured. Reading List (overview): early protest novels on labor history, such as Upton Sinclair's *The Jungle*, Meridel Le Sueur's Depression-era short stories from *Harvest*, the seminal work of Walker Evans, Grace Paley, Philip Levine, and similar writings that center on the changing position of the American worker. Responses to twentieth century and contemporary wars, including the anthology *Poetry Like Bread* and story collection *Redeployment*. Civil Rights includes work by Sonia Sanchez, LeRoi Jones, and others in *SOS: A Black Arts Movement Reader*, the novels of James Baldwin, poetry by Frank O'Hara, Audre Lorde, Muriel Rukeyser, and others. Rachel Carson's *Silent Spring* will be matched to the human cost of pesticide use, works that consider Chavez's United Farm Workers grape strike, Bill McKibben's *The End of Nature*, as well as issues of corporate farming and control that led to Occupy Wall Street and similar nationwide actions.

'ONE CANNOT REFUTE WHAT ONE HAS NOT THOROUGHLY UNDERSTOOD.'
↗ LEO STRAUSS Faculty

'It is time to cease belaboring the colleges for their shortcomings, and turn attention to 'the world.'
↗ ALVIN JOHNSON
First President and Founder

Clockwise from top left:

Al Gore speaking at Teen Vogue Summit at The New School, 2018

Researcher in the library of The New School for Social Research, 1960s

Library desk with stairway, 66 West 12th Street building, undated

Announcement for an exhibition of German posters, *Weimar-Nuremberg-Bonn: Art as a Political Weapon*, 1963

'MOTHER'
THE 'MASTER

MEETS BUILDER'

'There's a line in the picture where he snarls,
"Nobody tells me what to do." That's exactly
how I've felt all my life.'
↗ **MARLON BRANDO** Student

Bennett Cerf, publisher, editor, and a founder of the American publisher Random House, sends a courtesy copy of a new book to political appointee, cheerleader for urban highways, and 'master builder' Robert Moses. Moses writes back: 'I am returning the book you sent me. Aside from the fact that it is intemperate and inaccurate, it is also libelous. ... Sell this junk to someone else. Cordially, Robert Moses.'

    The book, seminal to the twentieth century, is *The Death and Life of American Cities* by Jane Jacobs. Jacobs, with no academic training as an urban planner, has nevertheless mounted an all-out campaign to stop LOMEX, the Lower Manhattan Expressway. The ten-lane superhighway proposes to connect the suburbs in New Jersey to the suburbs in Long Island, designating exits in Manhattan and Brooklyn, and carving the city and existing neighborhoods into isolated, polluted, impoverished, illogical fractions. Moses, as he has throughout his career, intends to relegate the inner city to corporate headquarters, crime and poverty, while expanding suburbia in perpetuity. In the single meeting between Jacobs and Moses, as she will recall to *Metropolis Magazine* in 2001, he grips the rail of a podium in Washington Square Park and howls: 'There is nobody against this—NOBODY, NOBODY, NOBODY, but a bunch of, a bunch of MOTHERS!'

    Jacobs draws vitriolic criticism throughout her career, but, despite her lack of academic degrees, she's embraced as faculty by The New School, where her activism and vision help to inspire a 2.0 in Urban Planning and Urban Policy.

    LOMEX, which was to be Moses' crowning achievement, never gets built.

Clockwise from top left:

▬▬▬ Jane Jacobs atttending a demonstration against the proposed Lower Manhattan Expressway, New York, 1962

▬▬▬ Berenice Abbott, *El at Hanover Square and Pearl Street*, 1936

▬▬▬ Social and urban activist and author Jane Jacobs during a protest, New York, 1964

1961

'My mother grew up with each of her children — whatever your age, that's the age she'd be when she listened to your stories. She never belittled our problems. It made for something permanent and reliable.'
↗ **ESTHER ROLLE** Student

'AND SO FROM THAT, I'VE ALWAYS BEEN FASCINATED WITH THE IDEA THAT COMPLEXITY CAN COME OUT OF SUCH SIMPLICITY.'
↗ **WILL WRIGHT** Student

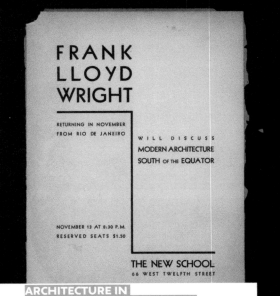

In 1923, The New School offers the first courses in urban planning and architecture. 'Architecture in American Civilization' seeks to 'understand the present position of architecture and city development in America and lay the basis for an intelligent attitude towards the future'. The course is taught by Lewis Mumford, a city planner, and an editor at the literary journal, *The Dial*. Later, Mumford will be a critic at *The New Yorker*. In his book *The Culture of Cities*, Mumford warns against an overemphasis on motorcars in the urban geography, and the disintegration of American cities. Controversial and prescient, *The Culture of Cities* lands Mumford on the April 18, 1938 cover of *Time* magazine.

ARCHITECTURE IN AMERICAN CIVILIZATION, 1923 LEWIS MUMFORD

The first six lectures will cover the historic course of architecture from the colonial dugout to the skyscraper: it will relate the material forms of American civilization to the places, the people, the occupations, the social institutions, the technical knowledge, and the myths by which they have been shaped. The next six lectures will examine the Metropolis, the Suburb, the Provincial Town, and the Region, considered as architectural wholes: and it will discuss the future of these units in the light of such initiatives as the Garden City Movement, housing, industrial decentralization, regional and city planning, elimination of the economic waste, preservation of natural resources, and the promotion of centers of arts and culture.

ARCHITECTURE AND DECORATION, 1931 FRANK LLOYD WRIGHT

American architecture today is in a stage of transition. New requirements, new advances in engineering, new materials have rendered obsolete the styles of 1900. Everywhere there is a tendency to create new styles through adaptation of the old, through amalgamation of various styles, or through sheer invention. There is now an 'international style' which has attracted wide interest, the keynote of which is functionalism. There are tendencies toward the creation of an 'American style'. The object of these lecture discussions is to explore the possibility of developing principles so clear and logical that the architect may proceed, unhampered by any style, to build beautifully and efficiently, and in harmony with the life of the time.

THE CONSUMER AND THE AUTOMOBILE, 1966 RALPH NADER

A special lecture by the author of *Unsafe at Any Speed*.

Clockwise from top left:

New School students inspect a model of the addition to the 66 West 12th Street building, 1955

The New School University Center

Announcement of a lecture by Frank Lloyd Wright, *circa* 1931

Berenice Abbott, *Patchin Place with Jefferson Market Court in Background*, 1937

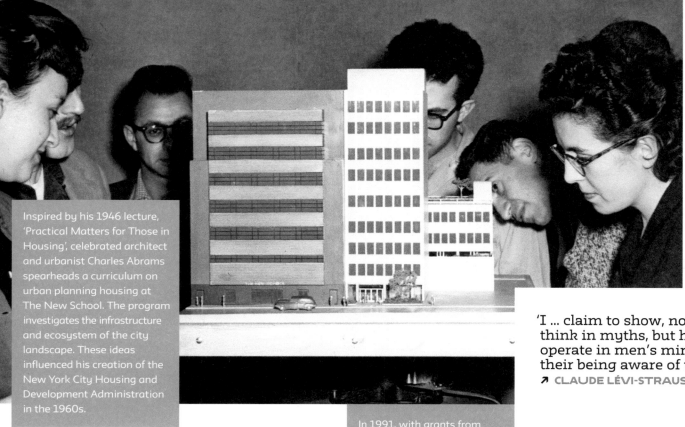

Inspired by his 1946 lecture, 'Practical Matters for Those in Housing', celebrated architect and urbanist Charles Abrams spearheads a curriculum on urban planning housing at The New School. The program investigates the infrastructure and ecosystem of the city landscape. These ideas influenced his creation of the New York City Housing and Development Administration in the 1960s.

'I ... claim to show, not how men think in myths, but how myths operate in men's minds without their being aware of the fact.'
↗ CLAUDE LÉVI-STRAUSS Faculty

In 1991, with grants from M. Kaplan, Revson, and the Andy Warhol Foundation, The New School's Graduate School of Management and Urban Policy opens the Environmental Simulation Center, which will employ computer modeling to assess development outcomes in New York City. The Sim Center offers unbiased applications of advanced, multifaceted simulations to further diplomacy, negotiations, and decision-making on land-use planning; the organization will go on from addressing contentious proposals in New York City parks and the broader urban landscape, to large-scale projects nationwide.

'A city ... is the pulsating product of the human hand and mind, reflecting man's history, his struggles for freedom, creativity, genius — and his selfishness and errors.'
↗ CHARLES ABRAMS Faculty

'I'VE ALWAYS BELIEVED THAT SERVICE TO OTHERS IS RENT WE PAY FOR OUR TIME ON THIS PLANET.'
↗ TONY CURTIS Student

'I think what most shocks me is that what we say publicly about mothers we would not dare say about any other group of people. Too many times to mention I have been at a checkout line in a store with a mother who is trying to cope with a crying child and after she leaves the cashier, who no doubt is a mother herself, will then proceed to bad mouth mothers to all within hearing range. In our culture there is public permission, and I say encouragement, to trash mothers.'
↗ SARA RUDDICK Faculty

'I'VE ALWAYS HAD THIS IN A KIND OF WORST-CASE DARK IMAGINATION. I WANT TO KNOW WHAT THE DARK FORM IN THE WINDOW IS. I WANT TO KNOW WHAT THE NOISE UNDER THE STAIRCASE IS.'

LISA UNGER Student

ANACHRONISMS IN OUR DYNAMIC AGE ... & THE EXTRAORDINARY REVOLUTION

SCHOOL WITH NEW IDEA OPENS TO-DAY

Intended Primarily for Grown-Ups

Practical Methods of Learning Rather Than Scientific Teach-

'I time my swims. Some days I swim way faster, and I don't know why. I notice it, even on a day-to-day basis. It's the same thing with playing guitar.'

↗ MARY HALVORSON Faculty

**THE RELATION OF EDUCATION TO SOCIAL PROGRESS, 1919
JAMES ROBINSON**

The object of this course is to consider the present deficiencies of education as a means of promoting social readjustment. It will include an analysis of the traditional elements in our current system, and attempt to distinguish between those that are vital and those that have become anachronisms in our dynamic age. The great additions to our knowledge ... made during the past quarter of a century will be reviewed, a matter which receives but slight attention in our colleges and universities, and account will be taken of the extraordinary revolution which has during the same period taken place in our social environment, since this, even if there had been no great increase in our knowledge of man, would have rendered a fundamental revision of our educational system essential. Lastly, an attempt will be made to determine the ways in which education should be readjusted so as to forward the reform of existing evils.

**AMERICA IS HARD TO FIND, 2018
JEREMY VARON**

Americans are supremely convinced of their nation's special promise, but also anxious, throughout history, that that promise is being squandered or unfulfilled. And they have bitterly disagreed over the nature of that promise—over what America is and should be. This course offers a theme-based engagement of post-World War II American history that seeks to make more navigable the great national conflicts of our day: those over war and peace; the balance of civil liberty and security; the status of America in the world; the meaning of pluralism; and the purpose and scope of government. We will explore the complexity of the defining events, figures, and debates of the recent past, focusing on the origins and evolution of the Cold War; anticommunism and the counter-subversive tradition; the African-American freedom struggle; the Vietnam War and opposition to it; New Left student and youth movements; New Right conservatism; the politics of globalization; and recent assertions of military power. ... We will listen to music, analyze films and images, read a graphic novel, and immerse ourselves in dialogue with the past.

'OUR HYPOCRISY IS TOO DEEP AND IMPULSIVE FOR US TO DETECT.'

↗ JAMES ROBINSON Founder

'The Constitution was essentially an economic document based upon the concept that the fundamental private rights of property are anterior to government and morally beyond the reach of popular majorities.'
↗ **CHARLES BEARD** Founder

'The thing that makes you exceptional, if you are at all, is inevitably that which must also make you lonely.'
↖ **LORRAINE HANSBERRY** Student

School Solely for Social Research to Open Here Monday

Faculty to Include Educators From Many Big Institutions; Will Aim to Turn Out New Type of Leader

'The study of history reveals that human progress has not been continuous and regular, but intermittent and spasmodic, often depending upon apparently accidental causes.'
↖ **CHARLES BEARD** Founder

Speaking to alumni, President Nicholas Murray Butler of Columbia University expresses his belief that the school must support the Congress and President Woodrow Wilson as the nation joins the fray of World War I. The United States, he explains, as of the declaration of war on Germany, is no longer neutral, and neither can be the university.

The issue of alumni relations, to President Butler, is delicate: in 1911, the dismissal of Professor J.E. Springarn (one of a group of professors who were ousted or who resigned for reasons of politics, academic freedom, educational philosophy, or all three) was viewed critically by alumni. A swiftly acting alumni coalition had published a pamphlet, which collected the correspondence between Butler and the banished professor, and decried the injustice of an institutional lord of higher learning:

He has stifled all manly independence and individuality wherever it has exhibited itself at college. All noble idealism, and all the graces of poetry and art have been shriveled by his brutal and triumphant power. He has made mechanical efficiency and administrative routine the goal of the university's endeavor. The nobler ends of academic life will never be served so long as this spokesman of materialism remains in power.

Four months after the meeting, Columbia University Professors James Cattell and Henry Dana, who publicly oppose the war and conscription, are dismissed. In the fervor that follows, Columbia University Professor Charles Beard resigns. Beard, in *The New York Times*, was negatively reviewed for his 1913 work, *An Economic Interpretation of the United States*, which 'sought to show that the founders of this Republic and the authors of its Constitution were a ring of land speculators who bestowed upon the country a body of organic law drawn up chiefly in the interest of their own pockets'. In stepping away from Columbia, Beard's stance is not in opposition to the war, but in support of free speech and protest, and

in the recognition of conscientious objector status for avowed pacifists. Columbia Professor James Robinson, who former President Theodore Roosevelt has condemned for his 'shameful perversion of historic truth', resigns not long after Beard.

Cattell's 1913 book, *University Control*, called for higher education that eliminated administration and trustees, and granted full power to faculty. While Cattell abandons his academic career, Thorstein Veblen, who had been in Washington working for the president to develop peaceable war settlements, joins the academic faction. In his 1918 work, *The Higher Learning in America*, Veblen finds particular potential in the American university, distinct from the tradition of Europe, and analyzes economic, class, and administrative constraints of the presumed model:

It appears, then, that the intrusion of business principles in the universities goes to weaken and retard the pursuit of learning, and therefore to defeat the ends for which a university is maintained. This result follows, primarily, from the substitution of impersonal, mechanical relations, standards and tests, in the place of personal conference, guidance and association between teachers and students; as also from the imposition of a mechanically standardized routine upon the members of the staff, whereby any disinterested preoccupation with scholarly or scientific inquiry is thrown into the background and falls into abeyance.

With surprising alacrity, Beard, Dana, Robinson, and Veblen go on to realize an ideological model of education in The New School, which opens in Chelsea, in 1919. The first course catalogue begins: 'The New School for Social Research is organized to meet the needs of intelligent men and women interested in the grave social, political, economic, and educational problems of the day.'

SIGNERS OF THE CALL

In 1936, The New School cosponsors the first session and exhibition of the American Artists' Congress, an organization of over 500 members that 'does not demand any political alignments', and states its mission solely as opposing 'war and fascism' and advocating for peace, democracy, and 'cultural progress'. The membership of the AAC is broadly defined, fine artist to commercial artist, and The New School and the New York School of Fine and Applied Art (later, Parsons) are represented heavily in the AAC 'signers of the call'. An incomplete list of artists representing the two schools (some are affiliated with both) tallies Peggy Bacon, Stuart Davis, Camilo Egas, Hugo Gellert, Dorothea Greenbaum, William Gropper, Rockwell Kent, Yasuo Kumiyoshi, Isamu Noguchi, Paul Strand, and William and Marguerite Zorach. The 1936 conference roster includes New Schoolers and New York Schoolers Stuart Davis, Rockwell Kent, Lewis Mumford, José Clemente Orozco, Ralph Pearson, and Meyer Schapiro.

Like The New School, the New York School of Fine and Applied Art is radical in origin. An 1878 splinter of the Art Students League of New York, the school, then called The Chase School, saw a second change of direction in 1902, when Robert Henri bested William Merritt Chase in a public struggle for ascendancy. Only two years later, Frank Alvah Parsons would become the school's Director. Parsons' approach to the arts was notably of the people, with an emphasis on advertising, design, and art as a living, rather than a tangential experience. 'Art is not for the few, for the talented, for the genius, for the rich, nor the church,' Parsons would say in 1920. 'Industry is the nation's life, art is the quality of beauty in expression, and industrial art is the cornerstone of our national art.'

Rockwell Kent, in his 1936 AAC address, argues that creative consciousness is inherently of conscience: 'Artists should be active in the movement against war, for artists, of all people in the world, are most concerned with life. It is by virtue of their love of life in all its manifestations, their love of the life-giving organisms, of the stars and the depths of the heavens toward which the living soul projects itself, of spring, summer, autumn, winter, because these are the seasons ... in all living creatures.'

'I happen to believe that most people — and this is where I differ from many of my contemporaries, or at least as they express themselves — I think that virtually every human being is dramatically interesting.'
↗ **LORRAINE HANSBERRY** Student

Clockwise from top left:

New School art class, 1960s

Chaim Gross with a student, 1950s

A classroom in the 66 West 12th Street building, *circa* 1951

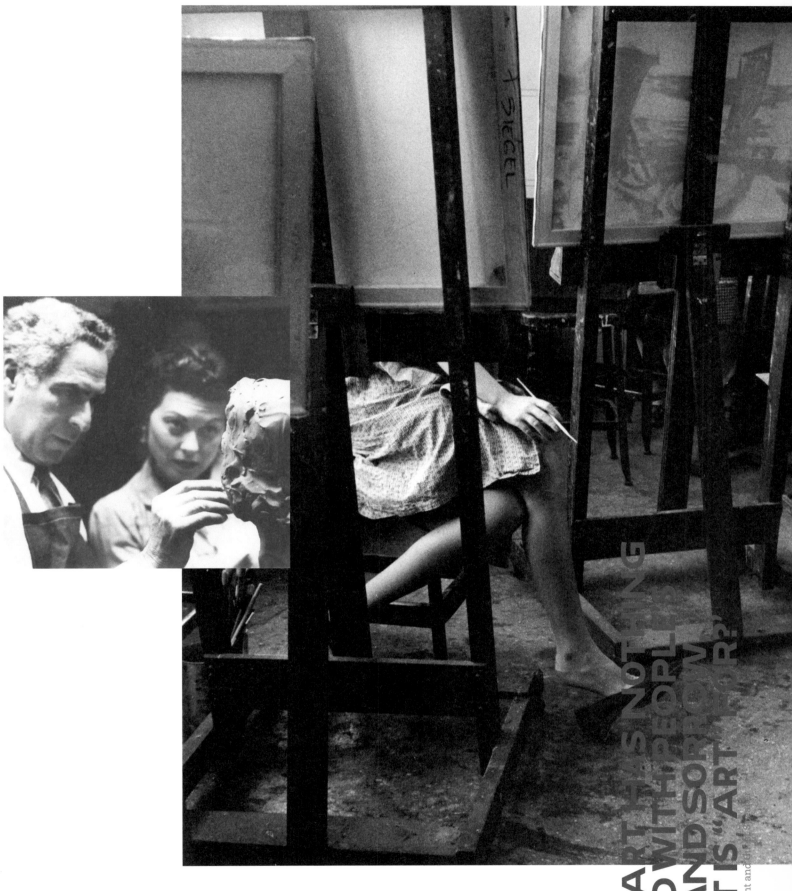

'IF MY ART HAS NOTHING
TO DO WITH PEOPLE'S
PAIN AND SORROW,
WHAT IS "ART" FOR?'
↗ AI WEIWEI Student and artist

'We urge the reconstruction of our school curricula to help root out those
narrow ambitions and ancient animosities that haunt and dominate
Europe and to replace them with a desire for cooperation. Our textbooks
in literature and the social sciences must be rewritten to eliminate
the glorification of war ... let us stress rather the heroes of peace.'
↗ AGNES DE LIMA New School Publicity Director

PROBLEMS OF EVERYDAY LIFE, 1938 KAREN HORNEY

The aim of the course is to show the unconscious motivations of frequent disturbances in our character and other attitudes, such as incapacity to make decisions, self-recrimination, ingratitude, etc., to show the difficulties in recognizing the underlying conflicts and in overcoming them.

1. The need to be perfect; its influences on self-confidence and efficiency.
2. Resentment against ties of limitations. Difficulty in making decisions.
3. Illusions of kindness, goodness, sincerity, unselfishness, rationality, superiority.
4. Self-recrimination; differentiation from helpful insight and the feeling of guilt; its function; its futility.
5. The tendency to put responsibility and blame on others.
6. Feeling unfairly treated.
7. Vulnerability in contact with others; fear of bluff and its discovery.
8. The feeling of not being wanted; timidity; loneliness.
9. The feeling of helplessness. Difficulty in accepting help.
10. Anxiety, helplessness, fatigue, resignation.
11. Attitudes toward sexuality and love.
12. Inhibitions toward work.

'It never entered my mind to teach in any other place in New York City than The New School, nor is it likely that any other school would have accepted me, since my work and ideas are controversial.'
↖ **JOHN CAGE** Student and Faculty

EXHIBITION

Prior to the retrospective concert on May 15, a selection of John Cage's scores will be exhibited at the Stable Gallery, 924 Seventh Avenue.

The preview will be held on Monday evening, May 5, from 9 to 12 p.m.

In 1951, at the height of his career, French couturier Christian Dior is a visiting designer at Parsons. During his time with students, he offers critiques of academic projects and shares his innovative construction techniques.

In February, 2015, The New School's Center for Public Scholarship hosts 'The Fear of Art'. The keynote speaker of the thirty-second Social Research conference, Ai Weiwei, is videoed in; at the time, he is forbidden by Chinese authorities to leave China. The human rights and censorship discussions draw a global representation of speakers and panelists: artists, writers, critics, activists, curators, editors, publishers, and lawmakers.

Clockwise from top left:

▬▬▬ Christian Dior visits Parsons School of Design, 1951

▬▬▬ Parsons School of Design, 1972–3

▬▬▬ Parsons School of Design student work, 1973

▬▬▬ Karen Horney teaching a class at the 66 West 12th Street building, 1930s

▬▬▬ Parsons School of Design student work, 1973

▬▬▬ Parsons School of Design student work, 1973

▬▬▬ Announcement for an exhibition of John Cage's musical scores, Stable Gallery, New York, 1958

In 1978, Parsons initiates a Masters of Fine Arts with concentrations in Painting, Sculpture, and Printmaking. The program is conceptualized on the Atelier model revisited throughout the century by Parsons and The New School, with fifty-six of sixty-four credit hours committed to the studio.

'Well, in high school, you see ... I started getting the art magazines. I started reading American Artist. You see, I was interested in commercial art. My only exposure to fine art had been those terrible Victorian paintings. That, to me, was fine art. Whereas commercial art was, you know, Norman Rockwell and all the stuff in the magazines. That stuff was so much more lively.'
↗ **RED GROOMS** Student

'The first stirrings of dissatisfaction and the first intimations of a better future are always found in works of art. The impregnation of the characteristically new art of a period with a sense of different values than those that prevail is the reason why the conservative finds art to be immoral and sordid, and is the reason why he resorts to the products of the past for esthetic satisfaction.'
↗ **JOHN DEWEY** Founding Faculty

LIFE

The five lightbox panels compile the 2,128 covers of *Life* magazine published from 1936 to 1996. *Searching for Africa in LIFE* evidences America's attitude toward Africa for a span of sixty years. The work, one of the four site-specific installations commissioned by The New School for the University Center, is unveiled in the Arnhold Forum Library. 'Throughout the magazine's sixty-year circulation, there were only a handful of covers depicting Africa,' explains the artist, Alfredo Jaar, at the ceremony, 'and those depictions are painful stereotypes which ignored a vast continent's cultural richness and racial diversity.' The year 1996, the end date of the reckoning, is concurrent with Jaar's inception of the work; *Life* magazine sputtered to an end four years later, in 2000.

'I am not naturally inclined to history or geography —maybe that's why I like to sing about it, because it helps me remember.'
↗ **SUFJAN STEVENS** Student

'Anyone can get dressed up and glamorous, but it is how people dress in their days off that are the most intriguing.'
↗ **ALEXANDER WANG** Student

Clockwise from top left:

▬▬▬▬ Alfredo Jaar, *Searching for Africa in LIFE* (detail), 1996 / 2014. Five color transparencies (Duratrans), Plexiglas. LED lightboxes. The New School Art Collection

▬▬▬▬ Alfredo Jaar, *Searching for Africa in LIFE* (detail), 1996 / 2014. Five color transparencies (Duratrans), Plexiglas. LED lightboxes. The New School Art Collection

'IT IS THE SURFACE I AM INTERESTED IN. BECAUSE THE SURFACE IS THE INSIDE.'

↗ **LISETTE MODEL** Faculty

THE QUESTION OF 'THE OTHER': HUMAN DIVERSITY IN MULTICULTURAL PERSPECTIVE, 1993
SUMITA CHAKRAVARTY

Issues of cultural diversity, of identity and difference, have emerged as among the most contentious of our time. They have been addressed by philosophers and political thinkers, artists and activists, whose contributions now constitute a rich legacy of thought on the dilemmas and paradoxes of the modern condition. Many of their works—by turns fascinating and poignant, angry and ambivalent—throw light on such topics as decolonization, ethnicity, the problem of diasporic peoples, the intermingling of cultures, and the transcendence of boundaries.

RETHINKING 'AFRICA': FROM DEVELOPMENT TO AFROCENTRISM, 2019
JACQUELIN KATANEKSZA

This course will investigate the epistemological foundations of development, the role of foreign interventions, and the foundational role of Africa in Western thought, in order to consider pathways into more Afrocentrically focused ways of being. From so-called natural disasters such as drought and famine, to the perception of 'failed states' and corrupt dictators, Africa is consistently represented as a place in need of 'outside' assistance. Through the Arab trans-Saharan and European transatlantic slave trades, to European colonialism, to post-World War II 'development', the relationship of Africa to the rest of the world has wavered between the twin pulls of exploitation and aid. Many scholars have asked whether foreign aid practices have actually done more harm than good on the continent. These scholars have been historicizing, politicizing, and destabilizing the seemingly stable discourse (and industry) of Western-style development. In this class we will draw on the work of scholars engaged in critical resistance to conventional development discourse to examine the role that foreign interventions on the continent play in contemporary economic, social, and political realities in Africa. We will go on to examine the foundational role of Africa in Western historical and philosophical thought, and various African sociopolitical visions of the future, looking specifically at indigenous knowledge systems as potential entry points into Afrocentric alternatives to development. We will develop skills to critically assess the historical effects of international intervention on the continent, asking what kinds of social realities are made possible, and which are possibly foreclosed, as a result of these practices.

The New School's Film, TV, and Radio Department is launched in 1948:
We expand these studies during a period when the informational arts of the world are under fire from many directions. It is not by chance that the sharp conflicts of our time come into focus in questions about these arts. Now, more than ever, the kind of spirit and mind that can make good movies and television and radio is exactly the kind of heart and brain the world needs to make truth prevail in all the arenas of human struggle and aspiration.

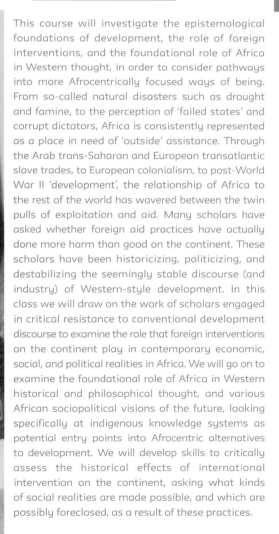

'Regardless of where many of us believe we land — in that field encumbered by not too much baggage or entirely too much — we all come from the same place, which is a road rutted by experience so banal, nearly remarkable, that memory tricks us into remembrance of it again and again, as if experience alone were not enough. What are we to do with such a life, one in which we are not left alone to events — love, shopping, and so forth — but to the holocaust of feeling that memory, misremembered or not, imposes on us?'

↗ **HILTON ALS** Student, Faculty and Honorary Degree Recipient

LIFE & VIBE

Life magazine seeks to reimagine itself, returning to regular circulation as a newspaper supplement. In *Life*'s second incarnation, 2004 to 2007, the Director of Photography is George Pitts, Parsons faculty, and the founding Director of Photography at *Vibe* magazine. *Vibe*, Pitts recalls to the Society of Publication Designers in 2009, 'enabled editors including myself to engage in an international discourse with a wide, disparate range of readers: the core fan base of hip-hop generation readers, popular music lovers, style and culture mavens, hipsters of all stripes, photography connoisseurs, serious musicologists, black culture militants, and scholars of all kinds'.

From 1998 to 2017, Pitts is integral to the study of photography at Parsons. During his two decades on campus, he serves as Director of Photographic Practices and Department Chair, and teaches popular courses such as 'Picturing Sexuality', ' Photography and Cinema', and 'Portraiture and Context'. Ryan McGinley, Pitts' former Parsons student, would remember his teaching, style, and creative philosophy at Pitts' 2017 memorial:

> When I was at Parsons in 2001, George taught a class called 'Nudity, Sexuality, and Beauty and Photography'. He was then Vibe magazine's photo director, so he held his class in his office after hours, since he was so busy. I took the elevator up, stepped out and walked through the doors of Vibe, with the two big lightboxes on either side, one of Mary J. Blige and the other of Nas. ... I learned that day about a German photographer who shot nude, handmade, life-size female dolls in the 1930s [Hans Bellmer]. The fact that we were learning about a surrealist photographer in a hip-hop office felt a bit contradictory, and I soon enough learned that was George's personality and artistry. George was about the aesthetics and cultures colliding. I was already halfway there by bringing my skateboard, punk rock, and graffiti style to the gay aesthetic. George was bringing refined dandyism and feminism to the pages of Vibe as their photo editor. We understood each other intuitively and immediately. It helped that I came to his first class wearing a yellow Cramps T-shirt. He took out his polaroid, shot my photo and said, 'The Cramps, huh? We're gonna get along just fine'.

'You have to find someone who believes in you and who will help you find that time where you don't have to think about a job but just making work.'
↗ **RYAN MCGINLEY** Student

In a 2013 interview with *WHACK!* magazine, Pitts offers an enduring word to future artists:

> Learn what your sensibility is about, and put as much of your essential self into your work as you can muster. Tap into as many dimensions of your talent as you can. Treat people with reverence, kindness, and compassion, including yourself. Learn as much from your mistakes as you do from your moments of so-called success. Cultivate your health, and sense of patience, realizing that it can take time for your full talent to come together eloquently.

In 2016, Pitts published his first, and only volume of poetry, *Partial Objects*, which compiled writings from *The Paris Review*, *The Partisan Review*, and other publications. In 'The Model', he writes:

> Before moving on to the final pictures, the models took a cigarette break, wandering brazenly without their skirts, with the odd bustles still attached to their waists, as the weather followed them, smitten by their daring, and the camera followed too, able to record on its own, suddenly free of the ventriloquist that directed its previous course of action.

THE MEANING OF MUSIC, 1934
CHARLES SEEGER

To the average educated American who has not been especially educated in music, the experience of music is not so much an abstract or philosophical, as a concrete, individual matter. Usually the basic criterion is personal feeling. Many people believe that increased musical knowledge leads to increased capacity to appreciate the varieties of musical experience. Musical values are to be sure dependent upon technical considerations, but they are to an equal extent dependent upon non-technical ones. In this approach the layman can be at least as proficient as the musician, provided he can bring to bear his own special aptitudes. Music needs this interest and support. This course, therefore, is designed for those who must, or can, approach music, even its technique, from a non-technical standpoint. Only on such a basis is it possible for musicians and laymen to meet upon fairly equal terms. There will be music each session.

HIP-HOP DANCING, 2004
JORGE PABON
(POPMASTER FABEL)

Learn two of the most exciting dance forms of the seventies funk movement: Popping and Locking. When these dances debuted on *Soul Train*, they took America by storm and influenced many early Hip-Hop dancers. Popping/Boogaloo style is a robotic dance form featuring both fluid and sharp angular movements that create illusions. Locking is a funky dance that incorporates points, wrist rolls, hand claps, and locks. We cover the foundations of the

'I had seen the Tennessee Williams works, all those plays that I was told were Williams. I found them interesting to look at, to listen to, but I didn't find them very compelling. I was compelled by 17, 18 years old. I'm learning. I did not reject them but didn't find them compelling. Yet I would go to a black church and I was turned completely out by the experience. And it was doing the same thing. It had text, it had music, it had different people dancing in the aisles, song. The text was quite elaborate'.
↗ **PAUL CARTER HARRISON** Student

Clockwise from top left:

Portrait of George Pitts.
Ryan McGinley, 2009

Cover of *Vibe* Magazine featuring Snoop Dogg.
September, 1993

Cover of *LIFE* Magazine featuring Jay-Z, November 2006

PICTURING SEXUALITY, 2016
GEORGE PITTS

This course examines the photographic representation of the female and male body from the nineteenth century to the present. The course is a passionate, analytical, and rigorous study of how the body has been depicted, perceived, and mediated in art via the many genres and diverse periods of photography. We will explore the evolution of the image of the body and sexuality in photography. The photography and films we will study include examples from the following contexts: nineteenth-century ethnographic and Victorian work; Modernist and global contemporary work; with a specific focus on Surrealism, fashion, documentary, portraiture, conceptual, and fine art practices throughout the world. Editorial photography, and cinema that overlaps historically with specific eras, will be viewed to enhance historical perspectives about those ideas associated with divergent aesthetics.

'So we are not as good as we should be, not as good as we could be. We will try to extend our grasp of 'other' mothers' lives. And perhaps when we do, we will find that some mothers, acting together and deliberately on behalf of all their children, can weaken just a little the forces of violence that are aimed against us and the forces of destruction that are sometimes aimed by us.'
↗ **SARA RUDDICK** Faculty

'WHENEVER I BECOME ABSORBED IN THE BEAUTY OF A FACE, IN THE EXCELLENCE OF A SINGLE FEATURE, I FEEL I'VE LOST WHAT'S REALLY THERE.'
↗ **RICHARD AVEDON** Student

'When I first wanted to take their picture, they would be antagonistic, but as soon as I would explain, or briefly explain what the pictures were for and what I intended, they were cooperative. There was one time when they weren't, when I was driven out, which was in South Carolina, and I made the mistake of being too conspicuous, I think, in my dress and in my appearance. I had a convertible and I had the top down; I was — this was early in the game — I learned — but I had been in the sun a lot and I was quite brown and I had a very bright-colored scarf, head scarf, which I had gotten in Europe. I had on some kind of jangly earrings, and I didn't realize what I must have looked like, and I went into this area, with my car loaded with stuff, and I literally frightened the people. They began dragging their kids away, and thought that I was going ... that I was a gypsy, only a modern gypsy in an automobile, and that I would come in and kidnap their children.'
↗ **MARION POST WOLCOTT** Student

'I can feel the music in me. I see dust and earth and rain and feet stomping. Sweat and good-good all over the stage. Sure, I may not know what the story is, but it has been sitting in my soul forever.'
↗ **DONNETTA LAVINIA GRAYS** Student and Faculty

'AFTER A WAR, CIVILIZATION FEELS LIKE A LUXURY, AND PEOPLE WENT TO THE NEW SCHOOL THE WAY YOU GO TO A PARTY, ALMOST LIKE GOING ABROAD. EDUCATION WAS CHIC AND SEXY IN THOSE DAYS. THE PEOPLE IN THE LOBBY OF THE NEW SCHOOL WERE EXCITED, EXPECTANT, DRESSED TO THE TEETH. THEY STRUCK POSES, EXAMINED ONE ANOTHER WITH APPROVAL. THEY HAD A BLIND DATE WITH CULTURE, AND ANYTHING COULD HAPPEN.'

↗ ANATOLE BROYARD Student and Faculty

TO BRING THE WORLD

1918

'WOMEN'S HISTORY IS THE PRIMARY TOOL FOR WOMEN'S EMANCIPATION.'

↗ **GERDA LERNER** Student and Faculty

Previous pages:

Patti Smith, 1970s

Clockwise from top left:

Social activist and philanthropist Dorothy Payne Whitney, *circa* 1910

Manhattan delegates march in the Woman Suffrage Party parade, New York, 1915

John Dewey, a philosopher and educational reformer associated with the inception of multiple schools, The New School among them, considers the place of the arts in 1932, late in his career, with a series of lectures delivered at Harvard University. Two years later, the lectures are collected in *Art as Experience*, in which Dewey concludes: 'Art is a mode of prediction not found in charts and statistics, and it insinuates possibilities of human relations not to be found in rule and precept, admonition and administration.'

WRITING OF FICTION: NOVEL, NOVELLA, SHORT STORY, 1975 MARGUERITE YOUNG

Fiction as the art of human nature in all its diversities, with emphasis on the beauty and power of language as the vehicle of personal expression; uses of metaphor, musical phrasing, and sentence structure, variations of style. Emphasis on poetic or artistic and psychological acclimatization of the writer toward the subject; close scrutiny of creative processes in each individual; choice and evaluation of material out of which fiction can evolve; assistance in organic handling of this material.

CONTEMPORARY MUSIC AND NIGHTLIFE IN NEW YORK CITY, 1981 LISA ROBINSON

For many New Yorkers, the city never sleeps. This course examines what goes on onstage and backstage in New York's top rock clubs, concert halls, dance clubs, and discos. How has the New York music scene changed? What makes the top recording artists choose to perform at only certain clubs? Is the recording industry responsive to the often outrageous creativity of the New York music scene? Who are the behind-the-scenes disk jockeys who decide what music New Yorkers dance to? How does the music nightlife influence fashion? Participants include Steve Rubell, former owner, Studio 54; Halston, fashion designer; Fran Lebowitz, author, *Metropolitan Life*, *Social Studies*; Neil Bogart, President, Boardwalk Entertainment Company; Jerry Brandt, Director, The Ritz; David Geffen, movie producer, President, Geffen Records; and surprise rock star guests. Included is a visit to one or more of New York's top clubs.

At twenty years old, Dorothy Payne Whitney (later Straight, then Elmhirst) is elected as the first President of the Junior League for the Promotion of Settlement Movements. She serves for two years, until 1909. She is one of the wealthiest women in the country, and her patronage of education, the arts, and political change will take her to the international presidency of the league in 1921, and to roles expanding women's freedom, the rights of Native Americans, philanthropy and war relief, and the founding and humanizing of academic institutions.

In 1914, with her husband Willard Straight (whom she married in 1911), and author Herbert Croly, she cofounds *The New Republic*. When anti-fascist faculty members are dismissed from Columbia University, and fellow professors resign in protest, she commits $10,000 a year for ten years to the proposal of a new school. The institution is the fruition of a conversation that she's been a part of since 1916, and her pledge disregards the admonition of her husband, who is wary of the radical cadre of academics. Advertised in December, 1918, in *The New Republic*, The New School 'is organized to meet the needs of intelligent men and women interested in the grave social, political, economic and educational problems of the day'. The copy will be reprised in the opening sentences of the first catalogue of courses.

Whitney intends the Junior League to offer The New School curriculum to its membership; she nearly resigns her presidency when the league, deeming the institution too overtly political, chooses Columbia University's women's college, Barnard, as a more appropriate educational satellite. Persisting in the principle of education for 'men and women', The New School asserts in its preliminary petition for funds and statement of purpose: 'The granting of the suffrage to women and the extension of women's interest into new and important spheres of public life will lead them to seek a better equipment both for power and service.' The 1920 passage of the Nineteenth Amendment to the United States Constitution will guarantee 26 million U.S. women the right to vote.

Enrollment for The New School's first semester is 70% women. In an advertising move that is perhaps sexist, perhaps directed toward student prospects who are primarily single, perhaps a disassociation with the Junior League and educational efforts borne of the women's movement (such as Chicago's Hull House), the school boasts the enrollment is '30% men'.

Through the 1920s, The New School chases enrollment in popular subject areas, developing an academic profile that extends well beyond the social sciences. The arts find robust student engagement, and The New School broadens its mission to political, educational, and creative actualization.

'IN ALL MY WORK, I'M INTERESTED IN TRYING TO UNDERSTAND THE HUMAN CONSEQUENCES OF GOVERNMENT POLICIES.'

↗ LAURA POITRAS Student

'ONLY IMAGINATIVE VISION ELICITS THE POSSIBILITIES THAT ARE INTERWOVEN WITHIN THE TEXTURE OF THE ACTUAL.'

↗ JOHN DEWEY Founding Faculty

September, 1946, a callout in the books section of The New York Times announces that W.H. Auden will be offering a course on Shakespeare at The New School. 'Mr. Auden has announced that in his course, which runs through both semesters, he proposes to read all Shakespeare's plays in chronological order'. The offering, held in the auditorium in the Joseph Urban building, is attended to capacity. Auden, who lives in the Greenwich Village, near the school, holds a discussion class on Saturday for credit students.

In the late 1950s, emerging Japanese composer Toshi Ichiyanagi enrolls in John Cage's signature New School course, Experimental Composition. Ichiyanagi's partner (his wife as of 1956), Yoko Ono, who also has classical music training, tags along to audit the class. While Ono and Ichiyanagi separate soon after, the three artists-composers will collaborate and exchange ideas from that time forth, in publication, music, and performance.

December, 1957, Robert Frost visits The New School to read some of his poems and 'reflect' upon them. He had lectured at the school in the 1930s.

'The ten male photographers with whom I was to work immediately put out their cigarette butts in my developer, spit in and hypoed it, probably peed in it. … Finally, I exploded — telling them I was there to stay.'
↗ **MARION POST WOLCOTT** Student

Whitney's first husband is a romantic figure of the day, a handsome, progressive idealist who has risen from humble missionary to international man of finance and influence; at the end of World War I, while serving in the U.S. armed forces in France, he dies of influenza. In December, 1925, dedicating a student center that she conceived and financed at Cornell University, his alma mater, Whitney speaks to her philosophy of the arts as a freeing influence in education: 'The arts intensify and dramatize life for us and include us in experience which might otherwise remain outside our range of knowledge and feeling. For that reason we welcome the theater here as basic to the life of this little society, and we trust that the other arts will also become the vehicles through which this community will get itself expressed'. While working toward the completion of the student center, Whitney meets and eventually marries another Cornell alumnus — a young Englishman named Leonard Elmhirst. Together, they go on to found Dartington Hall, a progressive school and center for the arts in Devon, England.

As of the early 1930s, Whitney is listed on The New School's Board of Directors. Now located in Greenwich Village, The New School is a convergence of academic and cultural pursuits, and a seemingly inexhaustible cohort of prominent faculty. Students study architecture with Frank Lloyd Wright; literature with W.H. Auden, Pearl Buck, and Robert Frost; art history with Horace Kallen and Meyer Schapiro; art with Thomas Hart Benton, Stuart Davis, Camilo Egas, Yasuo Kuniyoshi, José Clemente Orozco, Ralph Pearson, and Marguerite Zorach; photography with Berenice Abbott and Edward Steichen; music with Aaron Copland; and dance with Martha Graham and Doris Humphrey.

Into the 1960s, The New School, along with Greenwich Village, enter a golden age of thought and creativity. Whitney-Straight-Elmhirst continues to support and contribute to The New School, and to be a prominent figure until her death in 1968.

'I HAD TO FIGURE OUT HOW TO BRING THE WORLD INTO MY WORK.'
↗ BARBARA KRUGER Student

Clockwise from top left:

▬▬▬ John Cage, Yoko Ono, and David Tudor performing *Music Walk*. Tokyo, Japan, October 9, 1962

▬▬▬ Cellist and performance artist Charlotte Moorman and artist and composer Nam June Paik during a performance in New York, January 18, 1966

**WOMEN IN
THE AVANT-GARDE, 2019
TERRI GORDON**

This course examines the pivotal role of women in the European avant-garde movements of the twentieth century. Women are often seen as the models and muses of their male contemporaries in the groundbreaking movements of the twentieth century. Yet they were also creators and pioneers in their own right. In this course, we study the multiple ways in which women contributed to the twentieth-century vanguard, the personal and political stakes involved in forging new territory in art and culture, the pain and suffering that often attended their revolutionary efforts, and the artistic legacies they have left. Themes include the nexus of art and politics, sexuality and gender violence, war and madness, and suffering and creativity. We study Italian Futurism, German Expressionism, Dada, Surrealism, and other movements at the vanguard of European culture, politics, and art. The course covers the literary genres of poetry, prose, and drama and the artistic genres of painting, photography, collage, and photomontage. We also read 'founding' documents, such as manifestoes and political tracts.

NEW ATTITUDE

In 1927, literary critic, member of the Stieglitz circle, and Greenwich Village scenester Gorham Munson joins the faculty of The New School, where he will remain for over thirty years. In the fall of 1931, he offers two courses. In his 'A New Attitude Toward American Letters', he proposes to 'break free' from a literature dominated by the past or the present. In 'The Art of Writing Prose', he takes an editorial segment of his classes one step further: students will read and discuss their own work. Munson has no certainty as to the feasibility of a salon-style writing group in an academic setting, and in his 1949 how-to, *The Written Word*, which collects curricular material from two decades at The New School, he reflects upon the course that he viewed as a prototype: 'I planned to give it only once, but it met with unexpected popularity and I was urged to repeat it; I have repeated it ever since.'

The course is the first academic creative writing workshop; in 1934, Munson will adopt a more evolved course description. Since The New School's 1931 move to a dedicated, larger building, the curricular offerings have augmented lecture courses with 'workshops', which are experiential — learning by doing, rather than learning by study or observation. The New School's 1931 catalog boasts: 'Workshop courses are offered in architecture, art and design, drama, writing, music, dance, and marionettes.' Many of the workshop selections are arguably firsts, and, by 1934, the school has persisted in a vanguard of trials: workshops venture into, for example, graphic arts, photography, enameling, poster art, and physics.

Writing at The New School thrives; faculty, alumni, and former students are an encyclopedic representation of literature through the twentieth century. Adding areas of focus, the mid-century writing workshops produce hundreds if not thousands of well-published books, and the school publishes the literary journal *12th Street*, and two semiannual anthologies, *American Vanguard* and *New Voices*. (Anatole Broyard writes about the late 1940s, Greenwich Village, and the courses he took at The New School in his memoir *Kafka Was the Rage*.) At the same moment, James Baldwin and Tennessee Williams attend classes at The New School's Dramatic Workshop. A few notable mid-century students of writing at The New School include Madeleine L'Engle, Jack Kerouac, Mario Puzo, William Styron, and Sigrid De Lima, daughter of Alvin Johnson and Agnes De Lima, an early *New Republic* editor and Publicity Director for The New School, 1940–60. In 1953, *The Nation*'s literary critic observes: 'The New School has become the richest center of new fiction among all our colleges and universities.' Through the second half of the century, the school continues to draw extraordinary talents; a student of the 1960s sees course offerings by Amiri Baraka, Kay Boyle, Kenneth Koch, Robert Lowell, Frank O'Hara, and Marguerite Young.

'ONE WRITES TO MAKE A HOME FOR ONESELF, ON PAPER, IN TIME AND IN OTHERS' MINDS.'

↗ **ALFRED KAZIN** Faculty

LESSONS IN THE MODERN DANCE, 1931 DORIS HUMPHREY

This will be a practical course in the dance in which Miss Humphrey will give instruction in the fundamental principles and movements of the modern dance.

CONTEMPORARY NOVELISTS, 1931 GORHAM MUNSON

The novel is the great literary form of our age. Of comparatively recent growth, it is still seeking to fulfill its various possibilities. Conventions are made in it only to be loosened and abolished by a new generation of artists. This course of lectures aims to isolate the various exciting and often perplexing trends in the recent novel by a study of the individuals who exemplify these trends.

THE BOUNDS OF POETRY, 1931 ROBERT FROST

The method of this course, as appropriate to an inquiry into pure poetry, will be one of sounding for meanings, rather than one of general analysis. Some attention will be given to the parties of poetry, since the poet cannot create in isolation, without cooperation in the spirit; to sense and music in poetry; to the truth of the metaphor; to the capacity of poetry to transcend all boundaries. Because the truth about poetry is infinitely subtle, all formal requirements of the lecturer's procedure are excluded. The program of each session will _____ order that _____ eeds of his _____ the means

1931

'STORYTELLING REVEALS MEANING WITHOUT COMMITTING THE ERROR OF DEFINING IT.'
ⁿ HANNAH ARENDT Faculty

Clockwise from top left:

▬▬▬▬ *Styles for Writing*, book cover sculpture and proof designed by Jeremiah B. Lighter, *circa* 1972

▬▬▬▬ Class sessions, 1950s

THE STUDIO THEATRE
ERWIN PISCATOR, DIRECTOR

UNITY THROUGH THE DANCE

DANCE FESTIVAL
Presented By
MARIA LEY-PISCATOR

THE STUDIO THEATRE OF THE NEW SCHOOL

66 West Twelfth Street   May 28, 1943   New York

With the proliferation of creative writing Master's programs, and competing to retain its own celebrated faculty, in 1996, The New School and founding Creative Writing Director Robert Polito initiate a Master of Fine Arts program. Early faculty includes Hilton Als, Lucy Grealy, Amy Hempel, A.M. Homes, David Lehman, Rick Moody, George Plimpton, Francine Prose, Dani Shapiro, and Darcey Steinke. Early guests include A.A. Ammons, John Ashbery, Evan Boland, Kamau Brathwaite, Lucille Clifton, Robert Creeley, Allen Ginsberg, Louise Gluck, Daniel Halpern, Carolyn Kizer, Kenneth Koch, Stanley Kunitz, Philip Levine, Octavio Paz, Mark Strand, Charles Tomlinson, David Wagoner, and Eliot Weinberger.

BODY WORK, 1931
MARIA LEY-PISCATOR

Body training includes the study of every phrase of gesture in order to give the necessary foundation to the spoken work and to make the body the ready instrument of the mind.

ENGLISH POETRY FROM WYATT TO YEATS, 1934
NAT LOWELL

The poems are studied as poems and only a few are taken up at each meeting. The first half year goes as far as Pope, possibly including him. The second half year covers the late eighteenth century, the Romantics, the Victorians, and a few early moderns. The method is technical and poetic rather than scholarly.

In 1981, the ten-part series Conversations with Writers invites such notables as Richard Price, Louis Auchincloss, Bernadette Mayer, Stephen King, William S. Burroughs, Carlos Fuentes, Derek Walcott, Ishmael Reed, Quincy Troupe, Ann Beattie, Alice Notley, Toni Morrison, and Toni Cade Bambara.

In 1994, Barnes & Noble opens its first superstore, a six-story building at historic Union Square. The store invites New School writing professors to showcase recent publications. The sixth-floor event space is still used to feature work from New School professors, alumni, and students. The Riggio Honors program employs the space for the annual release of its award-winning literary magazine, and historical reprisal, *12th Street.*

alumni
PARSONS SCHOOL OF DESIGN
DECEMBER, 1961

'THE FUNCTION OF POETRY IS TO POINT OUT THAT THE SIGN IS NOT IDENTICAL TO THE REFERENT.'
↗ ROMAN JAKOBSON Faculty

Clockwise from top left:

Pictorial journalism class in the Thomas Hart Benton mural room of The New School, 1950

Program for *Unity Through the Dance* Dance Festival, presented by Maria Ley-Piscator, May 28, 1943

Alumni Parsons School of Design, December 1, 1961

**POETRY WORKSHOP,
FALL 1960–SPRING 1961
KENNETH KOCH**

Student poems are read in class and criticized in detail. Occasionally guest poets read and discuss their poetry. The work of modern poets writing in English and French is studied, to explore what they have discovered about language, imagery, and music that we can apply to our own work—for example, Yeats' use of symbols, William Carlos Williams' American idiom, John Betjeman's methods of writing parody, André Breton's surrealist metaphors, Henri Michaux's way of turning nightmares into mythology. The workshop is conducted on the assumption one needs not only criticism, but also the discovery of one's capabilities. Students are therefore encouraged to try their talents at various forms and genres (such as sestina, parody); there are also experiments in group composition.

**WRITERS ON WRITING, 2009
SIGRID NUNEZ**

More than any other artists, writers are often asked to state why they do what they do. In this class, in addition to reading creative work in different genres, we look at ways in which writers have described their work and the writer's place in society. Our reading includes manifestos, credos, journal entries, and interviews, as well as letters in which writers as mentors speak directly to other writers about their craft and beliefs. Students do exercises in which they write brief imitations of master writers, in

'If I had to qualify my work as a poet, I would say I was a ritual poet. I have been trying to manipulate the ancient roots of poetry in drama, chant, costume, magic and collective experience. My ritual site has been the bandstand, the concert stage, and more recently, the theater. Every performance is a ritual, every ritual an act of publishing.'
↗ **SEKOU SUNDIATA** Faculty

In 2016, following the success of her novel *Sweetbitter*, which she began while pursuing her MFA in Creative Writing, Stephanie Danler returns to The New School to recall with Helen Schulman—her graduate mentor and head of the fiction focus—the shaping of her *New York Times* bestseller.

Fall of 2018, Sigrid Nunez, a long-time faculty member of the MFA in Creative Writing Program at The New School, wins the National Book Award for her novel *The Friend*. She accepts the award at the National Book Awards ceremony, which is held annually at the Tishman Auditorium of The New School's Joseph Urban building.

The 2019 book party of The New School's MFA in Creative Writing hosts over fifty newly published books.

'Writing is ... being able to take something whole and fiercely alive that exists inside you in some unknowable combination of thought, feeling, physicality, and spirit, and to then store it like a genie in tense, tiny black symbols on a calm white page. If the wrong reader comes across the words, they will remain just words. But for the right readers, your vision blooms off the page and is absorbed into their minds like smoke, where it will re-form, whole and alive, fully adapted to its new environment.'
↗ **MARY GAITSKILL** Faculty

'A writer discovers what he knows as he knows it, i.e., as he makes it. No artist writes in order to objectify an 'idea' already formed. It is the poem or novel or story that quite precisely tells him what he didn't know he knew: he knows, that is, only in terms of his writing.'
↗ **GILBERT SORRENTINO** Faculty

A BEAUTIFUL CAT

'One ever feels his twoness — an American, a Negro; two souls, two thoughts, two unreconciled strivings; two warring ideals in one dark body, whose dogged strength alone keeps it from being torn asunder.'
↗ **W.E.B. DU BOIS** Faculty

Marlon Brando, in his copy of James Baldwin's 1961 collection of essays, *Nobody Knows My Name*, underlines the passage: 'The questions which one asks oneself begin, at last, to illuminate the world, and become one's key to the experience of others.' Years before, circa 1944, Brando was studying at The New School's Dramatic Workshop, and taking courses with University in Exile professors at The New School. In his copy of former faculty member Wilhelm Reich's *The Mass Psychology of Fascism* (published in the United States in 1946), Brando foreshadowed Baldwin in the margin: 'One cannot make the fascist harmless if ... one does not look for him in oneself.'

In Baldwin's 1963 work of nonfiction, *The Fire Next Time* (1963), Brando highlights: 'You were born into a society which spelled out with brutal clarity, and in as many ways as possible, that you were a worthless human being.'

As of the 1960s, Brando and Baldwin had been friends for two decades. They'd met at The New School in 1944, when both were taking classes with the Dramatic Workshop. Brando, at the workshop, was a disciple of Stella Adler, and Baldwin, still uncommitted to writing, was toying with acting or playwriting as a career, and seeking a partial reprieve in the progressive milieu of Greenwich Village. The friendship between the two artists would become lore to the culture of the 1940s through to the 1960s, and a nation reexamining its own histories and values. As Baldwin would write in 1966:

> I first met Marlon Brando in the spring of 1944, when, for reasons having to do with youth and confusion, I spent a lot of time hanging around Manhattan's New School for Social Research. Marlon was a member of the Dramatic Workshop of The New School and was then studying with Erwin Piscator. It was not long before we struck up a kind of laconic friendship — we were both very shy — and somewhat distrustfully informed each other of the shape of our futures: he was to become a great actor, I was to become a great writer.

Baldwin moves on from the Dramatic Workshop, which is too 'Method' for him: 'You really run into some kind of weird, psychotherapeutic class.' But he and Brando would stay in touch; they were briefly roommates, and Brando, well on his way to stardom, would spot Baldwin the finances to return from Parisian expatriation. Brando was, as Baldwin would write and repeat to his biographer, W.J. Weatherby, 'a beautiful cat'.

'It is almost 20 years since the end of World War II. The Army of the U.S. is now integrated. It is benefiting from the leadership of enlightened officers — black and white. The colossal incongruity of men who sought in the army of a democracy to indulge their petty prejudices, cloaking it in Army authority and imposing it on the backs of black soldiers to rob them of morale and dignity and the very democracy there were sworn to defend and die for — all this is disappearing.'

↗ **GEORGE NORFORD** Student

Clockwise from top left:

▬▬▬ Marlon Brando featured in *The New York Post*, August, 1950

▬▬▬ James Baldwin and Marlon Brando during the Civil Rights March on Washington for Jobs and Freedom, August 28, 1963

▬▬▬ Marlo Brando featured in *The New York Post*, August, 1950

▬▬▬ Marlon Brando featured in a magazine clipping, *circa* 1950

The New School for Social Research
66 West 12th St.
New York City 11

Course # 106   Final Examination   W. E. B. Du Bois

Fall Term 1948

The Negro In American History

1. Has the transplanting of Negroes from Africa to America been
    advantageous or disadvantageous ----

            (a) To the Negro ?

            (b) To the United States ?

2. If, in writing the history of the United States, the thoughts and
    actions of Negroes are omitted, does that seriously distort the
    picture?

3. What has been the part played by the Negro in the Labor Movement in
    the United States?

4. Was Reconstruction after the Civil War a disaster or a "noble
    experiment?".

5. If you had been alive, 1850 to 1860 how would you have tried to
    solve the slavery question?

On the cover of each examination book used, please print your
name, the course number, instructor's name and the type of credit
for which you are registered. Examination questions should be
returned with the examination book.

Clockwise from top left:

James Baldwin speaking at
'The Negro Writer's Vision
of America' conference.
Peter Moore, April 25, 1965

Panel at 'The Negro Writer's
Vision of America' conference.
Peter Moore, April 25, 1965

Window reflection of the poster for
'The Negro Writer's Vision of America'
conference. Peter Moore, April 25, 1965

Lorraine Hansberry, 1959

Brochure for 'The Negro Writer's
Vision of America' conference, held
at The New School, April 23–25, 1965

'The word "theater" comes from the Greek. It means the seeing place. It is the place people come to see the truth about life and the social situation.'
↗ **STELLA ADLER** Faculty

In a 1963 reunion of students from the Dramatic Workshop, James Baldwin, Marlon Brando, Harry Belafonte, and Sidney Poitier join the March on Washington for Jobs and Freedom.

The New School hosts a three-day conference, 'The Negro Writer's Vision of America'. The Spring 1965 event is dedicated to the memory of New School alumna Lorraine Hansberry. Baldwin is the keynote speaker. The eight-panel discussions advertise: 'James Baldwin, LeRoi Jones (Amiri Baraka), John O. Killens, Alice Childress, David Boroff, Truman Nelson, Richard Gilman, Gordon Rogoff, Rev. Milton A. Galamison, Frederick O'Neal, Paule Marshall. Many other outstanding writers, critics, and scholars.' The event convenes activists and participants from the 1963 March on Washington for Jobs and Freedom, as well as a group from later in 1963 (in which Baldwin was included), who demanded, from the stage of New York's Town Hall, that Christmas be declared a day of mourning for the four girls killed in a Birmingham church bombing.

A CONFERENCE ON

THE NEGRO WRITER'S VISION OF AMERICA

'YOU CAN CAGE THE SINGER BUT NOT THE SONG.'
↗ HARRY BELAFONTE Student

Final exam for W. E. B. Du Bois's *Negro in American History* course at The New School, 1948

A SCHOOL THAT IS A THEATER AND THAT IS A SCHOOL

In 1940, The New School welcomes Erwin Piscator and Maria Ley-Piscator and the Dramatic Workshop. Piscator, who has fled Nazi Germany, is a stage director, the founder of the Proletarian Theater in Berlin, a collaborator with Bertolt Brecht, and influential on a flourishing era of the European stage. Maria Ley, a dancer and choreographer who established herself in Berlin and Paris, shares creative origins with Piscator, her third husband, having worked on productions with Piscator's Berlin contemporary, Max Reinhardt.

While the Dramatic Workshop leaves The New School in the early 1950s, stops taking students, and sells the brand, Maria Ley—who had managed the Dramatic Workshop and directed its productions—returns to The New School in the early 1960s to form The Actors' Workshop. Ley moves on to faculty positions at other institutions, but teaches courses and lectures at The New School through the 1990s. The Actor's Workshop, and a second incarnation of the Dramatic Workshop, are variously upheld and revived by Ley's appearances and the faculty direction of Judith Malina, founder of the Living Theater. In the Stella Adler Theater Studio, 1971–3, The New School offers theater classes under the auspices of Stella Adler.

Harry Belafonte is the latest sensation in New York's jazz singing circles. Here he is with Sarah Vaughan at the Royal Roost where he recently made an auspicious debut. He is the discovery of Monte Kay, who heard him sing his own song, aptly titled *Recognition*, in a show at the New School's Dramatic Workshop. Belafonte has already had his Roost engagement extended from five to nine weeks. Records are in the offing.

THE CONTEMPORARY DRAMA, 1931
MARK VAN DOREN

While the emphasis in this course will be upon the current drama, certain historical backgrounds will be kept in mind for the sake of the light which they throw upon dramatic theory and practice in this or in any other generation. The point of departure in any given lecture will be a play or a playwright of current interest. In order, however, to arrive at definitions of the form, the point of view, and the material involved, some attention to dramatic tradition will be considered necessary. The general aim of the course is to stimulate and articulate intelligent discussion of what goes on in the theatre—to provide a vocabulary with which more can be said than 'I liked it' or 'I didn't like it'.

BACKSTAGE ON BROADWAY, 1981
HAROLD J. KENNEDY

A series of conversations with some of the theater's most distinguished personalities. Informal interviews with those performers, writers, and directors whose talent and experience have shaped the theater today.
→ Gloria Swanson
→ Walter Kerr
→ Helen Hayes
→ Eli Wallach and Anne Jackson
→ Arlene Francis
→ Hume Cronyn and Jessica Tandy

'Theatre today should be a radar—a detecting device that emits and focuses a powerful scanning beam on the universe; an alarm system—enabling us to discover social and psychic changes in time to prepare ourselves to cope with them.'
↗ **MARIA LEY-PISCATOR** Faculty

Clockwise from top left:

▬▬▬ Dramatic Workshop actor performing *The Flies, circa 1947*

▬▬▬ Harry Belafonte and Sarah Vaughan featured in *Metronome, March, 1949*

A THEATER

'EVERYONE, REAL OR INVENTED, DESERVES THE OPEN DESTINY OF LIFE.'

'My mother worked for a woman, Maria Ley-Piscator, who with her husband founded the Dramatic Workshop, which was connected to The New School. My mother did proofreading and typing and stuff for her, and as part of her payment, I was able to take acting classes there on Saturdays when I was ten.'
↗ ROBERT DE NIRO Student

'LIFE BEATS YOU DOWN AND CRUSHES THE SOUL AND ART REMINDS YOU THAT YOU HAVE ONE.'
↗ STELLA ADLER Faculty

'ONLY THE LIBERATION OF THE NATURAL CAPACITY FOR LOVE IN HUMAN BEINGS CAN MASTER THEIR SADISTIC DESTRUCTIVENESS.'

↗ WILHELM REICH Faculty

STAND-UP COMEDY WORKSHOP, 1988
SCOTT BLAKEMAN

A comprehensive examination of the art of writing, producing, and performing comic monologues. The underlying premise of the course is learning by doing. Students are expected to perform their own material regularly in front of the instructor and entire class, which critiques each piece of work for content, style, and delivery. Improvisational technique and traditional modes of comedy performance are emphasized to help students develop individual writing styles and strong stage personas. The course is intended to culminate with each student doing an actual audition at one of New York's leading comedy clubs.

'Imagine a street corner anywhere in the world, where those who live on the fringes of society gather to talk, to each other and to themselves, about life-changing events, missed opportunities, memory, loss and regret.'
↗ ROBERT ASHLEY Creator of DUST

'WE ONLY HAVE SO MANY FACES IN OUR POCKETS.'

↗ MARLON BRANDO Student

'Strange as it may sound, our task is not limited to individual productions. It is almost a matter of indifference how the single productions look, what weaknesses they suffer from, what flaws they contain, whether they are complete mistakes. Our goal is to supersede bourgeois theater in terms of philosophy, dramatic theory, technique and staging. We are fighting for a restructured theater, and this must follow the lines of the social revolution. So we shall probably fail again and again, in a sense, because of the inadequacies of the situation, and because this reconstruction cannot proceed in isolation. This much I have now realized.'

↗ **ERWIN PISCATOR** Faculty and Founder of the Dramatic Workshop

'Every now and then, when you're on stage, you hear the best sound a player can hear. It's a sound you can't get in movies or in television. It is the sound of a wonderful, deep silence that means you've hit them where they live.'

↗ **SHELLEY WINTERS** Student

Clockwise from top left:

Actors performing scene from *Shadow of a Gunman*, 1951

Dramatic Workshop playbills, 1940s

Contact prints of actors in the Dramatic Workshop, 1940s

Dramatic Workshop, The New School, 1940s

THE PEOPLE WE WANT TO BE

Vinnette Carroll, in 1948, is the first black woman to enroll in the Dramatic Workshop. In previous years, Carroll studied at The Actors Studio, which would one day arrive at The New School (1984) to launch its popular television show.

While attending The New School's Dramatic Workshop, Carroll, who has already earned her Master's in Psychology from New York University, pursues her doctorate in the same subject at Columbia University. In the early 1950s, Carroll steps away from her career as a clinical psychologist and joins the faculty of the High School of Performing Arts, a prestigious New York City public high school, where she teaches for the next decade, while furthering her career as an actor, playwright, and director.

Carroll has a celebrated career acting for film, television, and stage, winning an Obie in 1962, and an Emmy in 1964. In 1972, she's the first black woman to direct on Broadway; her 1976 show, *Your Arms Too Short to Box with God*, goes to Broadway three times. After advising for the New York State Council of the Arts, she initiates the Urban Arts Corps (UAC), a New York City production and education group that fosters the careers of hundreds of performers, including Cicely Tyson and Sherman Hemsley. The goal of the UAC, operational from 1955 to 1983, is to make arts accessible and culturally relevant to black, Hispanic, and urban communities.

ART AND MARXISM-LENINISM-MAO TSE TUNG THOUGHT, 1977
AMIRI BARAKA

The focus of this course is understanding the Revolutionary Aesthetic, the Marxist–Leninist definition and function of art versus the bourgeois definition and function. We use examples from this country and internationally, from the past and the present.

BARAKA AND REVOLUTIONARY THEATER, 2019
VICTOR PETERSON

The re-articulation of aesthetic praxis in the Black Arts Movement (BAM) of the 1960s has had a profound impact on art, theater, and performance today. This course discusses the work of the Black Arts Repertory Theater/School as well as the writings and plays of BAM writers and artists, most notably Amiri Baraka. Through these works, we will form our own concept of the 'revolutionary' or 'radical' and see how it applies to the work of that theater and other schools still running today.

'If the highest things are unknowable, then the highest capacity or virtue of man cannot be theoretical wisdom.'
↗ **LEO STRAUSS** Faculty

PSYCHOTHERAPY AS A SOCIAL INSTITUTION, 1964
PETER BERGER

Sociological presuppositions for the study of psychological phenomena. Psychological models and social-psychological reality in contemporary society. Psychotherapy as ideology and as institution. The social organization of psychotherapy and its relation with other institutions.

'White people have been so programmed into dealing in a certain way with us that they're not even aware of it. It makes it difficult for us, as artists, to be the people we want to be.'
↗ **VINNETTE CARROLL** Student

'CHILDREN SEE THINGS VERY WELL SOMETIMES— AND IDEALISTS EVEN BETTER.'
↗ **LORRAINE HANSBERRY** Student

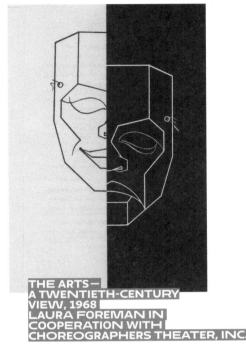

THE ARTS— A TWENTIETH-CENTURY VIEW, 1968 LAURA FOREMAN IN COOPERATION WITH CHOREOGRAPHERS THEATER, INC.

A series designed to explore topics of contemporary concern and controversy in the arts with leading representatives of music, dance, theater, film, literature, and the graphic arts.

→ Censorship and pornography: self-indulgence or self-expression?
Chairman: Hollis Alpert, Film Critic, *Saturday Review*; novelist and biographer Panel: Harold Greenwalk, PhD, President, National Psychological Association for Psychoanalysis; author, *The Call Girl* | Jack Kuney, Executive Director of Programming, Ch. 13 TV | John Watts, Director, Composers Theater; former Editor, *Manhattan East* newsp...

→ The Ar...
Chairm...
editor,...
Ossie...
Davies...
novelis...
colum...
Direct...
Alwin...
Dance...

→ Sexual...
Chairm...
psycho...
The Dr...
Square...
Health...

In 1965, Free Southern Theater, a traveling troupe of actors, recreates *Waiting for Godot* with a cast of African-American and white American actors. The group of actors perform at The New School after touring the most rural parts of Mississippi and Louisiana in an attempt to spread the message of the Civil Rights Movement to low-income African-American communities. In an attempt to help the nonprofit, The New School offers the school's space free of charge. Harry Belafonte, a former student at The New School's Dramatic Workshop, which supports and previews New York theater from community productions to Broadway, promotes and fundraises for the performance.

In 1984, a partnership with The Actors Studio signals The New School's initiation of a three-year MFA program in acting, directing, and playwriting, and recall the Dramatic Workshop of the mid-century. In 2013, The New School introduces a Bachelor of Fine Arts.

Dramatic Workshop OF THE NEW SCHOOL FOR SOCIAL RESEARCH ERWIN PISCATOR DIRECTOR 1948 1949 REPERTORY

'At the present time there is no dominant American mind. Our spirit is inarticulate, not a voice, but a chorus of many voices each singing a rather different tune. How to get order out of this cacophony is the question for all those who are concerned about those things which alone justify wealth and power, concerned about justice, the arts, literature, philosophy, science. What must, what shall this cacophony become, a unison or harmony?'
↗ **HORACE KALLEN** Founding Faculty

Clockwise from top left:

▬▬▬ Playbill for Free Southern Theater, *circa 1965*

▬▬▬ Dramatic Workshop of The New School for Social Research, *circa 1948*

▬▬▬ Vinnette Carroll, undated

▬▬▬ Drama students perform *Eugene Onegin*, 2018

FIELD TRIPS

A faculty member comes to an administrator with a course idea: music and magic mushrooms. The professor is John Cage, an American musician whose experimental compositions have made him a celebrity. The nation regards him as a comical digression and, simultaneously, reveres him as a genius. The Dean is Clara 'Woolie' Mayer, a foundation of the school, who has been on campus for forty years. At the time of Cage's proposal, she's Dean of the School of Philosophy and Liberal Arts, and Vice President of the University.

Cage, despite his perennial upstart status, has also been around campus for a long time, having first come to The New School as a student of global and contemporary music and composition. Among the courses and lectures that Cage attended were those of Henry Cowell, with whom Cage previously corresponded, and whose offerings, circa Cage's arrival, included: 'Music of Peasant Life', 'Folk Origins of Music', 'Music for the Church', 'Urban Music', 'Music of the Eighteenth-Century Lower Classes', 'The Place of Music in Society', 'Contemporary American Music', 'Music Systems of the World', 'Creative Music Today', and 'New Possibilities in Piano Playing'. Cage, briefly serving as Cowell's assistant, applied Cowell's compositional concepts to piano, as well as to sounds from sources other than musical instruments.

In the 1950s, Cage returned to The New School as faculty, teaching multiple courses, including his historical 'Experimental Composition'. In 'Advanced Composition', Cage taught alongside Cowell, who continued to guide The New School's approach to the study of music with a seemingly endless curiosity and dedication, and courses such as 'Music Systems of the World', 'Physico-Mathematical Theory of Composition', 'Musical Iconoclasts', and 'Teaching Children to Create Music'.

CREATIVE MUSIC IN AMERICA, 1941
HENRY COWELL

What is called the music of America is made up of a combination of influences from foreign countries together with musical practices which have through many generations become identified with the United States. Recent enrichments from many countries have strengthened the best foreign traditions. The rise of nationalism has sharpened appreciation of old native products. America has become the world's greatest musical land, but its people have not yet arrived at a knowledge of the musical styles, traditions, and clichés which it harbors. To become acquainted with these, and to discuss important native and foreign-born composers, is the purpose of the course. Musical illustrations are given, some of the composers appearing in person to explain and perform their works.

MAKE MUSIC NEW YORK, 2019
AARON FRIEDMAN,
DIANE RAGSDALE

In this course, students will take an active role in running Make Music New York, a free, citywide, outdoor musical celebration that has become the largest music event in the city's history. Each student will adopt one neighborhood to coordinate, and one participatory 'special project' to spearhead. By the end of the semester, students will have developed key skills in community organizing, grassroots fundraising, project management, music marketing and PR, festival production, and getting things done in NYC.

'I never left jazz. The relationship between structure and improvisation— that constant conversation and tension— I've always wanted in every genre and song that I perform.'
↗ LIZZ WRIGHT Student

'NO ARTIST IS AHEAD OF HIS TIME. HE IS HIS TIME; IT IS JUST THAT OTHERS ARE BEHIND THE TIMES.'
↗ MARTHA GRAHAM Faculty

'I DON'T DIG STAYING IN ONE GROOVE.'

— CHICO HAMILTON, Faculty

In May 1936, Henry Cowell, artistic radical and New School faculty member, is arrested on a "morals" charge for alleged contact with a seventeen-year-old boy. He pleads guilty, is sentenced to fifteen years' imprisonment, and remanded to San Quentin State Prison, where he continues to teach composition and write music. Alvin Johnson, President of The New School, as well as faculty members Cage, Aaron Copland, Charles Seeger, and others, petition for Cowell's release. Cowell returns to teach at The New School when he is granted parole in 1940. He is pardoned in 1942.

Clockwise from top left:

Contact sheet of various images related to classes at The New School. Pictured are performance artists Allan Kaprow and Robert Whitman, artist and composer George Brecht, composer John Cage, composer and poet Dick Higgins. Fred W. McDarrah, August 5, 1959

John Cage tuning a piano, 1957

Score for *Imaginary Landscape, No. 1.* John Cage, 1939

By the time of his visit to Mayer, Cage has not only gained recognition as a musician but as a specimen of an emerging generation. He's a radio and television regular, even appearing on game shows. In two years, he'll appear on *I've Got a Secret*, performing his iconic composition, *Water Walk*. On the Italian game show *Double or Nothing* (*Lascia o Raddoppia*) he'll be asked to list the twenty-four names of the white-spored agarics, as identified in Atkinson's *Studies of American Fungi*. Cage, self-assured, will offer to recite the list alphabetically, do so, and take the prize money.

While initially reluctant to endorse Cage's mushroom course, Mayer is swayed by the observational value of mushroom hunting. A creative and philosophical argument also speaks for the endeavor; the connection between random musical and artistic patterns, crucial to Cage's creative process, is paralleled by the growth patterns of mushrooms. As he'll explain while hunting mushrooms in Stony Point, New York: 'Our intention is to affirm this life, not to bring order out of chaos, nor to suggest improvements in creation, but simply to wake up to the very life we're living, which is so excellent once one gets one's mind and one's desires out of its way and lets it act of its own accord.'

Course no. 1289, 'Mushroom Identification', is first listed in Fall 1959. Cage is assisted in his preparations by horticulturalist Guy Nearing, and longtime collaborator and textile artist Lois Long, with whom Cage will later form the New York Mycological Society. The five-session seminar, simply put, will conduct 'Five field trips in the vicinity of New York City', and identifies Cage as an 'amateur mycologist'.

The course draws mushroom enthusiasts and Fluxus artists such as Alison Knowles and Dick Higgins, and the annual banquet makes the news: the culinary pages of *The New York Times*.

he New York Times.

COLLEGE STAGES MUSHROOM HUNT

10 in Course at New School Qualify as Mycophiles on Sloatsburg Jaunt

Special to The New York Times.

SLOATSBURG, N. Y., July 12—Ten mycophiles roamed the woods near here today in search of their love—mushrooms.

The expedition was an exercise in the newest course at the New School—mushroom hunting.

John Cage, the composer, conducts the hikes. He is an amateur mycologist, one interested in the study of fungi. Known for his experimental compositions in the area of musical sounds, he explained:

"As music sharpens the sense of audition, mushroom hunting sharpens the sense of vision and one's contact with nature."

He added that it was also a wonderful excuse for hiking.

However, naturalists have noted that although more than 700 types of mushroom have been proved edible, some species of the fungi can be extremely injurious to health. They warn that toadstools should not be gathered in the woods under the impression that they are the proper mushroom.

Advice for Amateurs

The group followed a brook in a damp wooded area. Guy Nearing, a spry 69-year-old naturalist, said that because of the dry weather yesterday mushrooms were more likely to be found in wet, dark places.

"It is just a coincidence that we do discover mushrooms," he said. "Mushrooms grow in a few hours and last only four or five days. You have to know where to look."

"They're exciting, exciting!" exclaimed Miss Margaret Nydes, a dress designer, commenting on the various colors of the mushrooms found.

"I'm a mycophagous," interjected Miss Lois Long, Mr. Cage's assistant in the course, while sniffing a fragrant black trumpet mushroom. "I like the colors and the shapes, but most of all I like to eat them."

"It's a challenge," observed Mr. Cage. "There is always the chance of making a mistake. That is the sport of mushroom hunting."

The fee for the course is $10. The course consists of five field trips. Yesterday's hike was the third. All the students consid-

Mycophiles (They Like Mus

Members of group from the New School on a hi mushrooms they found. From left they are Guy

Herbert Romanoff photographs specimens   M

U.C.L.A. EXPANDS ACCOUNTING COURSE

that the breadth a university education embark upon a car accountancy requi five-   five   study.'

DAY, JULY 13, 1959.

ns) Take to Woods

atsburg, N. Y., study some of the , John Cage and Miss Lois Long.

The New York Times (by Edward Hausner)
n Sherbloom views one on stump

BOATERS SAVED AT SEA

Jersey Coach and Son, Adrift
16 Hours, Picked Up

Special   rk Times.
                 July 11—

'MY HEAD IS A BONY GUITAR, STRUNG WITH TONGUES, PLUCKED BY FINGERS AND NAILS'

↗ **BOB KAUFMAN** Student

March, 2018: The Stone, an influential experimental performance space founded in 2005 by saxophonist, composer, and producer John Zorn, moves from the East Village to the ground-floor Glassbox Theater in The New School's College of Performing Arts. The move, which gives The Stone a larger space, is the culmination of an association that began five years before with 'The Stone Workshops at The New School', an artist residency program.

Clockwise from top left:

▬▬▬ Musical Theater Performance Lab for the College of the Performing Arts at The New School, 2017

▬▬▬ *The New York Times, July 13, 1959*

SOUNDAFFECTS

EXPERIMENTAL COMPOSITION, 1958
JOHN CAGE

A course in musical composition with technological, musicological, and philosophical aspects, open to those with or without previous training. Whereas conventional theories of harmony, counterpoint, and musical form are based on the pitch and frequency components of sound, this course offers problems and solutions in the field of composition based on other components of sound: duration, timbre, amplitude, and morphology; the course also encourages inventiveness. A full exposition of the contemporary musical scene in light of the work of Anton Webern, and present developments in music for magnetic tape (musique concrète: electronische musik).

ELECTRONIC MUSIC, 1959
RICHARD MAXFIELD

Music composed of sounds especially created by electronic techniques, without recourse to conventional musical instruments. A lecture course on a recent, radical, and controversial development in the art of music, which has had revolutionary impact on the contemporary musical scene. Examples from Krenek, Varèse, Cage, Stockhausen, and other composers are heard and analyzed. The course comprises a history of the technique; a discussion of its philosophic and aesthetic implications; an examination of related techniques, such as tape music and concrete music; and the specific approaches to electronic composition.

WASTE AND JUSTICE, 2019
TIMO RISSANEN, JOEL TOWERS

Students learn about the connections between waste, justice, design, and activism, both personally and politically. Throughout the course the concepts of waste and justice are examined as human constructs with impacts on each other. As the world's population increasingly urbanizes and the climate crisis worsens, the global economy risks breaching planetary boundaries with potentially irreversible consequences if societies continue to produce and consume at levels set by western standards. The course focuses on how issues of extractive production, linear consumption, and waste impact environmental justice communities, workers, and vulnerable populations, while demonstrating through innovative examples how these groups are crucial to the solutions. Economists such as Raworth and Max-Neef provide inspiring economic frameworks for ways forward. The course brings together experts from different fields to share innovative design solutions, advocacy campaigns, and scholarly research on waste and justice. The course suits students with a broad interest in sustainability and justice, and it has a bold goal: to empower and enable students to imagine unthinkable yet actionable futures.

'Creativity is the power to reject the past, to change the status quo, and to seek new potential. Simply put, aside from using one's imagination — perhaps more importantly — creativity is the power to act.'
↗ **AI WEIWEI** Student and Guest Speaker

'There are many prejudices about art, and first among them is that it is a skill and that there are definite rules.'
↗ **WOLF KAHN** Student

Clockwise from top left:

▬▬▬ Chinese activist and artist Ai Weiwei, 2017

 *SoundAffects*, an experiential public installation by Parsons School of Design students, 2011

'PERHAPS HOME IS NOT A PLACE BUT SIMPLY AN IRREVOCABLE CONDITION.'

↗ **JAMES BALDWIN** Student and Guest Speaker

'The idea of being a ritual poet and publishing through performance and recording did not come to me out of thin air. I got it from what I made of the Black Arts Movement, when I discovered the first poetry to set my imagination burning. It inspired the idea of making poetry records that had something greater than an archival shelf life, something that I could live with the way I live with my records. A temporal poetry that could fill and consume a living room.'

↗ **SEKOU SUNDIATA** Faculty

For one week in May, the corner of Fifth Avenue and 13th Street is morphed into an experience. Parsons, in cooperation with the digital design company Tellart, installs a white monolith in the midst of the downtown streetscape. The monolith collects temperature readings, video from multiple feeds, traffic and city noise, precipitation levels, rates of interference from mobile and cellular devices, and proximity information about bystanders and project onlookers. The incoming data is integrated by software that outputs a series of colorful, abstracted vertical bands and music. A falafel truck driving home for the day, for example, is recast as an intricate, exquisite tickling and grumbling of notes. The outputs are available onsite, online, or via mobile.

'This exploration', explains Joel Towers, Executive Dean of Parsons School of Design, 2009–19, 'is an invitation for the public to participate in the design of our cities, and will hopefully shed some light on the complexities of urban life. It's a tangible way to understand design's role in the world around us by looking at everyday occurrences in a different way'.

In 1959, Richard Maxfield, a former student of John Cage, teaches the first U.S. course in higher education dedicated exclusively to electronic music.

In 1969, Richard Goode, Murray Perahia, and Frederica von Stade graduate from the Mannes School of Music.

SoundAffects is recognized in a Core77 Design Award for 2012.

A four-semester project for The New School Master of Fine Arts in Creative Writing results in AshLab, which creates a 3D museum of John Ashbery's nineteenth-century Victorian residence in Hudson, New York. The museum may be explored by the objects in the home, or correlated poetry. The online environment is christened at The New School in April, 2014, with a public program of discussion and readings by participating faculty and students.

In 2018, the Mannes Orchestra performs with the Martha Graham Dance Company at the New York City Center. The performance selects from Graham repertoire pieces, *The Rite of Spring*, *Chronicle*, *Embattled Garden*, and *Panorama*, and features teen dancers from the New York City area. In addition to the original musical accompaniments by Norman Lloyd, Wallingford Riegger, Carlos Surinach, and Igor Stravinsky, staging includes iconic Graham set-design elements by Isamu Noguchi.

'I'D RATHER PROMOTE NEW YORK THAN ANYTHING ELSE IN THIS WORLD BECAUSE NEW YORK TO ME MEANS THE WORLD.'

↗ **DONNA KARAN** Student and Visiting Critic

THE FLUTE OF KRISHNA

'TO STOP THE FLOW OF MUSIC WOULD BE LIKE THE STOPPING OF TIME ITSELF INCREDIBLE AND INCONCEIVABLE.'

↗ AARON COPLAND

CONTEMPORARY AMERICAN MUSIC, 1933
HENRY COWELL

The course will consist of lectures on American musical tendencies and composers, copiously illustrated by composers and interpretive artists; of forums led by composers of different opinions who will discuss topics relative to their work and aims. ... Among the composers who will personally participate in the course are Lahn Adohmyan, Marion Bauer, John Becker, Russell Bennett, Evelyn Berckman, Nicolai Berezowsky, Marc Blitzstein, Henry Brant, Aaron Copland, Henry Cowell, Ruth Crawford, Richard Donovan, Vladimir Dukelsky, Lehman Engel, Vivian Fine, Rudolph Ganz, Rubin Goldmark, John Green, Howard Hanson, Roy Harris, Irwin Heilner, Bernard Hermann, Philip James, Wesley LaViolette, Daniel G. Mason, Max Meth, Jerome Moross, Harold Morris, Walter Piston, Quincey Porter, Wallingford Riegger, Dane Rudhyar, Carl Ruggies, Carlos Salzedo, Joseph Schillinger, Charles Seeger, Elie Siegmeister, Nicolas Slonimsky, David Stanley Smith, William G. Still, Mitya Stillman, Vanna Suesse, Bernard Wagenaar, Adolph Weiss.

EXPERIMENTAL RADIO STUDIO, 1948
MITCHELL JABLONS, NATHAN RUDICH

A study of advanced phases of radio production designed as a practical exploration of current production techniques and experimentation in new forms. A workshop for writers, directors, and actors. Actual programs will be recorded at each session, one or more for public broadcast.

This page:

Martha Graham, undated

From among her best students, Martha Graham chooses Thelma Biracree, Betty MacDonald, and Evelyn Sabin to form the original Graham Trio. On April 18, 1926, the three premiere as the Martha Graham Dance Group, in an early yet definitive exhibition of Graham's torso-wheeling style of modern dance. Sabin remains with Graham for four years, and subsequently performs and teaches within Graham's realm of influence; in 1934, at a private recital, the twenty-six-year-old dancer meets thirty-five-year-old pianist Leopold Mannes: they fall in love.

Mannes, the son of musicians and educators David and Clara Mannes, has successfully navigated the Depression by inventing a breakthrough process in color photography. The Kodak of the 1920s and 1930s is a trailblazer with a history of employing artists in business and technology. Sabin, in fact, had been immortalized by a Kodak film, perhaps the most advanced color processing to date, in her 1926 performance of Graham's *The Flute of Krishna*.

But Mannes, by the mid-1930s, is grappling with his future. His parents, in 1916, founded the Mannes School of Music, and he is, by his mother, a Damrosch, a son of 'America's First Family of Music'. In 1939, despite the assurance of a lucrative career at Kodak, and warnings from his friends and colleagues that he can't go back to music at forty years old, Mannes abandons Kodak to assume leadership of the Mannes School. He is the first President and Director of the College.

In July, 1940, Mannes and Sabin marry. A year later, as Sabin recovers from a stillbirth, Graham visits, asking that Sabin return to dance for the company. Graham has become a celebrated choreographer; she will soon begin work on her beloved ballet *Appalachian Spring* with former New School colleagues Isamu Noguchi and Aaron Copland; Noguchi is Graham's extraordinary designer (Noguchi designs a wooden rocking chair for the set, which Graham dances on, and which he later casts in bronze, one of a series of eight, and gifts to the New School Art Collection in honor of Martha Graham), and Copland will be awarded a Pulitzer Prize for his accompanying score. But Evelyn chooses Leopold. She wants to try to have another child, despite the medical uncertainty as to the couple's fertility. She will later remember, in an interview with biographer George Martin: 'I have had two inspirations in my life, Martha Graham and Leopold Mannes.' Sabin and Mannes will have two daughters.

Under Mannes' leadership, the Mannes School further augments its prestigious faculty and offerings, and sees many of its students achieve prominence, including Burt Bacharach, Richard Goode, Eugene Istomin, Anthony Newman, Murray Perahia, Eve Queler, George Rochberg, Julius Rudel, and Frederica von Stade. Through the 1970s and 1980s, alumni include Semyon Bychkov, Michel Camilo, JoAnn Falletta, Tim Page, Shulamit Ran, and Lara St. John.

In 1989, the Mannes School of Music joins The New School, complementing a conservatory practice with innovation and experimentation, and a curriculum that has led the way in the American idiom of jazz. *The New York Times* announces the merger with a capsule history of The New School and a callout to current Mannes faculty and guest artists Peter Serkin, Grant Johannesen, Yo-Yo Ma, and James Galway. While Mannes looks forward to broader curricular offerings and financial stability, the *Times* reports that the two schools intend to maintain Mannes's history and atmosphere.

OL·FOR·SOCIAL·RESEARCH··STUDY·FOR·COLOR

REATMENT · OF · THE · DANCE · STUDIO · · NEW · YORK · CIT

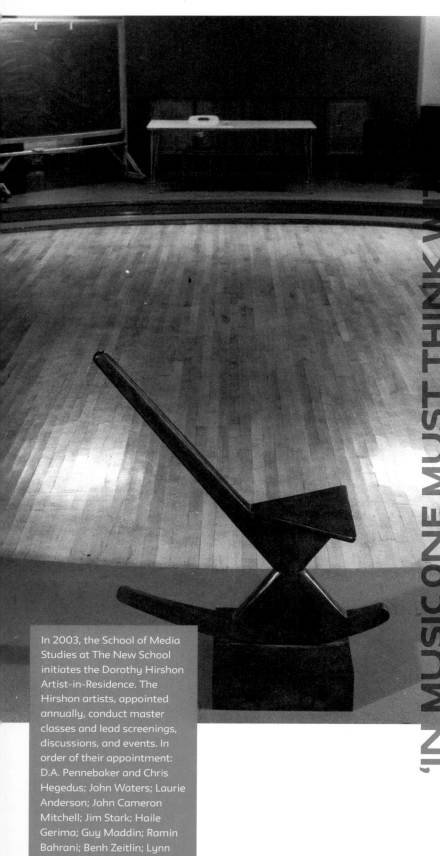

Marshall McLuhan, in the opening of his 1964 book *Understanding Media: The Extensions of Man*, coins the phrase, 'the medium is the message'. He writes: 'It is sometimes a bit of a shock to be reminded that, in operational and practical fact, the medium is the message. This is merely to say that the personal and social consequences of any medium … result from the new scale that is introduced into our affairs by each extension of ourselves, or by any new technology.' At Antioch College, in 1969, John Culkin, former Jesuit priest, media critic, and colleague of McLuhan, establishes the Center for Understanding Media, named after the McLuhan book; in 1975, the program moves to The New School, where the effect of media on individual and societal character has been a foundational academic investigation. With the arrival of the Center for Understanding Media, The New School initiates one of the first graduate degrees in media studies, with a Master of Arts in the subject.

'IN MUSIC ONE MUST THINK WITH THE HEART AND FEEL WITH THE BRAIN.'
↗ **GEORGE SZELL** Faculty

In 2003, the School of Media Studies at The New School initiates the Dorothy Hirshon Artist-in-Residence. The Hirshon artists, appointed annually, conduct master classes and lead screenings, discussions, and events. In order of their appointment: D.A. Pennebaker and Chris Hegedus; John Waters; Laurie Anderson; John Cameron Mitchell; Jim Stark; Haile Gerima; Guy Maddin; Ramin Bahrani; Benh Zeitlin; Lynn Hershman Leeson; Toni Dove; Jon Alpert and Keiko Tsuno; and Sean Baker.

'MY AMBITION WAS TO LIVE LIKE MUSIC.'
↗ **MARY GAITSKILL** Faculty

'Never has it had a more distinguished role to fulfill. Through mass communications — radio, television, and film — the theater has reached out to the smallest villages, has entertained and educated people. It has become a highly respectable and respected institution, financially and otherwise. But this is not all. The blueprint of the Dramatic Workshop was an even more vital one. 'Theatre as an instrument of better life' is not only as a mirror in which we see what we are and, sometimes, who we are, not only a polished substance that forms images for reflection, but also a speculum showing not only how men live, but how they ought to be. Whatever form it takes, any public performance is social. I would like to think that the implication of these words will spread throughout our culture in a clear way — with the understanding that everything is part of a whole.'
↗ **MARIA LEY-PISCATOR** Faculty and Director of the Dramatic Workshop

EXPERIMENTAL TELEVISION STUDIO, 1948
PAUL BELANGER

The study of television production techniques in all their aspects through practical demonstration. The evaluation of techniques of film, stage, and radio as applied to the new television medium. Specific problems arising from dramatic, musical film, and special events will be analyzed.

IMPROVISATIONAL ARTISTS LAB, 2019
JANE IRA BLOOM, JOSEPH GRIFASI

Your body, your voice, your music, your humor, and your fear. This is the DNA of an improvisational encounter and the departure point for [the] Improvisational Artists Lab. This collab[oration] between Jazz, Drama, and Mannes exp[lores the] reaches of how student performers [from these] disciplines interplay using the comm[on language] of improvisation. The course draws in[dividual] personal narratives through weekly e[xercises in] text, composition, soundscape, and m[ovement].

'Pull, pull on the contraction. Do not cave in. And the contraction is not a position. It is a movement into something. It is like a pebble thrown into the water, which makes rippling circles when it hits the water. The contraction moves.'
↗ **MARTHA GRAHAM** Faculty

'To me, objects are quite incidental and used only as a convenience. A pr[...] about something beyond that — something that permeates space. In 193[...] a rope, nothing else. It's not the rope that is the sculpture. but it is the sp[...] is the sculpture. It is an illusion of space. It is not flat like a painting see[...] a three-dimensional perspective. It bisects the theater space. Therefore, [...] into a spatial concept. And it is in that spatial concept that Martha move[...] In that sense, Martha is a sculptor herself.'
↗ **ISAMU NOGUCHI** Site-Specific Artist

'WE ALL LIVE IN A HOUSE ON FIRE,
NO FIRE DEPARTMENT TO CALL;
NO WAY OUT, JUST THE UPSTAIRS
WINDOW TO LOOK OUT OF WHILE
THE FIRE BURNS THE HOUSE DOWN
WITH US TRAPPED, LOCKED IN IT.'
↗ **TENNESSEE WILLIAMS** Student

DOOMSDAY

On January 9, The New School Board of Trustees considers the fundraising effort that was to have rescued the school, which is threatened by bankruptcy: in the last six months, they've raised almost nothing. Desperate, an ad hoc committee initiates secret meetings with New York University to explore a possible merger. Alvin Johnson, The New School's President Emeritus, acting with Hans Staudinger, a political thinker and scholar, and one of the original University in Exile professors brought to The New School in 1933, secure a $200,000 pledge from Joseph Schaffner, a department store tycoon and previous supporter of the school. The pledge is predicated on the condition that The New School remain autonomous from New York University. Johnson and Staudinger go on to raise an additional $240,000, staving off disaster. In a 'confidential' correspondence (sent to hundreds of recipients), Johnson characterizes the merger exploration as a plot, and a terminal solution: 'A merger with New York University is under discussion. That would be the end.' He signs off the letter with directions to respond via the contribution form and pre-addressed envelope.

When the trustees reconvene in March, the agenda is damage control: rumors of the merger have leaked, and New York University is afraid that it will be perceived as a bully and usurper in a failed annexation. The New School pens two press releases, which definitively place the blame on The New School's President, Henry David, whose resignation is announced in the first letter. On April 1, *The New York Times* succinctly dispenses with the subject: 'Although neither Dr. David nor the trustees elaborated on their policy differences, it is known that part of the conflict was over Dr. David's demand for a long-term budget.'

'All that we have in New York of magnetism, of opportunities to earn a living, of leadership, of the arts, of glamour, of convenience, of power to fulfill and assimilate our immigrants, of ability to repair our wounds and right our evils, depends on our great and wonderful criss-cross of relationships.'
↗ **JANE JACOBS** Faculty

'The whole problem with the world is that fools and fanatics are always so certain of themselves, but wiser people so full of doubts.'
↗ **BERTRAND RUSSELL** Faculty

| Previous pages: | Clockwise from top left: | | Entrance to 65 Fifth Avenue. Laima Turnley, *circa* 1969–1970 |

Philippe Halsman, *Dalí Atomicus*, 1948

The Graduate Center of The New School for Social Research, now The New School, 1969

The New School Bulletin, October, 1967

'One doesn't have to pursue unhappiness. It comes to you. You come into the world screaming. You cry when you're born because your lungs expand. You breathe. I think that's really kind of significant. You come into the world crying, and it's a sign that you're alive.'
↗ **JAMAICA KINCAID** Student

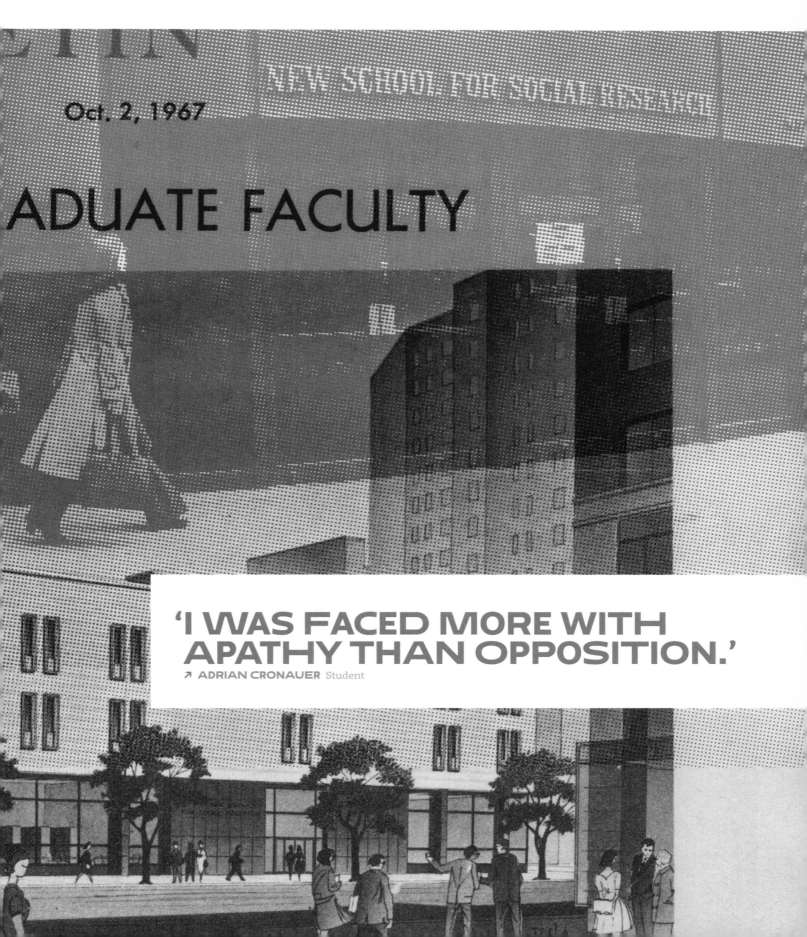

Oct. 2, 1967

NEW SCHOOL FOR SOCIAL RESEARCH

ADUATE FACULTY

'I WAS FACED MORE WITH APATHY THAN OPPOSITION.'
↗ **ADRIAN CRONAUER** Student

UNITED
AMERICAN
SCULPTORS
UNITED
EUROPE

Giuseppe Antonio Borgese, one of many exiled European scholars to teach at The New School as of the 1930s, publishes 'The Intellectual Origins of Fascism' in *Social Research*. Only in its fourth issue, The New School journal is already a weighty contributor to an international conversation, and deep concern, about global fascism. To aid scholars in their exodus from a Europe in political and social crisis, The New School has initiated its first degree programs — graduate degrees, not undergraduate degrees — to provide full-time faculty positions to an esteemed cohort of refugees. At The New School, the scholars forge a community and contend with the issues that challenge the world. Borgese seeks causation for fascism in culture, politics, and economics, dissects the relationship of Hitler to Mussolini, the Italian origin and the German ascendency, and issues a call to arms:

> *Germany is still a storage place for the pious safekeeping of mediaeval memories; Italy is still a peninsula jutting from the ancient world into the new. Involuntarily, but at highest speed, fascism is burning in both countries all the material of the past. ... The intellectuals of the new time, philosophers and poets, must reject sophistry and lies; they must think in terms of righteousness and truth, and of united Europe.*

'Race is not particularly interesting to me. Power is. Who has power and who doesn't. Slavery interests me because it's an incredible violation that has not stopped. It's necessary to talk about that. Race is a diversion.'
↗ **JAMAICA KINCAID** Student

Clockwise from top left:

Sculptures included in the exhibition *United American Sculptors*, 1939

Booklet for the exhibition, *United American Sculptors*, held at The New School, 1939

1939

'My family was reasonably liberal. Some kids I grew up with, their parents forced them to join the military, and my parents never, ever even brought it up. I imagine just looking at me, they were like "Not an army officer."

↗ MIKE DOUGHTY Student

'Life has been thrown into the world, light into darkness, the soul into the body. It expresses the original violence done to me in making me be where I am and what I am, the passivity of my choice-less emergence into an existing world which I did not make and whose law is not mine.'

↗ HANS JONAS Faculty

AMERICAN PROSE AND AMERICAN EXPERIENCE, 1941
ALFRED KAZIN

The aim of this course is to study the development of American prose from the close of the Civil War to the outbreak of World War II in terms of that period's most characteristic and most significant central idea—the theory of realism. Essentially, therefore, it is a study of the emergence, growth and decline of the modern spirit in America from the days when that spirit, speaking for the first time through Emerson and Whitman, proclaimed the supremacy of the democratic conscience and the obligation of the writer to a democratic society for which at times he provided political and spiritual leadership.

ETHNICS ON THE MOVE:
THE NEW YORK ITALIAN COMMUNITY, 1972
SILVANO M. TOMASI

A new awareness pervades the Italian community in the metropolitan area. The historical experience and the current variables affecting New York's Italians are analyzed. Interaction with majority

MONSTROSITY, METAMORPHOSIS, AND THE OTHER, 2007
SHELLEY JACKSON

The word 'monster' comes from the Latin for 'show'. But what is it that monsters show us? To see past the spectacle, we have to read closely and sometimes contrarily, examining how the 'other' is constructed (or deconstructed) via images of the monstrous, uncanny, and interstitial. Exhibits range from classic literary texts such as Kafka's 'The Metamorphosis', films including Tod Browning's still distributing *Freaks*, the science fiction of Philip Dick and James Tiptree Jr. to contemporary self-consciously 'monstrous' texts, like Severo Sarduy's *Cobra* and playwright Suzan-Lori Park's *Venus* that defiantly put themselves on exhibit. Selected essays, such as Donna Haraway's influential 'Cyborg Manifesto', offer both formal models and a language of ideas to help us draft our own arguments about the political and personal significance of the shifting image of the monster.

In 1939, Hans Speier oversees the publication of *War in Our Time*, which collects writings and lectures concerning the nature of fascism, and modes of resistance to fascism and fascist thinking. Many of the contributors to the work, edited by Speier, are members of The New School Graduate Faculty. Alvin Johnson writes the foreword. Speier is a member of the University in Exile, in addition to being a spy and an Allied propagandist.

In 2013, The New School establishes the Zolberg Institute on Migration and Mobility, which is named for New School Professor of Politics and University in Exile Professor Emeritus Aristide R. Zolberg, who passed away earlier that year. A Belgian of Jewish descent, Zolberg [...] a childhood in Nazi-[...] France by assuming [...] persona. The [...] warded, politically [...] nizationally active [...] ined The New School [...] Ary Zolberg was [...] grant to the United [...] ho became [...] voice for the rights [...] rants and for [...] istic approach [...] ration policy', [...] ered Archbishop [...] omasi at a memorial [...] ew School. 'I came to [...] n well—as a friend [...] ague—through [...] r for Migration [...] nd also through [...] ection to The New [...] where I taught many [...] o. I well remember [...] ssions Ary and I [...] e was working on [...] uld become one of [...] erworks, *A Nation* [...] n. This book lays [...] has become a [...] way to think about [...] tion policy'. The [...] supports a discussion [...] mics, policymaking, [...] ism in the area of [...] n and mobility.

THE TEACHING OF SLOGANS INTENDED TO BEFOG THE MIND OF WHATEVER KIND THEY MAY OBJECT TO

↗ FRANZ BOAS Faculty

THE MATSUNAGA AFFAIR

The National Endowment for the Arts (NEA) is under attack. A conservative Congress wants to defund the organization, and exercise its own judgement to decide what is art, and that which is deemed non-art (be it categorized as pornographic or political) may be suppressed by the government. Led by North Carolina Senator Jesse Helms, conservative forces are especially keen on withdrawing support for works by, for example, Andres Serrano, which they view as blasphemous, or Robert Mapplethorpe, which they view as extolling sinful homosexual practices in graphic detail.

On September 8, at the 1989 convocation, New School President Jonathan Fanton responds to the 'Culture Wars', and expansively asserts the university's commitment to free speech. On October 4, the school issues a 'Statement of Freedom of Artistic Expression' that has been adopted by the Board of Trustees. The document anticipates controversy on campus, but is uncompromising:

> *The university's responsibility for and dedication to securing the conditions in which freedom of expression can flourish extend to all forms of artistic expression, including the fine arts, design, literature, and the performance of drama, music, and dance.*

On October 18, the Parsons Galleries opens an exhibition of 350 works by Japanese designer Shin Matsunaga. On October 24, Associate Dean of Milano School of Management John M. Jeffries (PhD from The New School for Social Research), who is a person of color, pens an eloquent memorandum to President Fanton, questioning the university's inclusion of a 1983 advertisement that employs a blackface logo in the sale of the Japanese soda Calpis. It is a five-page letter, with an addendum of recent newspaper articles that address racial insensitivity, and racism, in Japan.

> *Following the fire drill ... on Thursday, October 19, 1989, I walked through Room One of the Exhibition Center to look at the Works of Shin Matsunaga, New York, 1989 exhibit. I was surprised to see that one of the displayed prints is a caricature based on a derogatory racial stereotype that was prevalent in American culture during the late nineteenth and early twentieth centuries. This particular piece of Matsunaga's work is indisputably derived from the depreciatory representations of African-American minstrels which were made most popular by Al Jolson's performances in blackface. ... It is a very offensive item.*

Jeffries cites Fanton's convocation speech, and 'the right to be free from intolerance', and doesn't argue against the display of controversial work; Jeffries speaks to the consciousness and intention of the print, and the choice to include the work in exhibition. The work is of no particular technical merit, and indicates no political awareness; it isn't making a statement, it's just oblivious racism. (The Calpis print isn't even representative of Matsunaga, who was merely interpreting an existing logo.) Case in point, Jeffries includes a newspaper clipping about Colgate's decision to change the name and blackface-figure logo for a toothpaste brand that racially stereotypes. Jeffries asks that a disclaimer be made available at the exhibition, or that the work be taken down. The Parsons Exhibition Committee declines both options, asserting that such acts would be editorial or censorious. President Fanton, after a meeting with Jeffries, also refuses to alter the exhibition.

On November 14, Sekou Sundiata, poet, performer, and the first Writer-in-Residence at The New School, visits the exhibit. Sundiata markers an X over the image, along with the comment 'This is racist bullshit'. Student organizations had been active in October, lobbying against institutionalized biases in race and gender, and with Sundiata's act, the campus erupts: a cross-hatch of images and criticisms soon cover the image. Defenders of the right to display the Matsunaga image see the acts as vandalism; those who oppose the display see the acts as protest.

On November 17, amidst tumult, the exhibition closes as per its schedule. Students and faculty, however, remain unsatisfied, and demand a full accounting from Fanton. Three days later, Lang Professor Ann Snitow writes a letter to Fanton; she is concerned about the direction the students are taking, but believes in their right to pursue action:

> *Why, I asked students, should the demands for more courses about black and third world people and for a more diverse student body and faculty take the form of a campaign against a racist representation? Had we got the target right? Were we perhaps displacing rage, losing sight of the potential for real changes at the university? Finally, Jonathan, I have three reasons for supporting the students in spite of all my doubts expressed here. First, though I wanted to argue with them, my recent work with them has made me feel that rich, polyphonic political conversation is currently possible as it was not two years ago. Second, I wanted to support Sekou,*

'I imagine one of the reasons people cling to their hates so stubbornly is because they sense, once hate is gone, they will be forced to deal with pain.'
↗ **JAMES BALDWIN** Student and Guest Speaker

The American Conscience, a show of approximately fifty paintings by contemporary artists, opens in March, 1964, at The New School Art Center. The curation spans thirty years to the present, featuring well-known paintings, such as Ben Shahn's *Passion of Sacco and Vanzetti,* and Robert Rauschenberg's elegiac Kennedy collage *Buffalo,* as well as considerations of abstraction in works by Paul Burlin and Robert Motherwell. 'Its greatest virtue is its variety,' writes *The New York Times* of the exhibition, 'there are not only such famous pictures as the Ben Shahn, but also typical work by Charles Burchfield, Edward Hopper, and other viewers of the American scene, and such more recent social comment classics as Jack Levine's *Gangster's Funeral* and Rico Lebrun's *Buchenwald Cart.* There are little known names (which for me included Wood Gaylor, Hella Moravec, Gyula Zilzer) for spice.' An October show at the Art Center displays sculpture by fifty modern artists; Lee Bontecou, Marisol Escobar, Alberto Giacometti, and Pablo Picasso are among the many influential figures who contribute work.

RITES OF PASSAGE, 1988
SEKOU SUNDIATA

This course investigates the rites of passage in American culture. We will examine the ways in which the culture prepares or fails to prepare its young for transition into the community of adult men and women. Using literature, the performing arts, and student writings as source material, we will look at the role of the Challenge, the Vision Quest, and the Initiation in rites of passage. The major themes to be explored are death, rebirth, and transformation as three basic aspects in the process of transition. Both a seminar and writing course, there will be required readings and writing assignments.

1989

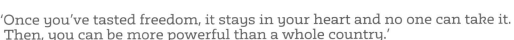

'Once you've tasted freedom, it stays in your heart and no one can take it. Then, you can be more powerful than a whole country.'
↗ **AI WEIWEI** Student and Guest Speaker

who ran the risk of being isolated by his act of angry response, an isolation that is part of the way racism operates. Third, I wanted to support the student effort to impress on the administration and on everybody that aggressive and heartfelt measures to bring a more diverse faculty and student body to the college must be taken — and soon.

Snitow and a group of faculty representatives meet with Fanton. On November 21, he publishes a letter to The New School community. While he personally finds the image 'deeply offensive and racist', he reprises his plea for free expression:

Let us not frame the issue as if freedom of expression and freedom from intolerance are incompatible or are enemies. They are both cherished values, and we should not have to choose which one we hold more dear. The question, I think, is how to use freedom of expression more vigorously in pursuit of a society free of prejudice and intolerance of all kinds. There are few people in this community who are not deeply torn over the issues the Matsunaga exhibit raises, on the one hand deeply committed to freedom of expression, on the other, passionate about the elimination of racism. ... It would be a sorry outcome if we let this episode divide us to the benefit of those who do not share our commitment to freedom of expression and to the search for a more just and humane society.

In the context of the 'Culture Wars', first *The Village Voice* and then *The New York Times* pick up the story. A series of protests follow on campus. The student body divides; some take Fanton's position. Sundiata is targeted with hate mail.

In five months' time, the NEA institutes what will come to be known as an 'obscenity clause', and instructs The New School to agree to the terms before receiving funding it was awarded for a courtyard renovation and installation by sculptor Martin Puryear. The New School refuses and, deploying many of Fanton's arguments from the Matsunaga Affair, files a suit against the NEA, winning a landmark battle three years later.

The Calpis logo, which was based on a 1924 work by German painter Otto Dunckel, is discontinued in July, 1990. John Jeffries remains faculty at The New School through 1997; Jonathan Fanton remains The New School President through 1999; Sekou Sundiata remains faculty until his death in 2007; Ann Snitow remains faculty as of 2019. Matsunaga, in an April 1990 letter to the Parsons Galleries, is apologetic for the Calpis work, and 'the trouble it caused'. In a 2004 reflection, 'The Calpis Incident at the New York Exhibit', Matsunaga disavows responsibility for the image, claims a Japanese historical context beyond American understanding, and laments that freedom of speech and public debate, enviable attributes of the 'American spirit', are not present, or even possible, in Japan.

'I knew it right away: I am a part of the feminist continuum. I am entering myself. The political radical that I was born to be was finding context, changing shape ... becoming female.'
↗ **ANI DIFRANCO** Student

SAYAR
NEW SCHOOL STUDENTS AND STAFF AGAINST RACISM

MEETING

Thursdays   ,at   7:45pm
GF Building 65 5th Ave.
Rm **209**

* Are you concerned about the institutionalized form of racism at The New School?

* Have you ever experienced an incident of direct or indirect racism at The New School?

* Do you feel that the **Eurocentrism** at The New School is a problem?

* Do you want to oversee the hiring of new minority faculty members.

* Do you feel that the curriculum and financial aid is racist towards Minority/Third World students?

* Are you concerned about the growing climate in The New School? AND IN NYC

* Help prepare for The Dec 2 intercollegiate Conference on Racism at CUNY

* The only voice that is heard and understood is the voice of collective action.

All Welcome
Parsons/Lang/GF/Managment / Sta

In 1990, a university diversity initiative resolves to address a lack of diversity in course curriculums, events, student body, and faculty and administrative representation at The New School. Six years after the adoption of the Diversity Initiative, students demand a more rigorous effort to foster diversity on campus. A student protest, the Mobilization, splits The New School community; the Mobilization spans months, with actions that include a nineteen-day hunger strike, sit-ins, die-ins, public forums, pamphlets and fliers, and a heated confrontation with New School President, Jonathan Fanton. The protests result in a commitment by the President's office to appoint five scholars of color to the Graduate Faculty, and a renewed pledge to seek diversity at The New School.

'WHEN YOU CHOOSE THE LESSER OF TWO EVILS, ALWAYS REMEMBER THAT IT IS STILL AN EVIL.'
MAX LERNER

AMERICAN DIALECTICS: ART IN NY, 2019
JED PERL

Since the end of World War II, art in New York has been animated by five powerful dialectical conflicts: between the artist and the public; abstraction and representation; romanticism and empiricism; spontaneity and reflection; nihilism and tradition. Nearly all of these conflicts originated in the earlier history of European modernism, and in 'American Dialectics' we will see how Old World ideas achieved a new weight, thrust, velocity, and impact as they were reshaped amid the exuberant forces of New York, the melting pot city. In a course that will range from Jackson Pollock, Willem de Kooning, and Joan Mitchell to Andy Warhol, Lee Bontecou, and Donald Judd, we will see how a variety of dialectical ways of thinking—ranging from Hegelian idealism to Kierkegaard's Either/Or to Hans Hofmann's Push/Pull—helped shape the artist's evolving sense of self and society in the rush-hour city of the postwar years. Readings will focus on writings by artists, critics, and other movers and shakers of the period, including Clement Greenberg, Harold Rosenberg, Peggy Guggenheim, Barnett Newman, Edwin Denby, Anni Albers, Grace Hartigan, Susan Sontag, Morton Feldman, and John Cage. Our exploration of overarching historical and theoretical forces will be grounded in close analysis of primary sources both visual and verbal. Where possible, classroom sessions will be supplemented by visits to galleries, museums, and relevant New York City landmarks. This exploration of developments in the visual arts in the decades after World War II will leave students with the theoretical and analytical tools needed to locate and interpret particular artistic developments within a broader social and historical context.

'I was born black and a female. I was born in a depression after one world war, and came into my adolescence during another, and while I was still in my teens the first atom bombs were dropped on human beings. I have been personally the victim of physical attack which was the offspring of racial and political hysteria. I have lost friends and relatives through cancer, lynching and war, drug addiction, alcoholism, mental illness — and I have come to maturity, as we all must, knowing that greed and malice, brutality, indifference, and, perhaps above all else, ignorance — abound in this world.'
↗ **LORRAINE HANSBERRY** Student

Clockwise from top left:

Susan Sontag.
Bob Adelman, 1981

Poster for a meeting of the New School Students and Staff Against Racism, 1989

Richard Griffith, Oscar Brand, Anita Sheer, Art Farmer, and Michael Benedict in the courtyard of The New School, 1963

Unidentified sculpture in the courtyard of The New School.
Peter Moore, 1964

A NEW UNIVERSITY PROFESSOR

Leonardo
El Greco
Caravaggio
Rembrandt

CLOSELY WATCHED TEXTS, 2008
LYNNE TILLMAN

In this class we read and watch a variety of texts: *The God of Nightmares*, a novel by Paula Fox; *The House of Mirth* by Edith Wharton; stories by Faulkner, Flannery O'Connor, and Denis Johnson, and essays by Primo Levi, Freud, and Virginia Woolf. We will also watch and read films: Alfred Hitchcock's *Rear Window*, for one, and make studio visits to contemporary artists. We will look at various texts in many ways, including how they question democratic ideas, principles, and concepts that are deployed inside an array of narratives. Reading closely helps us become better writers and thinkers; it is incumbent upon us to understand the mechanics and apparatus by which an essay, novel, story, film, or artwork comes to generate meanings. As there is no single definition of a close reading, what 'closely' means when we approach texts is, in a sense, ours to figure out.

1967

'Perhaps there is only one cardinal sin: impatience. Because of impatience we were driven out of Paradise, because of impatience we cannot return.'
↗ **W.H. AUDEN** Faculty

'SCIENCE IS ROOTED IN THE WILL TO TRUTH. WITH THE WILL TO TRUTH IT STANDS OR FALLS.'
↗ **MAX WERTHEIMER** Faculty

'I PREFER TO BE AT A PARTY WHERE A FIGHT MIGHT BREAK OUT.'
↗ **ROBERT GLASPER** Student

Hannah Arendt responds in *The New Yorker* to the controversy engendered by her five-part series, 'Eichmann in Jerusalem: Adolf Eichmann and the Banality of Evil', which first appeared in the magazine four years before:

> No one has ever doubted that truth and politics are on rather bad terms with each other, and no one, as far as I know, has ever counted truthfulness among the political virtues. Lies have always been regarded as necessary and justifiable tools not only of the politician's or the demagogue's but also of the statesman's trade. Why is that so? And what does it mean for the nature and the dignity of the political realm, on one side, and for the nature and the dignity of truth and truthfulness, on the other? Is it of the very essence of truth to be impotent and of the very essence of power to be deceitful?

In June, it is announced by *The New School Bulletin* that Arendt, formerly a professor at the University of Chicago and 'a celebrity of world-wide stature', will be joining the full-time faculty. The welcome chronicles two columns of her accomplishments. Arendt, who had previously taught high-profile courses at The New School in 1952, 1953, 1964, and 1965, will remain at The New School until her death in 1975. The New School establishes the Hannah Arendt Center in 2000; the center's foremost mission is to provide full online access to Arendt's digitized archive through The New School's Fogelman Library.

'It is, I think, a rather sad reflection on the present state of political science that our language does not distinguish between such key terms as power, strength, force, might, authority, and, finally, violence—all of which refer to distinct phenomena. To use them as synonyms not only indicates a certain deafness to linguistic meanings, which would be serious enough, but has resulted in a kind of blindness with respect to the realities they correspond to. Behind the apparent confusion lies a firm conviction that the most crucial political issue is, and always has been, the question of Who rules Whom? Only after one eliminates this disastrous reduction of public affairs to the business of dominion will the original data concerning human affairs appear or rather reappear in their authentic diversity.'

↗ HANNAH ARENDT Faculty

TERRORISM / WAR ON TERROR, 2019
JEREMY VARON

Long before September 11, 2001, the violence of non-state actors, frequently described as 'terrorism' by its opponents, was part of global political life. Since 9/11, and with the violence of ISIS, terrorism remains at the center of American politics and culture, evident in the anguish of U.S. policy, the securitization of everyday life, and various measures in the name of the 'war on terror'. This course takes an analytic, historical, theoretical, and critical view of the entire discourse on terrorism in the United States. … Is terrorism an especially extreme and reprehensible version of political violence? Or is it simply violence one does not like, no better or worse than other violence? The class then considers the varieties of violence called terrorism, from the deeds of Russia's Narodniks, to that of the 1960s-era Tupamaros and Weather Underground, to present-day proponents of national liberation. It next engages theories of 'cosmic war' as a frame to understand political violence, its redemptive promise, and its gross moral errors. The course looks finally at common practices to defeat terrorism, alert to how such efforts repeat the immoralities they seek to combat. Special attention will be given to U.S. detention policy as it pertains to detainees at Guantanamo and affects Muslim populations in the United States and worldwide. The course exists at a time of new 'terrorist' struggles germane to the United States—principally ISIS—as well as seemingly endless counterterrorist wars in Yemen,

Clockwise from top left:

▬▬▬ Hannah Arendt, undated

▬▬▬ Hannah Arendt at The New School, 1969

THE WORLD OF WORLD

In the fall of 2001, The New School's Julien J. Studley Graduate Program in International Affairs (GPIA) embarks on its first semester. Fifty students make up the rosters of four classes: 'Global Flows', 'Culture and Media in International Affairs', 'Comparative Development Experience', and the 'Practitioners Workshop'. Many of the students are not only new to the school but international, and new to the city.

9/11: students and faculty of the program witness the events at the World Trade Center — some through media, some by looking out their windows, some by looking up. Lower Manhattan is shut down. Military and police checkpoints span 14th Street, Houston Street, and Canal Street. New Schoolers, with other New Yorkers, mourn, volunteer, and respond politically, intellectually, and creatively. GPIA Professor Nina Khrushcheva, at the time of the attack, had been by The New School, jogging across Sixth Avenue when the second tower was hit; with a straight sight line to the World Trade Center, Khrushcheva watched events transpire. Khrushcheva volunteers at nearby St. Vincent's Hospital, and in her media class in the days that follow, she and her international students, with as much perspective as possible, analyze and discuss the post-9/11 news coverage. In 2019, Khrushcheva will remember:

> Because of the diversity of the GPIA's first group of students, we were able to grasp the potential perils of the globalized world. I learned as much from my students as they did from me, probably more. One of those lessons was that no event happens in a vacuum, policy decisions increasingly affect the world order. Equipped with this understanding our first-year graduates were particularly keen on jobs that can influence and improve policy making in America and abroad.

In the days, weeks, and months that follow 9/11, many students take time off from The New School, or change the course of their studies. Students of the GPIA remain. The attitude is steadfast: crisis is a call to action.

'Never feel self-pity, the most destructive emotion there is. How awful to be caught up in the terrible squirrel cage of self.'
↗ **MILLICENT FENWICK** Student

'The greatest benefit is if teachers are willing to present different interpretations or points of view. Students figure out for themselves what they want to take away; they put together their own understanding of the economy.'
↗ **FRANKLIN DELANO ROOSEVELT III** Student

'I don't think we have to have a personal relation to a life lost to understand that something terrible has taken place, especially in the context of war.'
↗ **JUDITH BUTLER** Guest Speaker

Looking down Sixth Avenue, 2016

WAR

'Today's milestone is human madness. Politics is a part of it, particularly in its lethal outbursts. Politics is not, as it was for Hannah Arendt, the field where human freedom is unfurled. The modern world, the world of world war, the Third World, the underground world of death that acts upon us, do not have the civilized splendor of the Greek city state. The modern political domain is massively, in totalitarian fashion, social, leveling, exhausting. Hence madness is a space of antisocial, apolitical, and paradoxically free individuation.'

↗ **JULIA KRISTEVA** Guest Speaker

POLITICAL ANTHROPOLOGY, 1963
ARTHUR J. VIDICH

A description and analysis of the traditional structure and bases of authority in a typical series of primitive and non-Western societies is presented to provide the basis for an understanding of the political effects of colonial and imperial penetration. Native politics is analyzed as a process of decomposition and internal revolution with an emphasis on nativism, resistance movements, changing distributions of power, and the emergence of new political myths. Special attention is paid to the groups, classes, and leaders who are crucial in effecting the transition to the politics of administration and the national state.

LAW AND TERRORISM, 2018
GLYNN TORRES-SPELLISCY

The conclusion of World War II led to a new era in international relations, one purportedly based on international law and human rights. In practice, however, states frequently ignore international legal requirements when the laws impede the pursuit of their own national interests. Since the catastrophic attacks on September 11, 2001, the United States has responded to security threats with policies and practices in its declared Global War on Terrorism that have challenged fundamental legal understandings. These policies have not so much disregarded international law as redefined it. This course focuses on the complex legal and domestic constitutional issues posed by the U.S. government's words and actions. Topics range from domestic issues, such as the U.S.A. Patriot Act, warrantless wiretapping, and indefinite detention, to international legal issues, such as the doctrine of preemption, the practice of 'extraordinary rendition', and the treatment of detainees in U.S. custody and control. Policies of the Bush and Obama administrations are compared and contrasted with respect to effects on the international legal order.

'TO THE SUM TOTAL OF MY LIFE BELONGS THE INSIGHT THAT THERE IS NO COMPLETE HOPELESSNESS.'

↗ **WILLY BRANDT** Honorary Degree Recipient

Robert Demeranville, in the GPIA's first class, is jogging along the Hudson River in New Jersey's Liberty State Park on September 11th. He is an onlooker as the hijacked planes strike the World Trade Center. Demeranville and others assist those who need immediate care as they arrive—fleeing Ground Zero—on boats from Manhattan. In 2004, after his graduation, Demeranville joins the United States Agency for International Development Office of Foreign Disaster Assistance as a Humanitarian Logistics Officer. Since joining USAID/OFDA, Demeranville has taken part in humanitarian aid efforts in Sudan, South Sudan, Hurricane Katrina, the Pakistan earthquake, Democratic Republic of the Congo, Myanmar for Cyclone Nargis, the West Africa Ebola crisis, the Haiti earthquake, the Chile earthquake, the Libya crisis, the Philippines for Super Typhoon Yolanda, the Nepal earthquake, the Mexico earthquake, Hurricane Matthew in the Caribbean, and, most recently, the Cyclone Idai response in Mozambique.

Immediately following 9/11, The New School turns over the courtyard and the second floor of the Eugene Lang building to St. Vincent's counselors as they assist families searching for loved ones. Much of Lower Manhattan is off-limits, and Student Services opens the Albert and Vera Academic Center to students who need a place to stay.

October, 2001, The New School Creative Writing Program co-hosts a Words to Comfort reading series in the Tishman Auditorium. The event raises money for the WTC Relief Fund and responds in poetry to the previous month. Readers include Claire Danes, Oscar Hijuelos, Rick Moody, Sharon Olds, Richard Price, and Lou Reed. In all, sixty readers—community members to NYPD officials—take the stage.

'THINGS CHANGE IN EVERY LIFE AND DISAPPEAR,
BUT IT IS THE PHOTOGRAPHS THAT REMAIN
FROM MY LIFE. THEY ARE WHAT I LOOKED AT,
FELL IN LOVE WITH (OR DIDN'T), AND NEVER FORGOT.
THERE ARE PICTURES OF MEN AND BOYS,
WOMEN AND GIRLS,
STATUES,
PENSIVE MONKEYS;
MOMENTS THAT TOOK MY BREATH AWAY,
ANGERED ME, MADE ME SMILE.'

↗ **CHARLES HARBUTT** Faculty

THE OBSCENITY CLAUSE

The National Endowment for the Arts (NEA) has granted The New School $45,000 toward the design of its courtyard and community garden, the only open space on campus. With an attack on the NEA led by Senators Jesse Helms and Alfonse D'Amato, the NEA leadership yields, and insists its grantees sign an 'obscenity clause' prior to the receipt of awarded funds. The clause is based on the 1991 Helms Amendment, which truncates the freedom of the NEA, but was not in play at the time of the 1990 grant selections. A conservative victory in the 'Culture Wars', the clause will allow politicians to decide what constitutes art. The thousands of grantees — among them, The New School, Shakespeare in the Park, and The Public Theater — balk. On their behalf, The New School's President, Jonathan Fanton, initiates legal action, and issues a five-page statement:

> *We believe the obscenity condition even as now interpreted, will continue to cause grant recipients to avoid producing controversial art for fear it will be seen as coming too close to the line that defines prohibited speech. ... It becomes more and more apparent that both the intent of the obscenity clause as adopted by Congress and its effect as implemented by the NEA is not to prevent government funds from being used to support obscenity. Rather, it is to suppress ideas and speech that the government finds dangerous or offensive.*

The tradition of a New School open area dates back to the first location of the school, 1919 to 1931, and the 'courtyard campus' of the London Terrace building in Chelsea. With the move to the Village, The New School renewed the concept in the 4,500-square-foot aperture between the iconic 12th Street building and the acquired building at 11th Street, an addition contiguous to the other side of the block. Since 1960, the 'courtyard' had played host to theatrical events, sculpture exhibitions,

'Unacknowledged leg
term for those poets ar
and political influence,
for America. The Unit
not provide for an op
Amendment does gua
often, it has been inc
writers, that have tak
opposition, conscient
dissent. ... When W.E.B
of the NAACP, he call
the pamphlets Tom P
American Revolution. \
such latent connection
figures and issues, inc
on civil disobedience, F
Lucretia Mott on the r
on war and empire,
society, Randolph Bou
and revolution, H.L. M
Norman Mailer and Gore Vidal on the Cold War.

jazz concerts, and creative, community, and political gatherings of all kinds. As part of the $2.6 million renovation of the 11th Street building, which is to house Eugene Lang, the school's newly established liberal arts college, American sculptor Martin Puryear has been commissioned to conceive of a space true to the evolving institution; Michael Van Valkenburgh, a landscape architect, who will work with Puryear. Toward fundraising, The New School has also sold a prized sculpture by Isamu Noguchi, a sculptor with a longstanding relation to the institution. Noguchi worked closely, over a thirty-year period, with Martha Graham, former New School faculty. A bronze cast of Noguchi's *Rocking Chair: Appalachian Spring*, as of 2019, remains in a fixed installation in the lobby at 12th Street; in honor of Graham, Noguchi gave the bronze, one of eight, to the New School. The original Rocking Chair design was used as a set piece for Graham's ballet, *Appalachian Spring*; the musical accompaniment for *Appalachian Spring*, by Aaron Copland, also New School faculty, was recognized in a Pulitzer Prize.

Facing judiciary defeat in 1991, the NEA backs off its demands, The New School declares victory, and the Vera List Courtyard moves toward a 1997 unveiling. Since then, limitations and assaults by the Congress on the NEA have been continuous.

'A conservative is a fellow who is standing athwart history and yelling "Stop!"'
↗ **WILLIAM F. BUCKLEY, JR.** Faculty

THE LONG QUEER 1990S, 2018
AMALLE DUBLON

The 1990s was a moment of aesthetic and critical foment for queer and trans life and politics. In New York, Los Angeles, and other U.S. cities, planned gentrification and rezoning—and resistance to them—had a lasting impact on a generation of artists and theorists, as well as the city's sexual, racial, and economic landscape. This course asks after the ongoing aesthetic and cultural inheritance of this period. We will study artists' interests in questions of social life, sexual and racial politics, space, and governance in the 1990s, as well as key concepts in critical race studies, black studies, queer and gender theory, and the economic left that emerged under the pressures of this period. Through artwork, critical writing, and archival material, we will trace how the notion of 'public sex' came into focus among queer and trans organizers, artists, and academics during a period of heightened response to HIV / AIDS, broken windows policing, and the 'clean-up' of areas of sexual commerce and recreation. How did entwined art and political practices yield legacies of performance art, printmaking, dance, and photography, as well as video, TV broadcast, and the beginnings of Internet-based work? We will explore the material and infrastructural histories that shaped queer and trans artistic production, such as mass movements against policing, the dot-com boom and the expansion of the Internet, the destruction of welfare, and the attack on state arts funding.

'You can't be a risk taker and expect to win each and every time. If you could control the future, then you wouldn't be taking any risks. And while failure leaves a bitter taste in your mouth, the sweetness of winning more than makes up for it.'
↗ **RUTH WESTHEIMER** Student

'A CIVILIZED SOCIETY IS ONE WHICH TOLERATES ECCENTRICITY TO THE POINT OF DOUBTFUL SANITY.'
↗ ROBERT FROST Faculty

'Democracy may mean something more than a theoretically absolute popular government, but it assuredly cannot mean anything less.'
↗ **HERBERT CROLY** Founder

1991

'The more superficial someone is, the more likely he will be to yield to Evil. That is the Banality of Evil.'
↗ **HANNAH ARENDT** Faculty

THE ELDERS' UPRISING

Since its inception in 1962, the Institute for Retired Professionals has been a thriving emblem of The New School's philosophy of experiential and lifelong learning. *The New York Times*, reporting on the group, details growing discord between the university and the membership. While The New School seeks to rejigger programming to encourage a more diverse curriculum and IRP student body, the group charges the school with limiting and diminishing offerings. With negotiations, the parties resolve their differences, and, as of 2019, there are over 300 members in the highly selective program, which has inspired upward of 500 similar academic models on campuses nationwide.

SOCIAL SECURITY, 1945
FRIEDA WUNDERLICH

The problem of security. Insurance, assistance, relief. Health insurance, workman's compensation, old age and disability insurance, unemployment insurance. Economic and social problems of wages. Minimum wages, fair wages, wage fixing by compulsory arbitration, family wages, sliding scales.

INTRODUCTION TO SOCIAL GERONTOLOGY, 1962
JESSE J. FRANKEL

A course of import to all age groups. ... The course consists of a series of lectures and discussions, using a multi-disciplinary approach, on the social and cultural problems of aging; that is, how older groups are affected by, and how they affect, social change. ...

FAMILY IN AMERICAN SOCIETY, 1963
LESTER SINGER

Analysis of the family in contemporary American society. The family is viewed as an institutional form, a social system in process, and as a socializing agency. The family patterns of a variety of other societies provide a perspective for analysis.

THE TWO WORLDS OF DR. SPOCK: CHILDREN AND SOCIETY, 1972

Dr. Benjamin Spock will deliver three lectures integrating the two major concerns of life—children and the social order in which they live. Topics include: present strains in middle-class child rearing; the relationship between rearing methods and the youth culture; the educational and political requirements for saving the world; the future of the family; future roles of father and mother.

1994

'Is it in part our thinking of age too as disaster that in some of us prompts new resistance and enterprise in later life? The disparaging view of age as useless and the positive implications of youth as dynamic have produced a variety of results: have hidden in some of our "senior citizens", have damned in others that confluence of widely distributed sources of individual experience, which is the long-lived, developed personality may become the flow of reasoned change, of considered reintegration of people, circumstances, events.'
↗ **CLARA MAYER** Dean, Vice President and Trustee

'THE GREAT THING ABOUT GETTING OLDER IS THAT YOU DON'T LOSE ALL THE OTHER AGES YOU'VE BEEN.'
↗ **MADELEINE L'ENGLE** Student

NEW SCHOOL BULLETIN
Vol. 23 No. 4   September 23, 1965

'One's lifework, I have learned, grows with the working and the living. Do it as if your life depended on it, and the first thing you know, you'll have made a life out of it.'
↖ **THERESA HELBURN** Faculty

In 1985, Franco Modigliani is awarded the Nobel Memorial Prize in Economics 'for pioneering studies of saving and financial markets'. An Italian prodigy conferred an honor by Benito Mussolini, Modigliani, due to racist legislation, was nevertheless forced to flee Italy with his family in 1938. In 1944, at The New School for Social Research, he completed his doctoral thesis, which he wrote under the advisement of Ukrainian-born Graduate Faculty Professor Jacob Marschak, and Russian-born Graduate Faculty Professor Abba Lerner.

In 2009, Teresa Ghilarducci is named, by *the U.S. News & World Report*, 'the Most Dangerous Woman in America', in relation to her newly released book *When I'm Sixty-Four: The Plot against Pensions and the Plan to Save Them*. The examination of the retirement dilemma is Ghilarducci's fourth book on the subject. At The New School, Ghilarducci is the Bernard L. and Irene Schwartz Professor of Economics and the Director of the Schwartz Center for Economic Policy Analysis (SCEPA) and the Retirement Equity Lab (ReLab).

'EDUCATION IS NOT PREPARATION FOR LIFE; EDUCATION IS LIFE ITSELF.'
↗ **JOHN DEWEY** Founding Faculty

'The idea is to die young as late as possible.'
↗ **ASHLEY MONTAGU** Faculty

'I think, at a child's birth, if a mother could ask a fairy godmother to endow it with the most useful gift, that gift should be curiosity.'
↖ **ELEANOR ROOSEVELT** Advisory Committee Member and Speaker

Clockwise from top left:

The New School Bulletin, September, 1965

English in Action class session, *circa 1964*

THE ART OF DANCE

For decades, perhaps half a century, an historic work of art, a treasure to New York and Latin America, has been sealed within a New School wall.

The work, restored and returned to view after a six-year process of planning and conservation, is unveiled at Parsons with a press release that explains: 'The 17-foot-long mural was commissioned by The New School, alongside works by José Clemente Orozco and Thomas Hart Benton, for its first building, an international style landmark by Joseph Urban.'

The mural, *Ecuadorian Festival* (oil on canvas, 1932), is an imaginative dance celebration by Camilo Egas, and a seminal example of Indigenismo, a movement of which Egas was a founder. The last of three murals commissioned for the Joseph Urban building, the dynamic figures fulfill a social conscientiousness and a global outlook. The painting is situated in a receiving area outside a dance studio known to the twenty-first century campus as 'The Martha Graham Dance Studio'. (The studio was dedicated to Martha Graham in 1962, the year the school inaugurated its Experimental Dance Center.)

In 1931, having lost its lease in Chelsea's London Terrace, The New School moved to its own building; there, the curriculum expanded to include dance, a subject that had been curtailed by space constraints. Urban's design for the dance studio was informed by New School faculty in dance—including Martha Graham and Doris Humphrey, both of whom would begin teaching at The New School in Spring of 1930, the last year in London Terrace. Humphrey and Graham were integral to the dance program for the next decade, and would retain ties with the school, returning for events and lectures; the workshop approach to teaching dance, pioneered at The New School, informed their educational models throughout their careers. Urban's design of the studio was also directed by his wife, Mary Porter Beegle, who

was dance faculty at Barnard College, and a writer, choreographer, director, and physical trainer for dance. As a performer, Beegle had been in Isadora Duncan's company; she would later work at The New School in public relations. The dance studio's circular configuration and wide bands of bright colors would be integrated into Egas' 1932 palette and composition: perpendicular movement and earth tones complement and contrast the swirling bursts of color.

At the time of the mural's completion, Egas had been teaching at The New School for three years. A year prior to his completion of *Ecuadorian Festival*, The New School had sponsored and exhibited his first solo show. As an artist, Egas had come of age in Ecuador, Spain, Paris, and Rome, pursuing an education in traditional and contemporary techniques and ideologies. Egas brought his sweeping capacities to The New School, where he was to remain for thirty-three years, initiating and directing the Art Workshop and subsequently directing the Art Department. He recruited a faculty contingent that included such luminaries as Berenice Abbott, Stuart Davis, Yasuo Kuniyoshi, and Lisette Model.

Egas died of cancer in 1962, and during one of the many subsequent renovations to the Urban building the mural was 'protected', only semi-successfully, through entombment within a wall. The matter was institutionally neglected until the 1990s, when there was a surge of interest in Egas. In 1994, Edward Sullivan, Professor and Chairman of the Art Department at New York University, penned a letter to Judith Friedlander, New School's Dean:

> I am writing to you now to congratulate you and The New School on your plans for restoring the Orozco murals. They are certainly one of the treasures of Mexican art in the U.S. However,

---

Clockwise from top left:

People sitting in the Caroline Tilden Bacon Room of The New School. Camilo Egas' mural painting, *Harvest in Ecuador*, can be seen on the back wall. Eliot Elisofon, 1940s

Barbara Morgan, *Doris Humphrey's The Matriarch*. 1938, estate stamped early 1990s. Gelatin silver print. 13 7/8 in. x 10 7/8 in. The New School Art Collection, Gift of Caitlin Morgan Sireci and Fiore Sireci, 2012

Barbara Morgan, *Martha Graham's Imperial Gesture*. 1938, printed late 1970s. Gelatin silver print. 13 7/8 in. x 10 7/8 in. The New School Art Collection, Gift of Caitlin Morgan Sireci and Fiore Sireci, 2012

'THE VALUE OF IMPERMANENCE IS TO CALL ATTENTION TO THE PERMANENT.'

↗ **STUART DAVIS** Faculty

'I keep coming back to qualities like empathy: think of the user and leave your body so you can really experience it from the other side.'
↗ **ROBERT VVONG** Student

128

'Youth is the season of the senses. Age passes through and beyond it, meets and survives the sorrows, the joys, and the boredom, lives once more in the young, reaches its values, when it is wise, in the course of long and varied experience of living. It is the task of the young, who are not too young, to help restore the continuity and the sense of life as a whole. Learn that misery like love neither comes only once nor lasts forever.'
↗ CLARA MAYER, Dean, Vice President, and Trustee

INTUITIVE DANCE AS MOVING MEDITATION, 2017
ASHLEY BRUNI

Focusing on the rituals and ceremonial dance practices of various lineages, students will learn techniques for deepening their physical expression and listening to the wisdom of the body. This exploration in embodied practice will provide a kinesthetic experience for understanding artistic impulse and discovering untapped creative potential. Students will engage in partner work to strengthen improvisational skills and moment-to-moment response, develop conscious listening skills, and probe the conditions of witnessing. Participants will benefit from an increased awareness of the space they occupy in relation to others, on the stage and off. Diverse genres of music and cross-cultural paradigms will play an integral role in class as students dynamically investigate primordial movements and subtleties of body language. Coursework will cover the increasingly mainstream ecstatic dance community and study the philosophies/practices of dance luminaries Gabrielle Roth, creator of the 5Rhythms movement practice, and Mary Starks Whitehouse, student of Martha Graham and founder of Authentic Movement.

BODILY ENGINEERING, 1931
MABEL ELSWORTH TODD

The posture and general physical appearance of the individual have been found to measurably affect mental attitudes. In order to achieve a complete adjustment to human affairs it is necessary to understand not only mortal behavior but bodily behavior as well. In this course the structure of the living body and the physical and psychological effects of the muscular balance in action will be studied.

this series of paintings is not the only masterpiece of Latin American art in the possession of The New School. I happened to visit today the mural (painted on canvas) on the lower level of the auditorium by the Ecuadorian painter Camilo Egas. This is an extremely important piece by one of the founders of modern art in Ecuador (who was associated with The New School for so many years). Unfortunately, the painting is in lamentable condition. ... In the context of Ecuadorian painting, this work by Egas has certainly as much importance as the Orozco murals. I would urge The New School to seriously consider saving this masterpiece. Before too long it will be too late.

Two smaller murals, a diptych by Egas located on the mezzanine level of the Urban building's theater, are freed from behind peg boards in 1996. The paintings, rolled up and removed at that time, were noted as missing within several years, and remain missing as of 2019.

In a 2011 interview with The New School, four months after *Ecuadorian Festival* is returned to public view, Michele Greet, art historian and author, discusses the emergence of Egas as an influential and prescient twentieth-century artist:

He worked in Rome and Spain and Paris and spent most of his life in New York City. So here's someone who's truly transnational, and bridging cultures, and ... there's new interest in his work as an example of what happens when these cultures come together at an exciting moment in the 1930s; but this is also what's happening in the contemporary art world now, with a focus on globalization, transnationalism, and multiculturalism.

Clockwise from top left:

▬▬▬ Ashley Bruni in the dance studio.
Elena Gorelik, 2018

▬▬▬ Camilo Egas working on his
Ecuadorian Festival mural, 1932

▬▬▬ Announcement of the dedication of the
dance studio as The Martha Graham Room.
The New School Bulletin. September, 1962

'A NATION THAT HAS NO MUSIC AND NO FAIRY TALES IS A TRAGEDY.'
↗ AI WEIWEI Student and Guest Speaker

DEDICATE MARTHA GRAHAM ROOM

The New School looked to both the past and the future on September 20 as it held special ceremonies marking the inauguration of its new Dance Forum and the dedication of the dance studio as The Martha Graham Room.

More than 150 leading figures in the dance world, education and the arts attended the event, which was chaired by August Heckscher, Special White House Consultant on the Arts and member of the New School Board of Trustees.

John Martin, retired dance critic of The New York Times, hailed Miss Graham's continuing contributions to America's cultural life. He reminded the gathering of the outstanding series of lectures and demonstrations on Dance Forms and Their Development that he, Miss Graham and Doris Humphrey offered at The New School in 1930-31.

A highlight of the reception was the announcement by sculptor Isamu Noguchi, that he will donate to The New School his bronze work, "Jocasta's Bed." The sculpture, originally conceived in 1946 as an element in his set for Miss Graham's ballet, "Night Journey," will be permanently placed in The Martha Graham Room.

Also participating in the reception program was Dr. Henry David, president of The New School, and Dr. William M. Birenbaum, deal. Among the many distinguished guests were Hanya Holm, Geoffrey Holder, Carl Van Vechten, Louise Nevelson, and Anthony Tudor, who will conduct several courses at The New School during the coming year.

1600 ATTEND SUMMER POETRY READINGS

The New School's first series of outdoor poetry readings in the Courtyard were enthusiastically received this summer. A total of 1600 persons attended the six readings, which were delivered by Marianne Moore, Stanley Kunitz, Alan Dugan, Leonie Adams, Kenneth Koch and Frank O'Hara. Although provisions were made for moving the readings indoors in case of inclement weather, this did not prove necessary. The readings were covered by WNDT, New York's new educational television station, which plans to televise part of the series this Fall. The success of this first venture augurs well for an expanded program of outdoor cultural activities at The New School next summer.

CO-BUILDER

As per the titular conceit, Alvin Johnson's *Pioneer's Progress* isn't a magnanimous sharing of recognition. In remembering his years as the Director and first President of The New School, Johnson mentions Clara Mayer just twice. But in her copy of the 1952 book, he inscribes: 'To my friend and co-builder of The New School'.

If not borne out by Johnson's memoir, the inscription is borne out by the historical record. Mayer worked alongside Johnson from 1924 until his retirement in 1945, remaining thereafter until 1961. Mayer had been a protégé of James Robinson, her professor at Barnard; in 1917, Robinson and a handful of professors fractured from Columbia University, which had taken a position that curtailed free speech, to form The New School. She followed Robinson, and in 1924, the young woman from a moneyed, influential family joined the Board of Directors. From that time forward, she would serve The New School as Assistant Director, Member of the Faculty Council, Associate Director, Member of the Executive Committee, Member of the Board of Trustees, Dean of the School of Philosophy and Liberal Arts, Dean of the University, and Vice President of the University. In an accounting of momentous occasions at The New School, it is difficult to open a file, dated to her office, that doesn't carry her stamp. She was actively involved in the recruitment of world-renowned faculty and lecturers, managing events and publicity, and maintaining relationships and correspondence with, for example, Berenice Abbott, John Cage, W.E.B. Du Bois, and Erich Fromm. In a personal letter, dated 1947, Albert Einstein thanked Mayer for her work in the 1930s to provide jobs and an intellectual community for scholars fleeing fascist and Nazi Europe. 'Very well,' wrote Einstein, did he know of 'the enormous contribution you and Dr. Johnson made to the rescue of the German professors through the University in Exile in those critical years and of the very large part you have played in making a fruitful place for them to work in this country'. In 1948, Mayer, who spoke, wrote, and translated German, was awarded an honorary Doctor of Letters from The New School.

In 1961, Henry David is appointed as the fourth President of The New School. President Emeritus Johnson is pleased with the choice, and writes to David: 'I am devoted to you.' But President David's first act is to fire Mayer, his longtime colleague, whom he sees as representative of an old guard, and as a competing center of power. David's brash act draws criticism from faculty—Henry Cowell, Alfred Kazin, Kenneth Koch, and others. The President has lost not only a primary administrator, but a crucial fiduciary officer and fundraiser. Within two years, David, having lost financial control of the school, is volunteering its carcass to New York University. Johnson, nearing ninety, rallies for a final victory, helping to secure the patrons necessary for the school's miraculous deliverance.

President David loses the little remaining support he has, and, in the mess that ensues, resigns the presidency. In her memoir, *The Manmade Wilderness* (1964), Mayer sets President Johnson and President David aside, and speaks to her pedagogical vision:

The role of education, as we conceive it, is to make actual what is potential in a given personality. Learning and teaching are essentially individual, in method and in aim: to self-development there is neither short cut nor assembly line. In the long run profoundly satisfying, it remains none the less an unremitting effort for discrimination, perspective, keen insights, clear values. If we are lucky, it goes on to the end of life.

As of 2019, Mayer is only known to have returned once after her professional departure: for an early 1970s Christmas party. Her papers, still in the process of digitization, are among the great treasures of The New School archive.

'Education is, after all, America's magic, as Ruth Benedict put it, and higher education is a major, perhaps the major, channel for social mobility. Today, the bourgeoisie may resent the students whom they cannot control, but they have invested enormously in them and tomorrow they may shift their loyalties in favor of their imperilled "children".
↗ STANLEY DIAMOND AND EDWARD J. NELL Faculty

Clockwise from top left:

Bernhard Mayer Memorial epitaph, 1928

Clara Mayer, undated

Letter from Clara Mayer to John Cage, June 18, 1958

CIVIL WARS; QUEER THEORY AND THE ARENAS OF ACTIVISM, 1994 ORGANIZED BY JULI CARSON AND MATTHEW EHRLICH WITH PANELISTS DOUGLAS CRIMP, C. LINDIWE EMOUNGU, SIMON LEUNG, LEE EDELMAN, JULIA SCHER, JOCELYN TAYLOR

Civil Wars: Queer Theory and the Arenas of Activism, an evening of panel discussions by distinguished practitioners in this field. Civil Wars will examine the application of academic theory to filmmaking, visual art, critical writings, and political activism. Focusing on the term 'civil'—as in civil war, civility, civil service, civil disobedience—the panelists will address society's view of appropriate parameters as central to the problems faced by the queer community and AIDS activists. As queer theory gains prominence within academia, increasing numbers of artists, filmmakers, and activists 'outside the ivory tower' apply queer studies as a vital part of their practice. Rather than adhering to a single agenda, queer theory has permitted the multiple voices of shifting identities to emerge. Civil Wars is essential education for all who are interested in the relationship of theory to practice and for all those engaged in understanding representation of identity in contemporary art.

ENLIGHTENED EXCHANGES, 2018 GINA WALKER

This course reads recently recovered published and private conversations between male and female thinkers that shed new light on women's participation in Enlightenment. We study the theological correspondence among Anna Maria van Schurman, Gisbertus Voetius, André Rivét, Jean de Labadie, and Bathsua Makin; Gabrielle Suchon's affinity for Spinoza, the philosophical interplay of René Descartes and Princess Elisabeth of Bohemia; Marie le Jars de Gournay's complex response to Michel de Montaigne; Marie Madeleine Jodin's political education in Diderot's library; the personal and intellectual communications between Damaris Cudworth and John Locke; Émilie du Châtelet and Voltaire; Margaret Cavendish and Francis Bacon; John Milton and Lucy Hutchinson. We consider women's idiosyncratic use of the Classical tradition in their engagement with canonical ideas, their reactions to each other, the new knowledge they produced, and the volatile public reception to 'the equality of the sexes'. We review contemporaneous and modern analyses of Poullain de la Barre's Cartesian argument that 'the mind has no sex' as a litmus test of the current diffusion of female intellectuals' works and reputations.

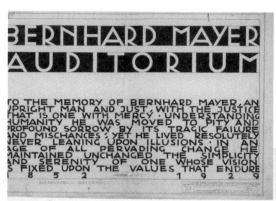

BERNHARD MAYER AUDITORIUM

1952

TO THE MEMORY OF BERNHARD MAYER, AN UPRIGHT MAN AND JUST, WITH THE JUSTICE THAT IS ONE WITH MERCY · UNDERSTANDING HUMANITY HE WAS MOVED TO PITY AND PROFOUND SORROW BY ITS TRAGIC FAILURE AND MISCHANCES · YET HE LIVED RESOLUTELY NEVER LEANING UPON ILLUSIONS · IN AN AGE OF ALL PERVADING CHANGE HE MAINTAINED UNCHANGED THE SIMPLICITY AND SERENITY OF ONE WHOSE VISION IS FIXED UPON THE VALUES THAT ENDURE 1852 · 1929

June 18, 1958

Mr. John Cage
RFD Willow Grove
Stoney Point, N.Y.

Dear John Cage:

You are one of the few people to whom money is really secondary, which makes me feel somewhat less unhappy about the size of the checks which you have been getting here. As teaching is at best a labor of love, perhaps it is of some relevance for me to tell you how much the association with you has meant to me personally as well as to the School.

Perhaps when you are teaching here this summer we may have the opportunity for an evening together, which I should appreciate.

Accept our many thanks for all that your work has contributed to the Music Department.

With warm regards,

Sincerely,

Clara W. Mayer
Vice President.

'Students come to The New School of their own volition because they want to know. This is a blessing to the teacher in many ways. New School students are the best of all question askers. They not only ask questions, they also make contributions of their own to the learning and the teaching process. They feel free and are encouraged to feel free, to bring their own experience and knowledge to bear upon the development of any point. In my classes I have often learned fundamental facts of greatest importance and in one or two cases I have persuaded students to publish in scientific journals, with much accruing benefit to the universe of knowledge. What more can a teacher say, than that he learns from his students? Another reason I like teaching at The New School is the warmth prevailing everywhere. Other schools are free, but at The New School warmth is added, and that makes a great deal of difference. There is a humanity and a cordiality at The New School which is unique. One feels welcome and free.'

↗ **ASHLEY MONTAGU** Faculty

THE PEOPLE PARADOX

The New School unveils the thirteenth site-specific work on the campus, *Pascal's Perfect Probability Pyramid & the People Paradox — The Predicament (PPPPPPP)*, by Agnes Denes. The work by Denes renders a 1980 drawing of *PPPPPPP* on a large scale. Denes' iconic pyramid of silhouetted figures is mapped as an eighteen-by-twenty-four-foot mural on the wall of the floor-through stairwell in the dining common in the new University Center.

In her 2008 book, *The Human Argument*, Denes considers individuals and their place in the pyramid: 'The magnificence of their collective accomplishments and the insignificance of the individual component are unmistakable. Not a single figure can walk away from the structure — they are the structure. They are the anatomy and the form and it is their illusions of freedom and the inescapability of the system that form the ultimate paradox.'

Denes hand drafted each of the original figures: black India ink on silk vellum. These figures were then digitally reproduced to monumental scale and placed on site. At the top of the pyramid, where the figures are spaced hairbreadths apart, the placements required painstaking perfection, as revisions were impossible. Bringing to the fore complicated issues of collective achievement, consumption, and individual sacrifice, the work hearkens to Denes' 1982 *Wheatfield — A Confrontation*, in which Denes planted two acres of wheat on a site two blocks from the Twin Towers that was valued at $4.5 billion. Denes' erstwhile wheatfield is also, as of 2019, approximately twelve blocks south of the post-9/11 *Irish Hunger Memorial*, a public arts work by Brian Tolle, an alumnus and former faculty of Parsons, and a site-specific artist of The New School Art Collection.

In 2019, on the eve of the fall centennial, Silvia Rocciolo, Curator of The New School Art Collection, considers *PPPPPPP* in the context of the school and its fine art holdings:

> In the dedication of her mural commission, Agnes Denes writes: 'read the figures, they are you'. I cannot think of a more apt summation of the extraordinary and unique body of works comprising The New School Art Collection, an ever-present reminder that art, in all its permutations, can be a radical act of community building. A vibrant articulation of the university's mission of education through free discourse and experimentation, the works highlight multiplicities of expression and sociopolitical and historical perspectives, and ultimately demonstrate how art, in all its permutations, can activate, engage, and lead to profound transformation. Read the figures, they are you.

'I AM NOT INFLUENCED BY OTHER HUMAN BEINGS. BUT I AM INSPIRED.'

↗ **ELAINE STRITCH** Student

'The fact that a cloud from a minor volcanic eruption in Iceland — a small disturbance in the complex mechanism of life on the Earth — can bring to a standstill the aerial traffic over an entire continent is a reminder of how, with all its power to transform nature, humankind remains just another species on the planet Earth.'

↗ **SLAVOJ ŽIŽEK** Faculty

'The paradox of education is precisely this — that as one begins to become conscious one begins to examine the society in which he is being educated.'
↗ **JAMES BALDWIN** Student and Guest Speaker

Previous pages:

Clara Mayer at Foreign Students' Tea, 1951

Clockwise from top left:

Agnes Denes, *Pascal's Perfect Probability Pyramid & the People Paradox – The Predicament*, 1980–2017. The New School Art Collection

I Stand in My Place with My Own Day Here: Site-Specific Art at The New School, edited by Frances Richard, a collaboration between The New School Art Collection and Parsons Curatorial Design Research Lab. Distributed by Duke University Press, 2019

'WHY IS IT SO UNUTTERABLY BENEFICIAL, THE THOUGHT THAT SOMEONE BESIDES MYSELF KNOWS ME?'

↗ KAREN HORNEY Faculty

Clockwise from top left:

Agnes Denes, Pascal's *Perfect Probability Pyramid & the People Paradox – The Predicament* (detail), 1980–2017. The New School Art Collection.

Vera List. undated

**PROBLEMS OF PEACE AND
THE LEAGUE OF NATIONS, 1920
JAMES ROBINSON, HARRY BARNES,
LEO WOLMAN, AND HORACE KALLEN**

This course will analyze the more important problems involved in the attempt to reconstruct international society on a stable and pacific basis. After an introductory lecture by Mr. Robinson, Mr. Barnes will discuss the development of modern nationalism and indicate the chief obstacles to peace contained therein. Mr. Robinson will then analyze the historic setting of internationalism and describe the psychological revolution which might make it possible to supplant the traditional notions of national sovereignty and to think in terms of international concepts. Mr. Wolman will give an exposition of the economic problems and forces relating to war and peace, with special reference to the economic background of the world war and the work of the Paris Peace Conference. Mr. Kallen will conclude the course with a discussion of the philosophical and political significance and implications of the proposed League of Nations, of the defects and merits of the specific league agreed upon by the Paris Conference, and of the nature and sources of the American opposition to the present proposed League of Nations.

In 1961, The New School's first Art Center-sponsored event, entitled 'Mechanism and Organism', premieres in the courtyard between the 12th and 11th Street buildings. Fifty American and European sculptors are exhibited. Each piece explores the changing relationship between man and machine in the modern city. The exhibit culminates in a roundtable discussion led by the Art Director of the Museum of Modern Art, Peter Selz.

In 2019, in concert with The New School centennial, The New School Art Collection and Parsons Curatorial Design Research Lab publishes *I Stand in My Place with My Own Day Here: Site-Specific Art at The New School*, edited by Frances Richard, with a foreword by Lydia Matthews and an introduction by Silvia Rocciolo and Eric Stark. In the 300-page monograph, upward of fifty esteemed writers consider the thirteen site-specific works of art realized for The New School. The works, central to The New School Art Collection, and distinguished by cultural and historical prominence, span a century of artists: Thomas Hart Benton, Agnes Denes, Camilo Egas, Gonzalo Fonseca, Alfredo Jaar, Glenn Ligon, Sol LeWitt, Rita McBride, Dave Muller, José Clemente Orozco, Martin Puryear and Michael Van Valkenburgh, Brian Tolle, and Kara Walker.

'NO AMOUNT OF SKILLFUL INVENTION CAN REPLACE THE ESSENTIAL ELEMENT OF IMAGINATION.'

↗ **EDWARD HOPPER** Student

'The secret to so many artists living so long is that every painting is a new adventure. So, you see, they're always looking ahead to something new and exciting. The secret is not to look back.'
↗ **NORMAN ROCKWELL** Student

'I CAN'T UNDERSTAND WHY PEOPLE ARE FRIGHTENED OF NEW IDEAS. I'M FRIGHTENED OF THE OLD ONES.'

↗ JOHN CAGE Student and Faculty

PEACE IS THE NEW

In the Spring of 1967, Students for a Democratic Society mobilize chapters at The New School and Columbia University. At Columbia, SDS students demand the university cease and disband research and investigation conducted on the behalf of the U.S. Department of Defense; SDS students at The New School demand that on April 13 the school cancel classes in solidarity with a scheduled national protest against the Vietnam War and the U.S. invasion of Cambodia. Both universities refuse. The New School's President, John Everett, contends that the school's established policy is one of political neutrality, and the demands made by the SDS chapter of The New School, he explains typify a 'confusion' that arises 'because we are wholly, deeply, and completely committed to the right of the human mind to be free'.

For three years, protests are ongoing at The New School and Columbia University. Students and faculty are arrested and injured. The responses of police officers, who also sustain injuries, range from calm and bureaucratic to brutal and arbitrary. Classes and academic pursuits are disrupted, campus buildings are occupied, and at The New School an 'Old New School' of the Graduate Faculty — émigrés who fled Europe prior to World War II — is pitted against student protest. A 1970 exposé in *The New York Review of Books*, 'The Old New School', by New School faculty members and protest organizers Stanley Diamond and Edward Nell, lays bare the hypocrisy of an old guard of University in Exile professors. Clashes between the aging professors and the radical baby boomers are vitriolic, but nevertheless full of pathos:

> The students seemed to have won a moral victory at the very moment the administration called in the police to clear premises that had been illegally occupied for a week. That is, while in the midst of a civil proceeding, the angry, resigned, and pressured administration resorted to immediate physical force. As the students walked out of the building to the waiting vans, through a cordon of police, under the puzzled eyes of the faculty, an authentically conservative political science professor wept. One distinguished philosopher in exile said to no one in particular, 'Now we've got the building back.' They've got the building, but the conflict over the character of the university is just beginning, and the struggle for the soul of the country goes on. As for the student strikers, they are moving their antiwar committees, seminars, and meetings out of The New School. This declaration of independence is a healthy thing and they have made their point. The Graduate Faculty of The New School was conceived in one crisis. Will it be reconceived in another?

'Understanding the limits of the dialogue possible in the elite but influential press is crucial to understanding our political lives.'
↗ **JANINE JACKSON** Student

'Don't let anybody tell you different, man: The main goal in life careerwise should always be to try to get paid to simply be yourself.'
↗ **KEVIN SMITH** Student

An exhibition designed and built in lieu of classes by the students of Parsons School of Design, as an expression of solidarity with the National Student Strike and a gift to the people of America, May, 1970

Previous pages:

▬▬▬ Parsons School of Design illustration student with lioness, 1948

Clockwise from top left:

▬▬▬ Poster for *Protest and Hope: An Exhibition of Sculpture, Painting, Drawing and Prints on Civil Rights and Vietnam*, 1967

▬▬▬ Poster for *Artists Against Nuclear Madness Present Dangerous Works*, 1982

▬▬▬ Class session with Tensegrity. Parsons School of Design Casey Coates Danson's student work, 1972–5

▬▬▬ "Students Stage a Peaceful Protest." *Courier Journal & Times,* May 24, 1970

▬▬▬ Booklet for the exhibition *My God! We're losing a great country*, 1970

DESIGN

'INSPIRATION SPRINGS MORE READILY FROM KNOWLEDGE THAN FROM IGNORANCE.'

↗ **HORACE KALLEN** Founding Faculty

1970

Students Stage a Peaceful Protest

By LANA ELLIS
Courier-Journal Staff Writer

Students at Parsons School of Design in New York demonstrated against the war, and no one was hurt. Like so many schools, Parsons suspended classes for the remainder of the school term, but once classes stopped the students worked harder than ever.

"Instead of burning buildings, we wanted to make a constructive statement," said Jane Snyder, organizer of the graphic peace offensive. Parsons, the alma mater of many of this country's leading fashion and furniture designers, illustrators and graphic artists, is usually the scene of a year-end exhibition of student accomplishments each May. The students chose to cancel their regular exhibit and prepare a visual protest instead.

"My God! We're Losing a Great Country" is the theme they chose to express their desire for peace and ecology. With the support of the faculty and administration, the students, led by the student council, worked for four days to prepare a graphic exhibit expressing their distress. Money for supplies came from the student council treasury and students' pockets.

The multi-room exhibits were a group effort with approval voted on by the students. "We have more unity in this school than there's ever been," said Miss Snyder.

Open to the public, the exhibit begins with a black room filled with lifesize plastic foam soldiers. Walking in the dark maze, a visitor must brush against and activate the soldiers. While music plays, photos are projected against the white figures.

Updated the Anthem

In the next room, students have contributed their original graphic designs. One is a book with each line of "The Star-Spangled Banner" brought up to date with modern photographs illustrating what the student believes the words mean today. One poster uses the words of a song from the musical, "South Pacific," to remind that "You have to be taught to hate and fear."

A small theater has been constructed where a 20-minute slide and music show

is presented. In a casket contains a

The Parsons' stu on their demonst letter plus round-President Nixon the event. The stu ticket money. Th graphed and blown poster. They rece telegram from a W tant saying the Pr attend. The ticket telegrams were re Secretary Walter woman Shirley Chi tary Robert Finch.

Miss Snyder's busy making pos other schools in materials donated dent funds, they've 6,000 posters a wee

The exhibit, wh on East 54th, mo New School for Sc museums, including expressed interest

One of the most colorful posters depicted symbols of peace.

'The basic thesis of gestalt theory might be formulated thus:
There are contexts in which what is happening in the whole
cannot be deduced from the characteristics of the separate
pieces, but conversely; what happens to part of the whole is,
in clearcut cases, determined by the laws of inner structure
of its whole.'
↗ MAX WERTHEIMER Faculty

BEAUTY AND USE, 1922
HORACE KALLEN

This course is an inquiry into the connection
between the fine arts and the other interests of the
community. Among the topics that will be discussed
are the soundness of the traditional distinction
between the beautiful and the useful; the various
conceptions of beauty; the sense of humor; the
nature of tragedy; what causes the formation and
the change of standards of taste; what are the
sources, the development and the qualities of such
... music, pure design, architecture,
... etry, the theatre and the
... ular attention will be given to
... and the specific differences
... nation of the artist, and to
... institutions as science, the
... try and the labor movement
... , the workmanship and the
... ious artists.

In March, 1970, in a brownstone down the street
from the Eugene Lang College entrance to The New School,
an accidental explosion is set off by members of the SDS
radical splinter, the Weather Underground, while members
of the group assemble nail bombs. (Since 1968, there had
been thousands of protest attacks—bombings, destruction
of property—all over the country.) Three Weathermen are
killed instantly, a third is crushed by the falling edifice of
the building, and the two Weathermen upstairs escape
without major injuries.

On May 4, 1970, at Kent State, national guardsmen
open fire on students, killing four and wounding nine. The
slogan, 'If you want to keep cool, go to the beach or the
New School', catches the attention of high school students,
who swarm to enlist in protest activities at The New School.
On May 7, 650 students at Parsons, which is in its first
semester as part of The New School, vote to suspend classes
'as an expression of solidarity with the National Student
Strike and as a dramatic indication of the loss of faith in
both the credibility and morality of the Nixon administration'.
Instead of protesting, Parsons students, with the support
of faculty, reconceive the 'travesty' of their graduating
exhibition as a group show that protests the war in Southeast
Asia: 'We are actively applying our time and talents
to further our opposition to the Indo-Chinese War and
the tragic events on some of the nation's campuses.'

For the May opening at Parsons, students send an
invitation to President Nixon; they include a round-trip
ticket, which they've paid for with their own money. The
White House declines, regretfully. The show, *My God,
We're Losing a Great Country*, moves to The New School
Art Center in June. In 1967, the Art Center, dedicated to
politically and historically engaged and often controversial
exhibitions, had mounted *Protest and Hope on Civil Rights
and Vietnam*.

'It is deeply comforting', remarks Art Center Director
Paul Mocsanyi in a press announcement, 'that in a world
where the mainstream of art betrays not the slightest
concern for human and moral values, the students of the
Parsons School of Design have created this exhibition.'
Mocsanyi would go on to hail the Parsons students as 'the
artistic spokesmen of their generation'.

The New School Art Center is located in the
Graduate Faculty building, which had been the site of the
school's most contentious protests. *The New York Times*,
in a June 13 review, announces: 'Peace is the New Design
at Parsons'.

POST-ELECTION
AMERICA SERIES, 2017

In response to the demand
information, for historical con
of then recent U.S. electio
consequences, The New Sch
14-week series of lectures by
called 'Post-Election Americ
led by experts in the topic a
sessions on the U.S. consti
law and policy, populism,
polarization, economic ineq
globalization, financialization
the future of health and per
change and environmental p
political economy of racial i
class politics, the urban-ru
political economy of the U.S.
is open to the public.
→ Introduction: Understandin
   with Will Milberg and Jessi
→ Race, class, and the urban-
   with Maya Wiley
→ U.S. Constitutional Law, wi
→ Political Polarization and I

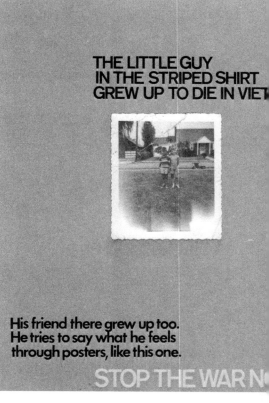

THE LITTLE GUY
IN THE STRIPED SHIRT
GREW UP TO DIE IN VIET

His friend there grew up too.
He tries to say what he feels
through posters, like this one.

STOP THE WAR N

'AND SO WE TURN THE PAGE
OVER / TO THINK OF STARTING.
THIS IS ALL THERE IS.'
↗ JOHN ASHBERY Guest Speaker

Clockwise from top left:

▬▬▬ Selection of student work
included in the exhibition,
*My God! We're Losing
a Great Country*, 1970

▬▬▬ *New York Daily News*,
April 23, 1970

GOD LOVE HOPE

Intended to coincide with spring break at U.S. colleges and universities, the first Earth Day takes place on April 22, 1970. Demonstrations and actions are held nationwide. A teach-in at Parsons addressing environmental sustainability is led by Stewart Brand, Merry Prankster, writer, activist, and the editor of the *Whole Earth Catalog*. Parsons, in its first semester with The New School, has simultaneously launched a Department of Environmental Design; The New School will not only offer courses and degrees, but will incubate environmental approaches to design in all sectors. By the end of 1970, the nonpartisan Earth Day movement results in the U.S. Environmental Protection Agency and the Clean Air, Clean Water, and Endangered Species Acts.

In February 1991, at its 13th Street gallery, Parsons opens a two-month exhibition, *Visual Perceptions: Twenty-Two African-American Designers Challenge Modern Stereotypes*. Curated by Roger Tucker, Michele Washington, and Fo Wilson, the exhibition 'seeks to raise consciousness and encourage the development of broader and more dimensional representations'. The exhibited designers are: Bill Allen, Gail Anderson, Darryl Beasly, Archie Boston, Keith Collins, Carl Davis, Seldon Dix, Gregory Grey, Ray Hooper, Eli Kinee, Ken McFarlin, Cheryl Miller, Reynolds Ruffin, Thom Shaw, Art Simms, Loretta Staples, Del Terrelonge, Ed Towles, Roger Tucker, Darryl Turner, Michele Washington, and Fo Wilson. 'The show', says co-curator Wilson, 'doesn't simply bring to light the presence of talented African-American graphic designers, it also asks the question: what role can the designer play in discouraging or perpetuating debasing cultural myths concerning any group of people?'

'American history contains much matter for pride and congratulation, and much matter for regret and humiliation.'
↗ **HERBERT CROLY** Founder

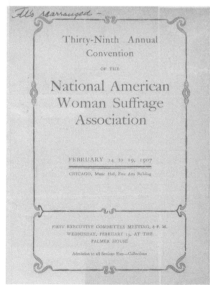

John Dewey, a thirty-five-year-old academic, boards a train bound for Chicago. It will be one of the last trains to run before the onset of the Pullman Strike, which will profoundly affect Dewey and the course of his research and perspective.

The nation is in the midst of a depression; strikes and unionization threaten the patriarchal dominion of industrial lords. Clashes between labor and ownership have broken out nationwide, with local, state, and federal authorities intervening on behalf of big money—sometimes with foot-dragging reluctance, sometimes with murderous enthusiasm. On the side of labor and social reform, there is an emergent optimism. A mere fifteen minutes speaking to a young rail proselytizer sends Dewey into a state of progressive rapture:

> I felt as if I had better resign my job teaching and follow him round till I got into life. One lost all sense of the right or wrong of things in admiration for his absolute almost fanatic sincerity and earnestness. ... I don't believe the world has seen but few times such a spectacle of magnificent, widespread union of men about a common interest as this strike evinces.

Clockwise from top left:

▬▬▬ Hull House community workshop poster, 1938

▬▬▬ John Dewey, 1946

▬▬▬ *Thirty-Ninth Annual Convention of the National American Woman Suffrage Association, 1907*

HULL-HOUSE COMMUNITY WORKSHOP

REGISTER NOW

FREE CLASSES
IN PAINTING-SCULPTURE
POTTERY-WEAVING-POSTER ART
ADULT CLASSES 7-10
CHILDREN'S CLASS 3:30

OR FURTHER INFORMATION WRITE OR PHONE HULL HOUSE
800 S. HALSTED ST. % ART DEPARTMENT PHONE MON. 6006

FEDERAL ART PROJECT-WPA-ILL.

'The need of a new institution which should be honestly free was actively discussed ... Beard and Robinson had resigned from their university in disgust with the oppressive action of the trustees, not actually directed against them but, as they saw it, vitally affecting them. John Dewey was in revolt against academic timidity and futility; Wesley Mitchell, although invulnerable as a statistical economist, was deeply discontented. ... The New School opened with éclat, for the spring term of 1919.'
↗ **ALVIN JOHNSON** First President and Founder

HABIT AND HISTORY, 1919
EMILY JAMES PUTNAM

The long predominance of habitual conduct over individual initiative in primitive society and in the early empires; the biological and social limitations which tend to foster habit and to develop it beyond its proper sphere; the technique of habit-breaking inaugurated by the Greeks and becoming a characteristic of western society; an effort to appraise the amount of excessive and undesirable habit in thought and action generally connected with such concepts as nationalism, religion, the status of women, etc.

'In the ultimate sense of education and of culture, there can be no conflicts. Education is the dynamic life process that makes us bearers and builders of culture; competent and independent contributors toward understanding life and carrying it forward on its various levels, physical, intellectual, and moral. When experimental physics turns up a fact in conflict with the body of physical doctrine, it is nothing more than a new and interesting problem, an area demanding more concentrated endeavor. Apparent culture conflicts are similar temporary stages on the way to a larger culture, a life with more content, individuals more capable of coping with it and enjoying life.'
↗ JULIE MEYER Faculty

'ANYONE WHO HAS BEGUN TO THINK, PLACES SOME PORTION OF THE WORLD IN JEOPARDY.'
↗ JOHN DEWEY Founding Faculty

Dewey is en route to the University of Chicago, where he will be a professor until his move to Columbia University in 1904. Upon his arrival in Chicago, the efforts of Hull House — an alms, outreach, and educational center — founded out of the women's movement, furthers his ideation of possibility. He will, in his lifetime, publish in the neighborhood of 700 articles and forty books. Among them: *The School and Society* (1899), *Democracy and Education* (1916), and *Schools of Tomorrow* (1915), which he co-writes with his daughter, Evelyn Dewey.

In 1919, when a splinter of Columbia University professors set out to form a 'New School', Dewey lends his name and principles of egalitarian and experiential learning. The time has come to render what is 'new'. One of the expatriated Columbia professors is James Robinson, who, in 2012, published *The New History*, which advocated for an active, socially conscious approach to history. In 1910, Theodore Roosevelt had put forth his presidential campaign platform with a call for a 'New Nationalism', whereas Woodrow Wilson put forth the winning platform, which called for 'New Freedom'. There was the religious movement of New Thought, the arts movements of New Sculpture and New Objectivity, and the 'New Woman' of the nineteenth-century women's movement—and, in 1918, *The New Republic* would publish an article by editor-in-chief and co-founder Herbert Croly that proposed and theorized an advancement in education that would take shape as a 'School of Social Research'.

Though Dewey declines several invitations to leave Columbia to join the insurgency, he does, after asking permission of Columbia's administration, teach several courses at The New School, and takes an increasing interest as the school gains students, credibility, and a place in American education and culture. He will return to The New School to celebrate his seventieth, eightieth, and ninetieth birthdays. For his ninetieth birthday, Dewey is saluted at events that span the better part of a week, but, above all, according to *The New York Times*, he honors the praise of New School's President Emeritus Alvin Johnson, who says that Dewey has helped liberate man from fear. 'The greatest protection against losing faith,' says Dewey, quoted in the *Times*, 'is to remember it means losing faith in ourselves. If we lose faith in human beings and human nature our outlook is sad indeed.'

This page:

Cover artwork by Keith Haring.
The New School Bulletin,
Spring, 1986

GAY AND LESBIAN HISTORY, 1996
JAMES C. WALLER

This summer, The New School examines gay and lesbian history at a crucial time when gay marriages and the ordination of gay clergy are making headlines nationwide. The growing field of gay and lesbian history is substantially altering our view of our civilization's past. To choose just two examples: the work of church historian John Boswell has shown that Western religious institutions' anti-homosexual ideology is a product of historical revisionism; likewise, the investigations of 'social constructionist' historians such as Jonathan Ned Katz and numerous others have indicated that familiar categories of human sexuality — including 'heterosexual' — may themselves be historically determined. In this course, James C. Waller uses major works of gay and lesbian history, biographical and autobiographical texts (including popular and mass-market works), and a few significant works of 'queer theory'.

'OUR FAITH IN THE PRESENT DIES OUT LONG BEFORE OUR FAITH IN THE FUTURE.'
↗ **RUTH BENEDICT** Student

NEW SCHOOLS FOR OLD

'Old myths, old gods, old heroes have never died. They are only sleeping at the bottom of our mind, waiting for our call. We have need for them. They represent the wisdom of our race.'
↗ **STANLEY KUNITZ** Guest Speaker

Evelyn Dewey publishes *New Schools for Old: The Regeneration of the Porter School*, which presents a model for education based on her transformation of a rural Missouri school into a community learning center. In 1915, she had published *Schools of To-morrow*, co-written with her father, John Dewey; where John Dewey's theories of education tended to be academic and philosophical, Evelyn Dewey was concerned with the practical implementation of progressive education. At the Porter School she had partnered with Elsie Clapp, who had been two years her senior at Barnard, and a graduate student of her father's at Columbia. Dewey, characterized by the *New York Herald* as one of Barnard's graduating 'militant suffragists and socialists', would be a political activist and a hands-on educational reformer whose impact would be felt nationally and globally for a century to come.

'Too often we're told that advocates of new policies are putting values of fairness above practical concerns, while supporters of laissez-faire are the ones who are serious about the economy. This isn't correct. For today's economy, the question is not whether we should help families with handouts; it's how to help families so they can thrive as workers and consumers. To boost long-term economic growth, businesses need a highly skilled workforce, ready and able to work. In today's economy, where most workers also have care responsibilities, this means we must find ways to address conflicts between work and life. These conflicts aren't trivial private travails; they're serious economic problems.'
↗ **HEATHER BOUSHEY** Student

1919

'History is, strictly speaking, the study of questions; the study of answers belongs to anthropology and sociology.'
↗ **W.H. AUDEN** Faculty

WOMEN IN NEW YORK, 1972
BETTY FRIEDAN

The relationship of women to the basic problem of the city today has not been understood or even explored by academicians, activists, policy makers, or even, in its larger implications, by women themselves. The course explores new and complex questions stemming from women's present situation in the city as it relates to basic city problems: poverty, violence, crime, pollution, schools, transportation, consumer exploitation, the housing, protection, and use of environmental and human resources, etc. Examination of new approaches, restructuring of institutions and innovations that might enhance the quality of life for men, women and children, as approached from the vantage point of women. Methods by which children are now virtually unrepresented in most crucial decisions of the city might be brought into the decision-making process, and the way their needs represent the interests and needs of a new will is further defined.

'I do not think that I am a natural-born mother. ... If I ever wanted to mother anyone, it was my father.'
↗ **ELEANOR ROOSEVELT** Advisory Committee Member and Speaker

'American education has a big lesson to learn ... what we need is not a certain system, nor a lot of new methods and equipment, but a direction, a conscious purpose. ... The development of a democracy demands that nothing be done to interfere with the fluidity of the population: there must be no barriers built between different groups and occupations; everything must be kept as open as possible to promote free and sympathetic communication. This demands common interests among all the people; and the strongest common interest between people widely separated by space and occupation is the evolution of their government to the satisfaction of them all. It is essential that the school, as the only instrument we possess for giving everyone the same experience in understanding the ideals and needs of a democracy and their own parts in it, keep pace with the government's progress.'
↗ **EVELYN DEWEY** Influential Educational Reformer and Activist

DESIGNING THE FUTURE

Parsons has 400 enrolled students, and is among the most prestigious art and design schools in the world. Albert Landa, Vice President of The New School, has just been told Parsons is on the brink of shutdown, but it doesn't make sense. Where's all the tuition money?

Harold Oram, a prominent fundraiser for educational and progressive causes, is on the phone. Landa is an active vice president, and he doesn't always go to the board of trustees to ask permission. Oram wants to know if The New School can bail Parsons out. No, Landa tells him, but there might be funds for a buyout.

In 1963, The New School narrowly averted its own sale to New York University. Since then, The New School has committed funds to renovate two buildings adjacent to its home building on 12th Street, and purchased Lanes Department Store at 65 Fifth Avenue (the site will eventually be a part of the twenty-first-century University Center). While Lanes was acquired at a bargain rate, through the interventions and generosity of New School patrons, Albert List and Stella Sweeting Fogelman, the school had put up half a million dollars to demonstrate its own solvency, and taken on substantial debt.

If The New School isn't the most solvent of prospective saviors for Parsons, the two schools parallel in origin, and Parsons' young Vice President, David Levy, is aggressively, even 'desperately', as he will recall in 2019, pursuing options that will keep Parsons alive. It was Levy who had allowed for the dire, if confidential, status of Parsons to reach Landa:

> After a rather fiery exchange, Dick Paget, the board's chairman, gave me a deadline of one month to find a merger partner and come to a credible agreement. Given the fact that we were on the cusp of the holiday season, this was a very tall order. I felt like the prince in a Grimm's fairy tale who has been told by the king that in order to marry the princess he must slay the dragon, walk through fire and bring back a treasure buried on the bottom of the ocean (or something like that). Clearly, Paget's view was that this was a futile or, at best, a Pyrrhic cause.

But Landa, after an exploratory meeting with Parsons, agrees with Levy's assessment: the design school's financial failings are the result of mismanagement. To Landa, it's nothing that couldn't be handled by bringing the tuition up to the rate of Parsons' competitors, and the appointment of a new academic dean. Landa takes the merger to The New School President, John Everett, who has been traveling. Landa is sure there's an opportunity, but unsure that Everett will agree. The New School, argues Landa, has been adding arts-related courses since its earliest years; the Parsons courses offer a huge block of academics The New School has always wanted, there's very little crossover, and the schools are linked historically and by radical disposition. Everett is all in, and the deal is done, Landa will later say, 'within weeks'.

The announcement is made on February 22, 1970. 'For some time now,' says President Everett, 'The New School has been considering suggestions that it should expand its offerings in the design field. Designers are becoming key people in our social structure and professional design education now more than ever requires that design students be exposed to the liberal arts and broad social perspectives.'

The news is coupled with a new Parsons offering: a four-year Bachelor of Fine Arts degree. For several years, Levy, who will become Parsons' Executive Dean, has been seeking additional income for Parsons by the adoption of the BFA, and, with the merger, opposition from an obstinate board is removed:

> I prepared a good deal of material to support the case for merger which, very importantly, included a set of spreadsheets and budget projections that clearly showed how Parsons could be break even or better within a year if properly managed. This was based, in part, on the fact that some months earlier I had written the curriculum, applied for and received BFA degree authority for Parsons from the New York State Department of Education. Achieving permission to grant degrees was extremely important to our merger prospects, because up to this time Parsons had been a three-year school offering only a certificate of graduation. Not only did this severely damage Parsons' competitive position against regional institutions such as Pratt, the School of Visual Arts, and others — most of which offered both undergraduate and graduate degrees — but it also deprived us of a fourth year of tuition income; in other words, granting this degree would be a vehicle for an automatic increase of 20–25% in gross revenue, as well as an overall enrollment increase based on an enhanced competitive position and larger applicant pool in the art school marketplace.

Clockwise from top left:

Listen to Me Chaise. Edward J. Wormley, after 1948

Hands constructing M.E.S.S. model. Joseph Marcella student work, 1970

Skyline from 66 West 12th Street building, 1970s

Stackable fiberglass chair. Joseph Marcella student work, 1970

'NEVER BE ASHAMED TO WRITE A MELODY THAT PEOPLE REMEMBER.'
↗ BURT BACHARACH Student

June, 1966. Leonard Baskin, class of 1949, is awarded an honorary Doctor of Fine Arts at The New School's thirtieth commencement ceremony.

At the time of its 1996 centennial, Parsons guest critics include Adri, Joseph Abboud, Jeffrey Banks, Donald Brooks, Marc Jacobs, Michael Kors, Isaac Mizrahi, Véronique Nichanian, Tracy Reese, Gloria Sachs, Anna Sui, and Donna Karan, who is awarded the Parsons annual outstanding achievement award in the centennial year. Guests in fine arts include Ross Bleckner, Mel Chin, Petah Coyne, Yvonne Jacquette, Rosalind Krauss, Robert Longo, Gracie Mansion, Matt Mullican, Robert Ryman, Kiki Smith, Jane Wilson, and Martha Wilson.

'A house is but the normal expression of one's intellectual concept of fitness and ... aesthetic ideal of what is beautiful.'
↗ FRANK ALVAH PARSONS
Director of the New York School of Fine and Applied Art and Parsons

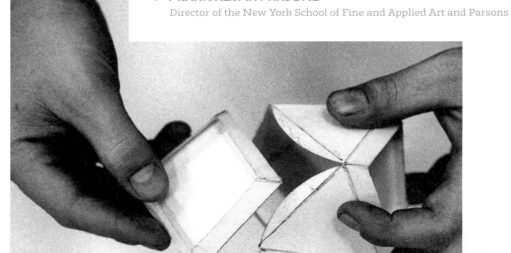

'I HOPE I AM THE ANTITHESIS OF DISPOSABLE FASHION.'
↗ **JASON WU** Student

'Perhaps our humanitarian interests are always there whether subtle or direct. The longer I continue my music practice, like a tree, it has its branches that grow and connect, sometimes break and ... regenerate.'
↗ **SUSIE IBARRA** Student

Students of Parsons and Milano, in collaboration with students from the Stevens Institute of Technology, design 'Empowerhouse' to compete in the U.S. Department of Energy's 2011 Solar Decathlon. Dozens of faculty members and over 200 students and multiple external partners — including Habitat for Humanity — contribute to the two-year project. The end result, a modular solar-powered residence that is practical, comfortable, community aware, and buildable, is selected as one of nineteen finalists to be prototyped and designed on the National Mall in Washington D.C. Students are entirely responsible for the execution of the construction. Finalist competitor teams hail from colleges and universities worldwide. Empowerhouse, which excels in engagement through its inventive use and innovation of NEW construction, competing against 90 percent of sustainability, and it includes the highest possible score, 100 of 100. Empowerhouse has leading scores in multiple categories; the innovative two-family home is built in cooperation with Habitat for Humanity, the world's largest developer in the United States, in Washington, D.C. The house wins the Washington, D.C. Mayor's Sustainability Award in 2012.

In the end is also a project, Parsons and Milano design reimagined orchestra gar ments, stretched out and versatile. In 2011, Marin Alsop, Music Director of the Baltimore Symphony Orchestra (BSO), sought out The New School for a contemporary hi-tech solution to orchestral wardrobe. In 2016, with materials donated by Under Armour, 400 new articles of wardrobe — outfitting 100 performers — debut

NEW FRONTIERS OF AMERICAN THOUGHT, 1933
HARRY A. OVERSTREET

It begins to be clear that forces of fundamental reconstruction are operating in America, as well as in the rest of the world, and that a new kind of social and spiritual pioneering is now in evidence. Every one of our major undertakings is affected by this vigor of new thinking, and the individual who wishes to escape the distressing effects of bewilderment in this rapidly changing world must achieve an orientation of himself with respect to the newly developing ideas. The time, in short, would seem to be at hand for an enlistment of ourselves in enterprises that are on the new frontiers of life.

FASHION UNBOUND, 2019
FRANCESCA GRANATA

[...] examines experimental fashion and [...] from the 1980s up to the present. It [...] ever-increasing challenge posed by [...] the art and fashion fields to the [...] of the body and of beauty, which [...] most successful articulations in the [...] twentieth-century high fashion. [...] way artists as well as designers [...] demarcations between the [...] of the body, the course questions [...] saw an explosion of grotesque [...] imagery articulating unsettling [...] which had been lurking just [...] surface throughout the twentieth [...] the questions we will ask are: Why is the [...] and 'perfect' body, which developed in the Western vocabulary as early as the Renaissance, so forcefully challenged by contemporary designers and artists? How can we read this proliferation of the grotesque in relation to changes in gender roles, attitudes to sexuality, and the AIDS crisis? How are theories of the posthuman influencing contemporary fashion and performance? We look at a range of media from the video and performance work of Leigh Bowery in collaboration with Charles Atlas and Michael Clark; to the dance performances by Merce Cunningham in collaboration with Rei Kawakubo of Comme des Garçons; to the experimental fashion shows staged by Alexander McQueen and Martin Margiela; to the more recent phenomenon of Lady Gaga. We also examine textiles' relation to the body as a second skin, a surface on which bodily borders are negotiated. Our readings will draw from fashion studies, art and design history, gender and sexuality studies, science studies, and medical anthropology. The seminar will pose a series of self-reflexive questions and exercises tying the readings to the students' own dress and design practices.

'THE WAY BACK IS ALWAYS SHORTER.'
↗ **MAYA DEREN** Student

Parsons brings to The New School a student body from thirty-six U.S. states, and twenty-one nations. Two years later, another fire sale lands The New School two more buildings on Fifth Avenue, just across the street from the former site of Lanes, which has become an expansion of the Graduate Faculty division. Mills College of New York City, threatened by a New York State revocation of accreditation, liquidates to The New School; Mills' 180 students finish out their degrees at courses offered by The New School and New York University. Mills is then disbanded, and, in 1972, Parsons moves in, leaving behind its Sutton Place location. It's a move from uptown to downtown: the Upper East Side to the teeming Greenwich Village of the 1970s, and an already illustrious faculty in art. (William Wegman, for example, is teaching fine arts in 1969, and Maurice Sendak, in 1973, is teaching book illustration.) In 1976, Parsons' enrollment has swelled from 594 to 933, and enrollment for evening courses, open to non-matriculated students, has ballooned from 250 to 2,000 students. The annual budget, $1.5 million in 1970, has grown to $4 million. David Levy, as Parsons' Dean, tells: 'Many of the things we gained you cannot verbalize. The point is that the range of courses we can now offer is extraordinary.'

In 2006, with the backing of New School President Bob Kerrey, The New School commences a curricular remodeling of Parsons. In 'Designing the Design School', The New School synchronizes Parsons with other areas of study, adds undergraduate and graduate degrees, increases full-time faculty from forty to 170, and consolidates the many isolated departments to five internal schools. The changes allow for a further integration of design, social change, and environmental consciousness throughout Parsons, and the emergence of new areas of study, such as the major in Journalism and Design (supported by the Knight Foundation) in Eugene Lang College, as well as new minors, which are made available to all undergraduates of the university. As of 2019, Parsons continues to expand upon its model of conscience in design, the arts, and academics, offering forty-seven degrees, non-degree and certificate programs.

'I get to challenge myself and kind of raise the standard for myself every season. Even the term 'fashion' is about change. It's about newness. And what that newness means is different every ten years, every five years.'
↗ **NICO RODRIGUEZ** Student

Clockwise from top left:

A flat-packed dwelling designed by Parsons students as part of a collaborative exchange program. Black River, Hällefors, Sweden, 2006

Parsons School of Design student work, 1976

A rooftop garden on a building in the Bronx designed and built by Parsons students in collaboration with the Neighborhood Coalition for Shelter, 2008

'SO THE DARKNESS SHALL BE THE LIGHT, AND THE STILLNESS THE DANCING.'

↗ T. S. ELIOT Faculty

1933

THE INSTITUTE FOR ADVANCED STUDY

School of Mathematics

Princeton, New Jersey

April 11, 1941

Dr. Jacob Billikopf
805 Bankers Securities Building
Philadelphia, Pennsylvania

Dear Dr. Billikopf:

    I am very gratified to hear that you are devoting part of your time and activities to the support of Dr. Johnson's University in Exile. I am convinced of the high value of this institution which enabled a considerable number of prominent creative personalities from Europe to work in their special fields and to give an interested public occasion to attend their lectures. In this way, Dr. Johnson made a great contribution to the intellectual life of the United States, saved valuable intellectual forces from decay and last, but not least, avoided undesirable professional competition with the American teaching profession.

    Hoping that you will be successful in your efforts, I remain, with kindest regards,

        Sincerely yours,

(SIGNED)   ALBERT EINSTEIN

        Professor Albert Einstein

'The Nazi party penetrated nearly all strata of society. … The establishment of dictatorship made it possible for them to shift to other political affiliations as they had done in the past. Too late it was realized that they had lived up to the German proverb: *Nur die allergrössten Kälber wählen ihren Metzger selber* (Only the most stupid calves vote for their own butcher).'
↗ **FRIEDA WUNDERLICH** Faculty

Germany's Enabling Act gives dictator status to Hitler. To gain the parliamentary adoption of 'The Law to Remedy the Distress of the People', Hitler's forces detain eighty-one Communists and twenty-six Social Democrats, preventing them from taking part in the vote. Crushed by a decade of a struggling economy, class inequities, and global depression, German democracy has come to an end.

Hitler placates fears, assuring the nation that the federal states will not be done away with: 'The government will make use of these powers only insofar as they are essential for carrying out vitally necessary measures. ... The number of cases in which an internal necessity exists for having recourse to such law is in itself a limited one.'

Throughout the world, critics of German fascism fear the worst. Alvin Johnson, President of The New School, who frequently travels to Germany, had expressed the January before that Germany was a 'land of Nazis'. With Hitler's ascendance, an April 1 national boycott and picket of Jewish businesses precedes, by six days, the adoption of the Civil Service Restoration Act, which dismisses non-Aryans from positions as civil servants, government officers or representatives, judges, and professors. Johnson writes to New School Press Director, Agnes De Lima: 'Among the German professors who are being ousted, many are my personal friends. I'm setting out to find money, if I can, to get ten or a dozen of them to the U.S. to set up a German university in exile.'

The Rockefeller Foundation has already initiated steps toward interventions, and Johnson, after gathering financial backing, heads uptown for a meeting. Johnson recalls his en route preparations in his memoir, *Pioneer's Progress* (1952):

As I rode in the bus to Rockefeller Center, on a bright and hopeful morning, I revised my ideas. I could get fifteen scholars as easily as five. I revised my ideas again as the elevator shot me up to the Foundation offices. I'd ask for twenty-five. President Raymond Fosdick was so cordial I found it easy to put my case. French liberal and Jewish professors, refugee scholars from Germany, were in deadly peril. Many of them had been engaged in research projects financed by the Foundation.

Their fate was of profound interest to the Foundation. But the Foundation could do nothing for them, except perhaps supply them with money, which the Germans would grab. The New School, however, could issue invitations that would give those scholars non-quota visas to America for themselves and their families. ... Fosdick heard me through patiently. 'How many could you take care of?' he asked. To my own surprise I answered, 'It would not be worthwhile to go ahead with this project unless we are prepared to take care of a hundred,' 'I shall have to consult my trustees,' said Fosdick. 'I can do it by telephone and give you an answer in three days.' But the next day he called me up. The trustees had approved and I could go ahead immediately.

Through 1945, 300 scholars are rescued through the efforts of the Rockefeller Foundation and The New School, which employs 181 of the scholars as faculty. Finding professorial posts for the scholars is difficult because many of the scholars are new to the English language, many are Jewish, and one, Frieda Wunderlich, is a woman. Writing on her behalf in 1933, Harvard economist Joseph Schumpeter explains that her 'case is still more difficult than that of the other economists who have been dismissed because she is a woman, which fact very much restricts the range of possible employment'.

Of the 181, a handful remain as permanent faculty at The New School. Wunderlich is the single woman among them. The group, which form the Graduate Faculty, are employed as a mainstay of the university's first degree programs: PhDs offered in Philosophy and Social Sciences. For the Fall 1934 debut semester of The New School for Social Research, ten full-time professors are listed, with 'other appointments' to be 'announced later'. The ten: Karl Brandt, Gerhard Colm, Arthur Feiler, Eduard Heimann, Hermann Kantorowicz, Emil Lederer, Hans Speier, Erich von Hornbostel, Max Wertheimer, and Frieda Wunderlich.

A statement as to the founding of the Graduate Faculty and The New School for Social Research is included in the first catalogue offered by the department:

As a non-political educational institution The New School can offer no comment on the political expediency of the ethical justification of a policy pursued by a foreign nation. As an American institution, however, The New School is under obligation to express by word and act its own faith in the value of academic liberty. Without freedom of inquiry and teaching in the higher educational institutions there can be no intellectual freedom in society at large; and without intellectual freedom the democratic system under which we live cannot long endure. ... We have often sinned, and shall, we fear, often sin against the principle of tolerance, but we are aware of our guilt. In the realm of education our offences become less frequent. We all agree that real education begins where racial, religious, and political intolerance ends.

In extending its hospitality to a group of the German professors who have been displaced, The New School conceives itself as acting in the capacity of a representative of American institutions, in the first instance, and, ultimately, of American Democracy.

The next year, a constitution is adopted by the Graduate Faculty, and ratified by The New School:

The Graduate Faculty of Political and Social Science of The New School for Social Research is founded upon the principles of academic freedom and the rights and duties implicit in freedom of thought, inquiry, teaching, and publication.

Previous pages:

Marble copy of a Roman sculpture, *Aphrodite of Cyrene*, given to New School Director Alvin Johnson by architect Joseph Urban, 1930s

Opposite

Letter from Albert Einstein to Dr. Jacob Billikopf, April 11, 1941

BUFFALO NEWS
OCTOBER 23, 1937

AMERICA SHOULD

THANK DICTATORS

America," Noted Writer Tells Stalin, Mussolini and Hitler. Adding Such Fine Blood to Our Human Stock."

WITH this wave of emigration, as with the Pilgrims, the Huguenots and the Jews from Brazil, the glory lies not in the occasional man of exceptional eminence, like Carl Schurz, but in the myriad of sturdy men and women who have done their part as useful, progressive, constructive citizens —who have given always to America and the world more than they have taken out of it.

Then came a half-century during which we let the milk be watered. Steamship companies had perceived the profit in the steerage. They plastered Europe with alluring advertisements which made it appear that our fruit trees bore diamonds and our rivers ran molten gold. Corporations, looking for common labor at cheap prices,

The World War ended that era. We restricted immigration; we established strict regulations to cut off the congenitally shiftless, the ignorant, the diseased. Still, we needed something to restore the balance, for immigration downward by the of 40 years between 18_ and 1920. We could not have but that something on our own initiative. We didn't have to. Lenin, Stalin, Mussolini and Hitler performed the service for us.

LENIN was the first of our unwitting benefactors when he sank with Russian Russian intellectuals. Some died in the Revolution, some faded out through hardship and privation.

war ended that its members had lived from infancy. In the biological sense of the phrase, this is still first-class blood. And those who carry it have been marrying and increasing among us.

Still better, perhaps, for the long purposes of our breed, are those Russian physicians, lawyers, engineers and scientific men who could not tolerate the Bolshevik dictatorship and got out. They found the new world singularly inhospitable, it is true. The physicians—some of them among the best in Europe —could not practice here. The bar of language, the regulations against granting licenses to aliens, prevented.

They went to work at anything they could find. A group of them, under contract, actually dug graves in New York

was procurator of the Holy Synod in 1917 was by 1921 a dishwasher in the Hotel Pennsylvania, New York. The Russian lawyers, like the doctors, took the first work that offered itself. In New York and Philadelphia, circumstances led most of them to adopt house painting as a trade. Some of them have branched out as reasonably successful contractors, have married native-born women, are educating children in our public schools.

Science and engineering speak a universal language; most of the Russian emigres who followed these professions have done reasonably well. One, Igor Sikorsky, designer of airplanes, has rendered us brilliant service. And these fine strains are becoming blood of our blood—thanks to Lenin and Stalin.

Our gifts from Mussolini have come not in one Christmas basket, but gradually. Ever since the March on Rome, Italians who believe that the state is made for man, not man for the state, have preferred exile to conformity, and have chosen the United States as the atmosphere in which they can breathe most freely. Some of them, like Count Sforza, were eminent in Italy. All of them have in their genes such qualities as the Huguenots and the Forty-eighters have contributed to the American stock.

Finally, Hitler. He has held power for less than five years; yet already he has served us better than many an American to whom we have raised monuments. No group of immigrant exiles known to our national history has boasted so high an intelligence quota and character rating as the "Nordic" Germans and Jewish Germans who have come to us during the last four years.

Albert Einstein heads the list as he would head any list chosen for pure intellect.

THE distinguished scholars and philosophers who are grouped in the University in Exile at New York, the professors scattered among our established schools and universities, the scientific men at work in our laboratories—they have brought families or will marry here and breed their superior qualities into the new American stock.

Just for one example: A German company making a scientific specialty depended almost for its existence on the uncanny skill of a certain research worker. Came the Nazi revolution

In 1937, Thomas Mann, upon the occasion of the Graduate Faculty's fourth year, visits The New School. Considered the best living German novelist, and perhaps the German conscience, Mann's third visit to the United States is heralded by the press. Addressing his New School audience, Mann remarks:

This youngest American institution of higher learning is in an interesting way connected with a strange incident that happened at, or I should rather say was inflicted on the oldest German university, Heidelberg. There, the great lecture hall ... bore the inscription: 'To the Living Spirit!' This inscription — unbelievable as it seems — has been removed from the building. Thus the regime has declared that there is — for the time being — no home for the living spirit in Germany's universities. Now I suggest that your faculty take these words and make them your motto, to indicate that the living spirit, driven from Germany, has found a home in this country.

In a 1979 lecture to the Department of Psychology, Mary Henle, who joined the Graduate Faculty in 1946, will explain: 'This story helps us understand why the University in Exile was popularly known as "Little Heidelberg on 12th Street".'

In 1942, the university, which through the 1930s hosted no fewer than thirteen Italian scholars fleeing fascism, establishes the École Libre des Hautes Études as an exile university for French and Belgian scholars fleeing Nazi rule. General de Gaulle recognizes the École Libre des Hautes Études as the only university of a 'Free France'. In 1945, the American Council for Émigrés (ACE) is initiated by Else and Hans Staudinger; Else is the Program Director of ACE, and Hans, who escaped Nazi arrest in 1934, is the Dean of the Graduate Faculty of Political and Social Science at The New School. ACE helps find jobs in the United States for over 3,000 scientists and scholars; the program is supported by Paul Tillich and Eleanor Roosevelt. The Graduate Seminars, established by the Graduate Faculty as a progressive think tank and discussion series, continues today in The New School's online media platform Public Seminar; the University in Exile continues in The New University in Exile Consortium, a globally oriented initiative to assist imperiled scholars.

'The discipline of the Third Reich is toadyism and not freedom. Its anti-Semitism and its inflammatory nationalist propaganda are narrow mindedness and not intellectual breadth. Fascism is intellectual slavery.'
↗ **WILLY BRANDT** Honorary Degree Recipient

'You who are students here have a history to be proud of. In a sense it goes back to Heidelberg, founded in 1386, but it has the newness of The New School.'
↗ **MARY HENLE** Faculty

Newspaper clippings,
Buffalo New York News,
October 23, 1937

'SECULARIZATION', 1968
PETER BERGER

An inquiry into the evidence for and against the
thesis of progressive secularization in modern
society. Emphasis will be placed on the question
of the secularization of consciousness.

German Immigrants Scattered Over U. S. In Effort To Give Them New Start In Li[...]

(Second of Two Articles)

(By Lydia Gray Shaw—Associated
Press Feature Service Writer)

New York—Five hundred immigrants, fleeing Nazism, landed in New York the other day.

Most were in family groups, loaded with possessions. Few were single men, almost none single women. But some were children, sent on ahead by parents not yet able to finance their own journeys.

What was to become of them? How would these aliens find their place in a strange country.

One learns the answer at the crowded headquarters of the National Coordinating Committee for Aid to Refugees and Emigrants Coming from Germany. Its job is to help make these Germans and Austrians (and Italians, too, under new arrangements) self-supporting.

First, committee workers try to persuade refugees to pass on through New York to regions where better opportunities lie. Most of the newcomers are from small towns and are happier away from a city. But fully a third of them have remained in New York.

Farmer Lost in City

There was the German farmer who, with his wife, was established in a New York apartment. After a few weeks, he wouldn't eat. He wouldn't go outdoors. The committee, on the advice of a psychiatrist, found a place for him on a Connecticut farm. Once moved he was happy.

Some refugees have been sent as far west as Washington. Others are farming successfully in Virginia and Kentucky.

Some need temporary loans to tide them over, or help them get started in a new business, but most of them need advice—which takes hours of the skilled counselors' time.

If possible, the refugee is kept in the type of work he did at home, or in an allied field. Sometimes a hobby, like photography or designing, may yield him a living.

Occasionally training for a new kind of job is necessary, especially in the case of lawyers, who are not accustomed to English law which is the basis of practice in the United States. Usually German lawyers are advised to study bookkeeping and accounting. Wherever possible, retraining is carried on by existing agencies. Trade schools, WPA classes in English public school [...]

Many professors are easily placed in American universities. The University in Exile, established in downtown Manhattan for refugee scholars, takes others. This year it has added three Austrians.

Night Schools Help

Doctors and dentists find the state examinations their greatest stumbling block. The committee helps them find temporary work while they are studying English at night preparatory to taking the examinations.

A woman physician works all day as a servant and goes to school at night.

Some types of workers are always in demand. "We have far more [...]

Chemists usually can find jobs, particularly in the dye industry, for which Germany is famous. Laboratory technicians in the soap, perfume, and textile industries are also reported easy to place.

Many German Jews are employed as mechanics, watchmakers, and instrument makers.

A fortunate few of the refugees have managed to bring a small amount of capital with them. The committee helps them choose a place to set up shop, preferably the kind they operated in the old country.

One, who opened a junk shop in New York, now employs from 15 to 20 men. Another is manufacturing candy.

[...]man immigrants have brough[...] One man has set up a ski fac[...] tory near Boston. Another [...] and manufactures ski costum[...]

Two Germans who invent[...] materials, one an acid-resista[...] ber hose and another a new [...] carbon paper, have brough[...] processes into the United St[...]

What effect will this imm[...] have on America? Nobody [...] Doubtless the country will [...] much from the scholars, lik[...] stein and Lederer, the sta[...] like Benes and Bruening.

Government officials [...] refugees will be absorbed by [...] other immigrants. It's an [...] ual problem. And most of [...]

Immigrants—new style—see New York's skyline for the first time

'We Americans can eat and the red points have gone back to the Devil, leaving it to the good old honest Dollar to regulate our consuming fires. All through the war we were the best fed people under the sun. Now we will have to look to our buttons. And shall we not be universally admired for our sleek plumpness, like Little Jack Horner? ... Well, you say, what can we do about it? Could we find food, even by stinting ourselves savagely, for all those hungry people?'

↗ **ALVIN JOHNSON** First President and Founder

Prompted by success and a growing student body, The New School celebrates its fiftieth anniversary in 1969. Promotional materials for the event boast that at fifty years the school has registered 1.5 million students. The 1984 celebration of the fiftieth anniversary of the University in Exile culminates in a convocation in Berlin, where Richard von Weizsäcker, President of the Federal Republic of Germany, is awarded an honorary degree by New School President Jonathan Fanton. In 2009, for the seventy-fifth anniversary of the University in Exile, The New School returns to Berlin, where New School President Bob Kerrey awards an honorary degree to German Chancellor Angela Merkel. Additionally, The New School announces the Alvin Johnson–University in Exile Memorial Fellowship Fund; the scholarship will cover tuition and provide stipends for exceptional German students pursuing graduate degrees at The New School for Social Research.

Since 1992, The New School's Transregional Center for Democratic Studies (TCDS) has held a Democracy & Diversity Institute for graduate students every summer in Poland. From 1999 to 2015, the institute held a winter session in South Africa. The flagship programs exemplify the TCDS mission: 'an interdisciplinary examination of democratic theory and practice, with the principle of open, rational, public debate by citizens at its core'. Since its first project—the East and Central Europe Program, initiated in 1990—TCDS tallies 1,700-plus graduates from fifty-plus nations.

'I walk in my American streets and it is such a Sunday afternoon as writers and makers of movies exist on ... sunshine and the autumn, just hinting that it is almost its time. And the people—some so carefully dressed, as to define the day only as Sunday, and others so terribly casual. There is a peace that is supposed to come on such Sundays; it is hard to believe that my nation prepares for war. I think that Germany must have known such Sundays. God help us.'

↗ **LORRAINE HANSBERRY** Student

Clockwise from top left:

▬▬▬ Newspaper clipping, *North Adams Transcript*, November 22, 1933

▬▬▬ University in Exile faculty, 1933

ECONOMIC HETERODOXY

In 2003, Argentine President Néstor Kirchner and Senator Cristina Fernández de Kirchner (who is also Argentina's first lady, and the future President of Argentina) stop at The New School as part of their visit to New York City and the United Nations General Assembly; they are joined by Nobel Laureate Joseph Stiglitz for an economic policy discussion, which is moderated by New School President Bob Kerrey. The site of the event, The New School's Orozco Room, places them at the center of José Clemente Orozco's *Delphic Circle* murals; the 1931 pentaptych dramatically summons a global struggle for equity in governance. During the proceedings, President Kirchner asserts that as long as there are hungry Argentinians, Argentina will not pay off its international debt; a powerful statement by Senator Fernández leads President Kerrey (recently a U.S. presidential hopeful) to observe: 'I'm glad I'm not running against her.' Six members of the Argentine Cabinet attend the lunch reception that follows.

In 2004, President Kirchner and *New York Times* columnist and Nobel Laureate Paul Krugman have a public conversation that considers Argentina's successful handling of its recent economic crisis. President Kirchner speaks with clear-headed perspective about the greed and influence of foreign lenders: 'let me say a word on behalf of international financial consultants. They're not necessarily evil; sometimes they really are just stupid.' The New School event, hosted by the Graduate Program in International Affairs (GPIA), is organized by a new university body, the Argentina Observatory, which makes for the beginnings of the Observatory on Latin America (OLA), instituted in 2006. In June 2010, three months before his hospitalization and subsequent death due to cardiac arrest, President Kirchner, at The New School, gives his final foreign speech, which will inspire New School Trustee Julien Studley to found and support the President Néstor Kirchner Fellowship. The fellowship will sponsor public lectures on annual themes, and support academic fellows from Latin American and Caribbean countries.

Since 2006, the OLA has held upward of 150 events, with more than 6,000 students taking part. The goals of the OLA, to watch, understand, and provide a forum for discussion 'about the processes of social reform occurring in the Western Hemisphere', are pursued through five major programs: the President Néstor Kirchner Fellowship, Building Bicentennials, the Cuba Program, Design and Development, and Latin America on the Move.

'We are paid to think, to teach, to communicate, to learn ... it's a great privilege. First of course it's not always easy to get the employment to give you that privilege but assuming that one makes that transition into academic life, then the main advice is not just to appreciate it but to be self-conscious about how to maximize the values you have in this relatively privileged way of being an adult in this world.'
↗ **IRA KATZNELSON** Faculty

ARE WE GOOD NEIGHBORS? 1939
HANS SIMONS, CHAIRMAN

Speakers of different viewpoints discuss frankly and critically the possibilities of a Pan-American policy in the economic, the cultural, and diplomatic fields, stressing the relations between the Latin American countries and the United States. Representative Latin Americans are also expected to take part in the discussions. The aim of the course is to investigate the background and bases of inter-American relations, to clarify prejudices and to replace propaganda by sober evaluation, in order to answer the question of what should be the policy of 'good neighbors'.

→ Continental cooperation: Hans Simons.
→ The historical background of the Pan American movement: Samuel Guy Inman.
→ Inter-American cultural exchange: Stephen Duggan.
→ Inter-American trade relations: Chester L. Jones.
→ Cultural achievements in South America: Mrs. Irma G. Labastille.
→ Inter-American press relations: Leland Stowe.
→ Mexico: Frank Tannenbaum.
→ Argentina: F. Schwartz Artune.
→ Brazil: Herman G. James.
→ Spanish influence in South America: Fernando de los Ríos.
→ Chile: speaker to be announced.
→ The economic factors in inter-American relations: Earle K. James.
→ The legal aspects of Pan Americanism: Edwin Borchard.
→ The role of diplomacy in inter-American relations: William R. Castle.
→ Lesson to be drawn: Hans Simons.

'Ever since I moved to New York in 1987 and, without conscious plan, walked eastward from Greenwich Village on yet another "exploratory mission" in the new (to me) city, I have been trying to understand how, in one of the oldest quarters of an American city, a new form of urban community seemed to be emerging, and I have been trying to visualize the future in the tenements of the past.'
↗ **JANET ABU-LUGHOD** Faculty

'Yes, I believe in economic heterodoxy; I believe fundamentally that if a juncture is agreed upon within a strategic project framework, there can be different answers that can work and that in many cases, it is necessary to respond to the situation of each particular country.'
↗ **NÉSTOR KIRCHNER** Guest Lecturer

In 2002, The New School initiates the International Field Program (IFP), which is open to undergraduate Juniors and Seniors, Master's and PhD students, and continuing education students. In cooperation with the GPIA, the IFP, as of 2019, has sent approximately 2,000 students to thirty countries. The immersive nine-week programs put students on the frontline of activism and governance, policy change, community development, urban planning, citizen journalism, and international questions of social and economic justice. In 2019, IFP country sites are the Balkans, Brazil, Cuba, Ethiopia, and South Africa.

September, 2006, 'Expectations and Experiences for the Latin American Region' is held in The New School's Orozco Room. Co-organized by Michael Cohen and directed and introduced by Cristina Fernández de Kirchner (Senator and First Lady of Argentina), the discussion group includes Marco Aurelio García (advisor to the President of Brazil), David Choquehuanca Céspedes (Minister of Bolivian Foreign Affairs), Bernardo Álvarez Herrera (Venezuela's Ambassador to the United States), and Heraldo Muñoz (Chile's Ambassador to the United Nations). Choquehuanca, of an indigenous community, leads with two thoughts: this is the first room in New York he's been in where the people in the pictures look like him; his people have waited 500 years to speak in university forums.

'I don't think we have theorized sufficiently about what happens when we 'live together' in fieldwork. We are observing as we participate. Living together produces, over time, shared conversations, memories, and affections for people we have known in common. ... My experience of having developed these affections across differences is not unique. Fieldwork is a particularly intense and perhaps peculiar way of learning and being in the world, but every intimate relationship, if you think about it, involves bridging differences.'
↗ **LILA ABU-LUGHOD** Daughter of Faculty Member Janet Abu-Lughod

Clockwise from top left:

José Clemente Orozco, *Science, Labor and Art.* New School mural. 1930–1931. The New School Art Collection

José Clemente Orozco working on mural with assistant. 1930. The New School Art Collection

'EVERYTHING IS ARRANGED SO THAT IT BE THIS WAY, THIS IS WHAT IS CALLED CULTURE.'

↗ JACQUES DERRIDA Honorary Degree Recipient

HAVANA STUDIO: HISTORIC PRESERVATION AND URBAN STRATEGY, 2019
MICHAEL A. COHEN AND ANTHONY TUNG

This studio course will focus on the analysis of threats to Havana's heritage in the wider context of building an urban strategy. Cuba and particularly the metropolitan area of Havana are experiencing rapid change, including economic liberalization, arrival of new technologies, and global flows including tourism. Meanwhile, the cityscape of Havana has come to wide attention among architects, historians, and urban preservationists for several reasons. Firstly, it has been somewhat frozen in time since the Cuban Revolution of 1959 and has not been affected by such common urban practices as cutting highways through existing neighborhoods, or leveling deteriorated communities for the construction of out-of-scale large modern housing blocks. This has generally left intact a rich 400-year-old architectural legacy reflecting the wealth accumulated while Havana was the principal embarkation point for the Treasure Fleets of Colonial Spain and later as one of the world's major sources of raw sugar. Nevertheless, the frozen cityscape has come to be an environment of severe physical hardship for the occupants of gravely degenerating structures (at least 500 buildings collapse each year) amid widely failing infrastructure. Such slum-like conditions pock-mark the cityscape. Will a wave of much-needed economic revitalization bring with it the destruction of this singular environment? Or can Havana develop policies that support concurrently its economic growth, social justice, and the conservation of its heritage? Students will learn and apply techniques to assess urban heritage and key elements such as infrastructure, spatial form, and local and neighborhood management. This course will be offered within the Cities and Social Justice concentration of the Graduate Program in International Affairs (GPIA) and will include visiting specialists on specific aspects of these challenges. The course will include a two-week workshop in Havana.

FEMINIZATION OF MIGRATION, 2019
JANVIEVE WILLIAMS COMRIE

International migration in Latin America and the Caribbean has contributed to highlighting a salient feature of current migration processes: its feminization. This is commonplace in public opinion, but the specificity of migration and its consequences for women remains largely ignored and thus unknown. This course addresses and deepens this issue in the context of the United States. This course will explore, through migration literature, case studies, guest lectures, and site visits, the multiple intersections between gender and migration, and how women have captured, communicated, and resisted through different artistic expressions—from poems and stories, to theater and visual arts. In recent years, a growing level of attention, body of arts, literature, and political activism has appeared, showing how patterns, systems, and structures are fundamentally gendered; how migration policies affect men and women differently both in the process of emigration and immigration.

'The utopias of a better world and a more just society have to do with words, with the generation of dreams, with imagination, with a very important identity that overcomes languages and is the identity of the human condition, to be able to recognize our own image in every fellow man, in a different age. I believe that the key to our time lies in this respect for diversity.'
↗ **CRISTINA FERNÁNDEZ DE KIRCHNER** Guest Speaker

URBAN SOCIOLOGY, 1988
JANET ABU-LUGHOD

The course explores three defining characteristics of cities: population growth and density, socio-political hierarchy and spatial differentiation, and imperial control over their hinterlands. These variables are traced from the origin of cities to the contemporary metropolitan United States, the chief focus of the course. American cities are characterized today by the coexistence of many ways of life; as physical and social space are increasingly detached, residents connect selectively to the city through ethnicity, race, family, social class, gender, place of origin, and recency of arrival. The course familiarizes the students with a variety of methods used to study cities and their neighborhoods and offers an introductory experience in doing fieldwork in an urban area.

'The shocking contrast between the well-nourished and the hungry in the world demonstrates every day that fundamental human rights begin with the right to live.'
↗ **WILLY BRANDT** Honorary Degree Recipient

'Climate change knows no borders. It will not stop before the Pacific islands and the whole of the international community here has to shoulder a responsibility to bring about a sustainable development.'
↗ **ANGELA MERKEL** Honorary Degree Recipient

Clockwise from top left:

José Clemente Orozco, *Homecoming of the Worker of the New Day and Struggle in the Orient.* New School mural, 1930–1931. The New School Art Collection

José Clemente Orozco, *Struggle in the Occident* or *Carrillo Puerto & Lenin* (detail), 1930–1931. The New School Art Collection

VIGILANCE IS NOT VIGILANT ENOUGH

1939

'From the ownership of women the concept of ownership extends itself to include the products of their industry, and so there arises the ownership of things as well as of persons.'
↗ **THORSTEIN VEBLEN** Founder

FEMINIST DILEMMAS, 2019
MIRIAM TICKTIN

This course will explore current dilemmas in feminist theory and politics. For instance, topics include the #MeToo movement, women of color theories of care, femonationalism, intersections of feminism and disability studies, 'law and order feminism', TERF feminists and trans politics, and queer feminism. By tacking back and forth between theory and the way the history of theory helps us to illuminate current debates, we will learn about the potential and limits of feminist politics, theory, and methods. This course will satisfy requirements in Perspectives for Anthropology students.

Frieda Wunderlich, the only woman of the original Graduate Faculty, is appointed as the Dean of New School's Graduate Faculty of Political and Social Science. She is believed to be the first female academic dean in secular higher education, and the first female dean of a U.S. graduate school. Upon Wunderlich's unanimous election to the position by her colleagues, The New School President, Alvin Johnson, welcomes her to the role:

> Dr. Wunderlich's work in a succession of important educational and governmental positions in Germany prior to 1933 made her one of the first ranking women of that country. In contrast to the present status of women, which restricts them to the lower paid and less important positions, Dr. Wunderlich's career embodied far-sighted social policy based on scholarly training in economics, on experience in social work that began with the administration of a whole district during the World War, and on practical politics in both elective governmental posts and trade unions and other politically important groups.

Wunderlich publishes five books in the United States, and multiple articles. Her field is the rise and effects of Nazism: the economic and social crisis that led to the failure of socialism, the appeal of Aryanism, and the role of women, increasingly limited in a fascist state. In The New School's journal *Social Research*, for example, she publishes 'New Aspects of Unemployment in Germany' (February, 1934), 'Women's Work in Germany' (August, 1935), and 'Education in Nazi Germany' (September, 1937), in which she writes:

> What value does this new generation receive in exchange? Will they really have more honor, more courage, more heroism? No courage is necessary to fall in line and to march; cringing, not courage, has emerged as the selective process. Political reliability means suppression of one's views for the sake of a career. The outspoken child is stigmatized as politically unreliable and is denied secondary education; the student, the professor, face something more serious. To find heroism in

READING WORD BY WORD, 2006
FRANCINE PROSE

Throughout history, written language has been used to create masterpieces and to pump out propaganda, to delight and delude, to reveal and obscure the truth. But unless we read closely—word by word, line by line, sentence by sentence—it can be hard to tell the difference. In this class, we close-read the short stories of great writers, brilliant stylists—Joyce and Cheever, Mansfield and O'Connor, Beckett and Bowles, etc.—whose work rewards this sort of reading, writers whose fiction cannot be fully understood unless we read it with this sort of intense attention and careful scrutiny. We also study this week's issue of *The New Yorker* and today's copy of *The New York Times* as we look at the ways in which words are used to convey information and insight, to transmit truth and beauty, and to form and transform our vision of the world.

'The status of nonmarried female scholars was probably higher in the United States than in Germany, but it certainly was peculiar. Male scholars viewed female scholars either as nonentities or nun-like, above academic life (because most are powerless), or, on the contrary, as extremely thorny, dangerous, manipulative people who had to be handled with caution. Dr. Wunderlich's male colleagues generally viewed her in the last category, partly because she had the loyalty of a major administration, partly because she stimulated loyalty and devotion in various people, and partly because of her extremely strong character, her great persistence and her willingness to wait a long time to achieve important goals.'
↗ **FELICIA JOHNSON DEYRUP** Faculty

Clockwise from top left:

■■■■■ Gina Luria Walker, Professor of Women's Studies and Director of The Center of The New Historia at The New School, 2017

■■■■ Frieda Wunderlich, undated

'THE WORLD DOESN'T LIKE INDEPENDENT WOMEN, WHY, I DON'T KNOW, BUT I DON'T CARE.'

↗ **BERENICE ABBOTT** Faculty

Clockwise from top left:

████████ Text on the back of preceding photograph

████████ Frieda Wunderlich and New School student Stina Thornell, October, 1953

'After a century of struggle for the rights of women and their growing position of equality with men and participation in all phases of public life, a sudden turn in the opposite direction has taken place in Germany. According to the National Socialist doctrine, woman is too precious to participate in public life and she is unfit to share in the same employment with men. Woman must realize that her special mission is to bear children and care for the home, and she must concentrate on these tasks. How far will it be possible to realize this ideal? The revolution which started the women's movement and knit women together in a close sisterhood fighting for a new status in society was not only a spiritual one. ... The development in Germany is a blow to the general women's movement which cannot but affect women in all countries of the world.'
↗ **FRIEDA WUNDERLICH** Faculty

'The only heroine that women of my generation grew up with was Joan of Arc — and we all knew what end she came to.'
↗ **GERDA LERNER** Faculty

Germany today means going to the concentration camps. With liberty lost as a moral force, with the suppression of individual development, with human minds stiffened into a single pattern, with human reason eliminated as a factor in education, the outcome will be an irresponsible, unquestioning mass without personal originality, and unadapted to a changing world. The nation kills its heroes and free spirits. Slavery never resulted in heroism, thus the system undermines itself. Internal contradiction annihilates the aim for which it fights.

And yet, inspired by hatred against the Western world, trained only for war through an excellent technique of drill and command, ready to fight where democracy tries to persuade, this great steamroller of collectivism threatens the Western democracies with the concentrated power of a highly gifted nation. It is a terrific danger which nations still enjoying their liberty are not prepared to meet. Eternal vigilance is not vigilant enough.

Exiled scholars scattered throughout the world will fight to prevent the spread of the disaster. In silent community with those who could not leave the countries of dictatorship, in open community with those who gave them hospitality, they will continue to work to maintain mankind's eternal right to freedom.

Mrs. Stina Thornell from Sweden who holds one of AAUW's (American Association of University Women, Washington, D.C.) grants and is studying at the New School, consulting with Dr. Wunderlich.
October 1953

YOU GONNA GIVE 'EM A CLASS IN HOW TO SCUFFLE?

Clockwise from top left:

New School students listening to jazz in the Thomas Hart Benton mural room, December, 1955

Count Basie, guest at a Marshall Stearns course on jazz in the Thomas Hart Benton mural room, December 1, 1955

New School Jazz Program 1992–93

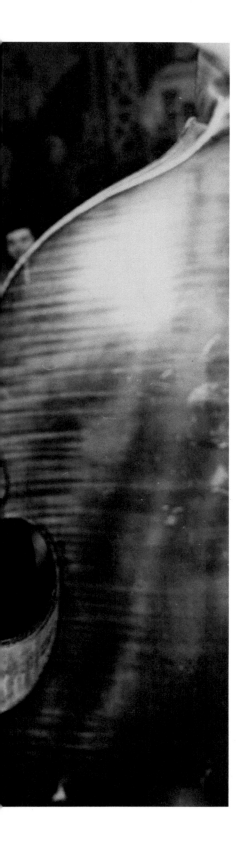

The New School offers the first college-level course devoted to the history of jazz. The fifteen sessions of 'Jazz: The Music of America' approach the subject with a narrative of musicology. The weekly topics proceed: Beginnings; The Blues; Ragtime; Jazz in America; The Evolution of Jazz; King Oliver; Jazz in Europe; New Orleans Jazz; Louis Armstrong; Duke Ellington; Swing; Big Bands; Vocal; Boogie-Woogie; The Future.

While the course is The New School's first in-depth treatment of jazz, New School lectures have been offered on the subject since 1933, and jazz dance has been offered at the Dramatic Workshop since its inception in 1940.

Robert Goffin, who instructs 'The Music of America', is a Belgian lawyer, poet, and jazz historian. As the author of *Aux Frontières du Jazz*, Goffin is credited as having published the first book to significantly investigate the formation of jazz. He is supported in the teaching of the course by Leonard Feather, a British composer and music journalist.

While The New School maintains a place of prominence in experimental and contemporary music—folk to jazz to experimental to Fluxus to contemporary classical—the school is hesitant to enter the arena of conservatories; New York City already has Juilliard and Mannes. But, in September, 1984, Parsons Executive Dean David Levy drafts a letter to New School President Jonathan Fanton, 'Re: Proposal for a BFA Curriculum in Jazz at The New School / Parsons'. Levy writes:

> As you know, I have thought for some time about the possibility of the university developing a music program (or even a music division), and while the general idea remains appealing, a traditional approach (i.e. one that would place us in competition with existing conservatories such as Juilliard, Mannes, or Manhattan) is probably a mistake. However, none of these institutions is doing adequate work in jazz; certainly none has reached out in a significant way to tap the incredible resource of this city; a move that would distinguish any program achieving genuine access to New York's unparalleled jazz community.

'Jazz has already played an important part in the fight for human freedom. It is the music of freedom, freedom of individuals and of races. It is the great art of democracy, irreconcilable with the philosophy of the dictators. It is high time for America to be aware of this, and to prepare to establish this power all though the world. Jazz can be a universal instrument in the accomplishment of a bloodless victory.'
↗ **ROBERT GOFFIN** Faculty

'A composer knows that music is written by human beings for human begins and that music is a continuation of life, not something separated from it.'
↗ **HANS EISLER** Faculty

'All great music is contemporary. If it's still alive and kicking, then it's contemporary. If it fades away, it was a period piece. It had its moment, and that was it.'
↗ **STEVE REICH** Faculty

October, 1933: Johanna Beyer's *Three Songs for Soprano* is performed at The New School. That year, or the year after, Beyer begins taking classes with The New School's sage of contemporary music, Henry Cowell. A groundbreaking experimental composer, Beyer, who also holds two degrees from the Mannes School of Music, debuts *Music of the Spheres* in 1938; the work is the first known score for electronic instruments by a woman composer.

Courses in the history of jazz are a mainstay of The New School's curriculum as of 1942. Marshall Stearns, who in 1952 founds the library and research archive, the Institute of Jazz Studies, initiates his popular and influential New School course in 1954; 'The Role of Jazz in American Culture' investigates its subject matter with 'films, field trips, rare recordings, and guest appearances of prominent musicians'. The course runs until 1961; for Stearns' 1955 lecture on 'Kansas City and the Count', none other than Count Basie himself performs. Musicians, musical instruments, students, and onlookers pack the classroom. The audience is surrounded by the muralled walls of Thomas Hart Benton's historic site-specific work America Today.

'I try by the end to have them open up and be able to take risks – to play more vividly, to just give 100 percent of who you are as a musician.'
↗ **JOANN FALLETTA** Student and Guest Artist

Levy lays out his plan: jazz at The New School would build on 'existing resources such as our Guitar Study Center', and borrow from 'the model of Parsons School of Design, in which the resource of the best professional practitioners are fully used as faculty'. The program would also have the advantage of the school's associations with jazz musicians and professionals, and its longstanding calendar of jazz events. The letter also names as a resource Arnie Lawrence, the popular jazz saxophonist and jazz educator, who could help bring jazz to The New School: 'He has worked closely with virtually every major living jazz player, and maintains close ties with most of them.' Lawrence will later co-found the program.

Hank O'Neal, a music producer, author, and philanthropist active in jazz and its communities, reviews the proposal and writes to Albert Landa, Vice President of The New School. O'Neal is straightforward: his studio musicians haven't been taught, and he's never seen a conservatory musician with the skills to play jazz professionally. That said, the soon-to-be board member of the School of Jazz can't help but exhibit a tempered enthusiasm: 'The messenger brought the proposal on Wednesday afternoon; I first saw it at 7:00 and gave it a very hurried reading. A very well-known jazz musician, Zoot Sims, arrived with his wife at 7:30 for dinner. I told Zoot about the proposal and ... he said simply: "You gonna give 'em a class in how to scuffle?"'

Despite a cascade of corrections concerning the proposal, O'Neal can envision the program, and has a sense of The New School's role in the enterprise: 'What I'm saying is that if The New School wants to do something in jazz education it should have the courage to do something different, something innovative.'

In 1986, The New School forms the School of Jazz and Contemporary Music, with a philosophy of artistry, foundational learning, and a faculty of artist-as-mentors.

JAZZ, THE MUSIC OF AMERICA, 1942 ROBERT GOFFIN, ASSISTED BY LEONARD FEATHER

The lectures are illustrated by records and instruments. Each session includes discussion in which the following eminent jazz musicians and critics participate, subject to the convenience of their professional engagements: Red Allen, Albert Ammons, Louis Armstrong, Count Basie, Sidney Bechet, Benny Carter, Dave Dexter, Jimmy Dorsey, Tommy Dorsey, Duke Ellington, Benny Goodman, John Henry Hammond, W.C. Handy, Earl Hines, Billie Holiday, Harry James, Gene Krupa, Jimmie Lunceford, Glen Miller, William Russell, Eddie Sauter, Raymond Scott, Artie Shaw, George Simon, Charles Edward Smith, Eddie South, Barry Ulanov.

'So long as the human spirit thrives on this planet, music in some living form will accompany and sustain it and give it expressive meaning.'
↗ **AARON COPLAND** Faculty

Clockwise from top left:

▬▬▬ Reggie Workman teaches a jazz ensemble at The New School, 2016

▬▬▬ Book jacket for *Giants of Jazz*. Jacket design and illustrations by Parsons School of Design alumnus Robert Galster, circa 1957

BY
STUDS TERKEL
SKETCHES BY
ROBERT GALSTER

• LOUIS ARMSTRONG • BESSIE SMITH
ECKE • FATS WALLER • DUKE ELLINGTON
DMAN • COUNT BASIE • BILLIE HOLIDAY
MAN • STAN KENTON • DIZZY GILLESPIE

STUDS TERKEL

GIANTS OF JAZZ

CROWELL

'To stand up on the stage is to say to many people: look at me. How can you do that without speaking the only truth you know?'
↗ **JUDITH MALINA** Student and Faculty

THE ROLE OF JAZZ IN AMERICAN CULTURE: A SEMINAR, 1957
MARSHALL STEARNS
GIVEN IN COOPERATION WITH THE INSTITUTE OF JAZZ STUDIES

This course explores the penetrating and varied insights into American culture afforded by a study of jazz, along the lines of the students' interests. Jazz is considered from the point of view of music, history, literature, psychology, linguistics, sociology, anthropology, folklore. Discussion and evaluation of specific areas of study, including folkways of the jazz environment; the linguistics of jive; analyses of theories, styles, eras and their influences; the psychology of the individual jazzman; the problems in jazz fiction; historical research through newspaper files and interviews; the sociology of rock and roll; jazz abroad; West African music in the New World.

POLITICS OF IMPROV, 2019
DANIELLE GOLDMAN

This course analyzes how, if at all, improvisation can be understood as a politically meaningful practice. In addition to viewing a range of performances, students survey recent literature on improvised dance, assessing the various ways that improvisation has been lauded in the field of dance studies. But we'll also look beyond typical configurations of dance. The course frequently turns to jazz and jazz studies, where one finds a vast and rigorous analysis of improvisation, and often a more exacting look at race, gender, and the politics of U.S. performance during the 1960s and 1970s.

NEW YORK CITY COMPOSERS, 2019
MARY HALVORSON

A new ensemble performing the compositions of modern New York City-based artists. Music will

In 1956, the Mannes School of Music offers the first U.S. college-level major in the study of guitar. In 1962, the Berklee School of Music follows with a degree offering. In 1987, Mannes is the first American institution of higher education to grant in-residence status to a guitar ensemble.

1963: 'Al Cohn and Zoot Sims Quintet to play in New School Courtyard: Al Cohn and Zoot Sims, two great tenor saxophonists, will bring their quintet to ... the second "Jazz IS Music" concert in The New School's Summer Arts Festival.'

Following a 1969 New School performance of his work, Steve Reich teaches at The New School for three years, which is believed to be Reich's longest-term academic association as faculty. He wins the Pulitzer Prize for music in 2009.

In 2018, as part of an ongoing project to preserve the legacy of the legendary composer Philip Glass, the College of Performing Arts initiates the Philip Glass Institute (PGI), with the Philip Glass Ensemble in residence. 'My own legacy flourished in a wide garden of music going on all at the same time,' says Glass, who continues: 'In my lifetime, I was contemporaneous with all kinds of music, and I rejoiced in it. In terms of range and variety of modern music, it is important to be unafflicted by prejudice. The music stands by itself. At the new PGI, we can prioritize a curriculum which doesn't require critical approval of any period or style. Young composers need to be true to their voices. 'Coming up' can be very independent, and this is what will be guiding our work at The New School.'

Lisa Bielawa, vocalist, composer, and longstanding member of the Philip Glass Ensemble, is announced as the first Composer-in-Residence and Chief Curator of the Institute.

YOU WHO WILL CARRY THE BURDEN

Volume 1 of *The New School Bulletin*, dated October, 1943, announces a course of study that will make degrees accessible to U.S. veterans returning from World War II. 'The program', the *Bulletin* explains, 'is one of the first practical proposals put forward to meet the crisis in liberal education brought about by the war.' The undergraduate degrees will be the first offered by the school. Speaking alongside Alvin Johnson, New School President, and Clara Mayer, Dean of the School of Philosophy and Liberal Arts, Dean Hans Simons of the School of Politics expresses optimism that the returning soldiers will bring a heightened awareness to the national perspective:

> All of us are going to ask, why did we have to fight — what did we fight for? The real answer to these questions must come from society as a whole. But it will be composed of the answers millions of individuals are able and willing to give.

The *Bulletin* takes stock of The New School's first twenty-four years, celebrating the ten-year anniversary of the University in Exile, providing and expounding upon the calendar of current courses and lectures, and announcing the latest issue of *Social Research*, as well as faculty art shows by Berenice Abbott, José de Creeft, Camilo Egas, Stanley William Hayter, Yasuo Kuniyoshi, and Louis Schanker. Among other highlights are performances and a new division, 'a Radio Workshop for the radio actor, announcer, and director', from the Dramatic Workshop.

In 1972, The New School establishes the Freshman Year Program, which offers advanced high school seniors the opportunity to complete their first year of college before enrolling, as sophomores, in a more traditional college or university program. Three years later, The New School introduces a full four-year program, the Seminar College; the Seminar College is basal to Eugene Lang College, which The New School dedicates in 1985. Counter to a normative history of colleges and universities, The New School's first undergraduate degrees are offered long after the school's first graduate degrees; with a curricular identity already in place, the formation of Eugene Lang College is met with excitement and optimism.

Eugene Lang, the college's benefactor, was born in 1919, the year of The New School's founding. In 1981, Lang founded the I Have A Dream Foundation; in 1996, for his contributions to education and social causes, President Bill Clinton would award Lang the Presidential Medal of Freedom; in 2012, five years prior to his death, Lang would hold, according to Swarthmore College, thirty-eight honorary degrees. October 1985, in his heartfelt founder's address of Eugene Lang College, Lang speaks to a vision that takes up the ideological mission of education set forth by the founders of The New School in 1919:

> For me, for my family, this is an awesome, incredible — and deeply sentimental — occasion. ... It seems so eminently appropriate and fortunate that the newly titled college should be embraced by The New School. Where else could one find all the circumstances of an outstanding tradition of educational innovation and enterprise, a richness of faculty and educational resources inviting more intensive employment, a vibrant seminar college ready for a quantum leap into the future? ... What will the Seminar College, under its new name, become? Building upon the character of its past, I see the college growing steadily for some years with many more students, each eager to extend horizons of academic enterprise, with their teachers no less eager to teach and to encourage them. I see a college whose focus is clearly directed to individual student development. As envisaged, that means small classes, working in the seminar format, calculated to stimulate intellectual interaction among students, and between student and teacher. It means broad curricular scope and flexibility so that, under sustained faculty guidance, students can create study programs related to individual objectives and abilities. It means a curriculum that will enable students to draw enriching vitality and educational adventure from the cultural and sociological aspects of New York City. ... In recent months, my family and I have heard many kind words and have rejoiced in some wonderful, heartwarming reactions to our commitment. We have been excited by the enthusiasm with which all constituencies of The New School have clasped the fledgling college to their collective bosom. However, beyond joy and excitement, my family feels a humility and profound gratitude. Our hopes for Eugene Lang College, and its transcendently important mission, rest with administrators who will give it purpose. Our family commitment, however it be recognized today, truly counts for very little. You who will carry the burden will give it real meaning.

'The cure for capitalism's failing would require that a government would have to rise above the interests of one class alone.'
↗ **ROBERT HEILBRONER** Student

Clockwise from top left:

▬▬▬ Students gather in the courtyard of The New School, 1973

▬▬▬ Entrepreneur, philanthropist and New School Life Trustee, Eugene M. Lang, 1985

▬▬▬ Author, professor, social activist, and feminist bell hooks speaks at The New School's Eugene Lang College of Liberal Arts, 2013

THE HEART AND BRAIN OF WRITING POETRY, 1987
SEKOU SUNDIATA

Raw material for poems can be gathered from innumerable personal sources. Those sources can be generally categorized as conscious and unconscious. Although they may appear as opposites in conflict or unrelated factors in daily living, the integration of thinking and feeling is possible through language and can be powerfully realized in poetry. The possibility of uncovering and creating meaning is what makes art, is what gives poetry its reason and poets their due. There are also sources beyond the self that can provide a rich pool of material for poems: current events, marriages, funerals, children at play, etc. Interpreted through the poet's own sensibilities, these sources can be transformed into meaningful poems that speak to the writer's interpretation of contemporary life. This course will explore the use of both personal and extrapersonal sources as thematic sources for writing poems.

'If a man feels very deeply about the war, or any sorrow or gladness, his feeling should be symbolized in his expression, no matter what medium he chooses.'
↗ **YASUO KUNIYOSHI** Faculty

'First of all, welcome — parents, grandparents, siblings, cousins, and every member of every kind of extended family. So, here you are at last, class of 2010, about to graduate. But from what? First of all, of course, from a lifetime of being students. This is a major identity shift, with intimations, perhaps, of an identity crisis. From now on, even if graduate school intervenes for a few years, you're in charge of your education — that intricate process by which the mind, the heart, and the soul are trained to examine themselves thoroughly and encounter the world honorably.'
↖ **MARGO JEFFERSON** Faculty

Eugene Lang College welcomes its first Scholar-in-Residence, bell hooks, in the Fall of 2013. During her tenure she leads and participates in dozens of lectures, courses, public events, and forums.

As of 2019, The New School's veterans' degree program, initiated in 1943, continues in the Bachelor's Program for Adults and Transfer Students, known on campus as BPATS.

'A CLASSIC BOOK IS ONE THAT DOESN'T HAVE TO BE WRITTEN AGAIN.'
↗ **W.E.B. DU BOIS** Faculty

WHAT ARE
DOING ABOUT

'WE ARE A RACE OF
ARTISTS. WHAT ARE
WE DOING ABOUT IT?'

↗ **SHIRLEY GRAHAM DU BOIS**
Co-Collaborator for The Negro
in American History Lecture Series

In 2019, The New School
community takes part in
'400 Years of Inequality',
a diverse coalition of persons
and organizations that
observes the 1619 arrival
of the first slave ships in
Jamestown as a principal
marker in America's ongoing
struggle with inequality.
The coalition calls on
everyone to resist a history
of inequities and recognize
the quadricentennial.

Clockwise from top left:

▬▬▬ Several thousand marchers parade
on Fifth Avenue in protest of the
East St. Louis riots. W.E.B. Du Bois
is shown third from right, in the
second row, July 28, 1917

▬▬▬ Lorna Simpson, *IS*, 1991. Toned
gelatin silver print, 24 in. x 20 in.
New York, The New School Art
Collection

WE IT?

'EDUCATION MUST NOT SIMPLY TEACH WORK – IT MUST TEACH LIFE.'

↗ W.E.B. DU BOIS Faculty

THE NEGRO IN AMERICAN HISTORY, 1948
W.E.B. DU BOIS, CHAIRMAN
GUEST LECTURERS, INCLUDING
IRENE DIGGS,
JOHN HOPE FRANKLIN,
E. FRANKLIN FRAZIER,
SHIRLEY GRAHAM,
CHARLES H. THOMPSON,
RAYFORD W. LOGAN,
HUGH H. SMYTHE,
LORENZO J. GREENE

This course follows the development of America's relations with Europe and Africa in the seventeenth and eighteenth centuries. This is followed by a study of the New World between 1400 and 1700 and the American Revolutionary War with England; a treatment of the economic, social, and political development of the United States; the influence of slave labor and the Cotton Kingdom and the Civil War. Reconstruction is viewed as the struggles between democracy and Big Business in a South dominated by land monopoly and caste. There follows an inquiry into the part played by Negroes in the social and economic development of the nation during the nineteenth century, including the lives of men like Frederick Douglass and Booker T. Washington and the Negro as writer and subject in American literature. The development of capitalism and imperialism in the twentieth century, covering both world wars and the Depression, is considered from the point of view of Negro workers and thinkers.

DEATH OF COOL, 2019
JESSICA GLASSCOCK

With beginnings in the avant-garde art world and African-American minstrelsy, the consumption of subculture has been a driving force in fashion since the nineteenth century. This course will examine the interaction between fashion and subculture from its early modern origins into the advent of the ever-multiplying streetstyle tribes of the late twentieth century. Topics to be covered include the bohemian artists of the late nineteenth century, and the rise of African-American subculture as exemplified by jazz and the Zoot Suiter. In the second half of the twentieth century, the chemical aesthetics of the psychedelic hippie movement of the 1960s and the apocalypse of punk in the 1970s will be examined as both subcultural expression and fashion inspiration. Through readings of primary texts and critical theory and the viewing of exploitative and documentary film, the relationship between mainstream fashion and the culture of 'cool' will be explored.

A 1947 study conducted by the Social Science Research Council, a major nonprofit organization, finds no formal African studies programs in the United States. Since the early twentieth century, at historically black colleges and universities there have been courses in Americans of African heritage, as well as the history of Africa and the United States, but, in 1953, the U.S. Department of Education concludes that historically black higher education has made principal 'the important mission of providing education for teachers, ministers, lawyers, and doctors for the black population in a racially segregated society'.

After World War II, returning soldiers who have gained a more worldly outlook (some have been to Africa and fought alongside African soldiers) and who have been somewhat integrated, are interested in the subject. Eighty years old and emerging from academic retirement, W.E.B. Du Bois fashions a 1948 course for The New School, which, along with a course at Northwestern University, will be the first like it at an historically white university. The guest lecturers are a callout of Du Bois' oeuvre and the leading thinkers and Civil Rights activists of the day.

1948

'The maker or "creative artist" goes his own way, independent and uncoercible, not to be tamed to society's uses, not be harnessed in social rule. But the tradition does not accept this liberty of the artist at its face value; it will not take it for what it seems to be. Spokesmen of the tradition interpret the artist's mysterious gift as but a different bondage, as a direct subjection to a different, a supernatural, power. Calling this subjection Inspiration or Possession, they have pronounced it good or evil as occasion prompted or need required; but always good or evil as a power alien, uncompromising, and rebellious, a thing to be respected but tabooed, or else to be watched and checked and overcome and tamed, by force and by fraud if necessary.'

↗ HORACE KALLEN Founding Faculty

'COME ON. I DON'T HAVE ANY PROBLEM VIOLATING MY OWN INSIGHTS IN PRACTICE.'

↗ **SLAVOJ ŽIŽEK** Faculty

THE YELLOW CURTAIN

Only weeks before, Edward Jewell of *The New York Times* had lauded Joseph Urban and Thomas Hart Benton for their work in The New School building at 12th Street. The building, designed and architected by Urban, was the relocated and first dedicated home of the university. Benton's mural, *America Today*, was one of three site-specific murals on the premises. On January 25, 1931, a multi-panel mural by José Clemente Orozco is the second mural covered by Jewell. The murals by the renowned Mexican painter are 'disappointing' and 'a melee of fragments'.

The Times publishes three letters that object to the criticisms, and Alvin Johnson, the school's President, sets the criticisms aside as political; one of the panels portrays the Russian Revolution, and depicts Vladimir Lenin, Joseph Stalin, and the Red Army. Johnson is committed to artistic freedom, and insists the murals are not a political endorsement by the school, and that only a 'dunce' would think they were. In 1942, Orozco confirmed Johnson's view: 'I had been given absolute freedom in my work; it was a school for investigation, not for submission.' Johnson's estimation of creative freedom, in practice and as an aspirational ideal, are the scholarly terrain of Horace Kallen, a founder of The New School who is formative to the school's curricular development in the arts and philosophy. (In all, Kallen would be on the faculty roster for fifty-four years, teaching his last course in 1973.) In 1942, accumulating research from twenty-three years of teaching at The New School, Kallen opens his two-volume investigation, *Art in Freedom*, with a plea for creative autonomy:

> According to an ancient tradition, the 'creative' artist possesses a liberty denied to other men. His skill and workmanship may be of the best, or may not be at all. But he is not a poet or maker because of skill and workmanship. He is a poet or maker because he is able to make things which no skill can attain and no workmanship encompass.

With the end of World War II, Johnson's ability to resist political and financial criticism of the Orozco work is strained (he denies that the murals have cost the school backers). World War II is supplanted by the Cold War, and Johnson writes a pamphlet, which he completes the year after his official retirement in 1945, seeking to deflect Red Scare denunciations of Orozco's subject matter. But the pamphlet isn't convincing enough to stem McCarthyism and a Western mobilization against Joseph Stalin, who is already responsible for more deaths than Adolf Hitler, and the murals are a recurring blot on the reputation of the school.

In 1947, New York State demands that educators sign an oath of allegiance to the American and State constitutions. Clara Mayer, Dean of The New School, reluctantly asks faculty for their compliance. In 1949, Orozco dies, and with Johnson's influence fading, ten years of criticism and internal dissent about the murals leads the Board of Trustees to a compromise position; while the artistic merit of the panels is not in question, the Soviet panel will be covered for some occasions; the works are not to be destroyed. In 1953, the aging Alumni Association of the Graduate Faculty issues a statement that 'the murals on the fifth floor represent primarily propaganda and are inappropriate in a place devoted to science and teaching'.

The Soviet panel of the Orozco murals is then semi-permanently covered by what has come to be known as 'The Yellow Curtain'. The curtain immediately sparks student organization and protest, which results in a tortured public and personal embarrassment for the school. In 1955, not letting the story go, Hans Simons of *The New York Post* editorializes:

> The murals have been there since 1930; they survived the indigestion of the Nazi–Soviet pact. Libertarians who loathe communism ... managed to admire art, swallow their food, and remember that in a democracy one can distinguish between art, politics, the right of the artist to be politically wrong, and the duty of everyone to be tolerant, not to say adult.

The yellow curtain is quietly dismantled in 1956 or 1957, and in 1962, the 'Orozco Room' is returned to the roster of classrooms.

S T U D E N T S

W A N T E D

To join committee protesting curtaining of mural in Orozco Room

Call ORegon 3-7344 11:00 A:M to 1:00 P:M
Jack Heilweil   (Mon. to Fri.)

'"Emergencies" have always been the pretext on which the safeguards of individual liberty have been eroded.'
↗ FRIEDRICH HAYEK Student

SEVEN

SUNDAY

EVENINGS

OF

POETRY

■

THE NEW SCHOOL
66 W. 12 STREET
NEW YORK 11

Under the direction of
JEAN STARR UNTERMEYER
and LEONIE ADAMS

Reading of poems
with commentary, by the poets

Feb. 25   CARL SANDBURG
Mar. 4   WILLIAM CARLOS WILLIAMS
Mar. 11   EDITH SITWELL
Mar. 18   PADRAIC and MARY COLUM
Apr. 1   e.e. cummings
Apr. 8   JOHN BERRYMAN
          ROBERT FITZGERALD
          WINFIELD TOWNLEY SCOTT
Apr. 15   LEONIE ADAMS
          JEAN STARR UNTERMEYER

Time: 8:30-10:10 P.M.
Series subscription: $8.50

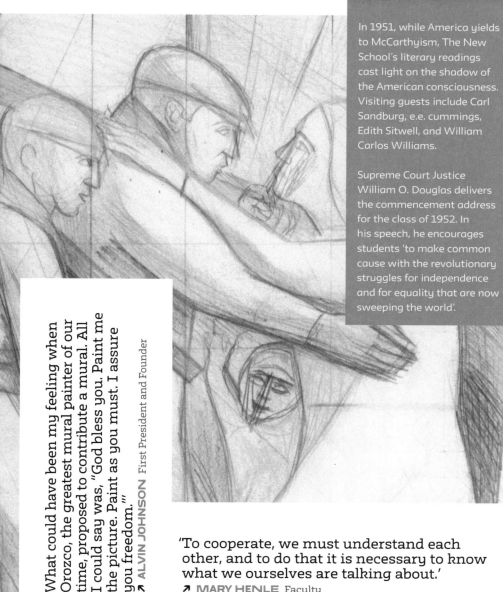

In 1951, while America yields to McCarthyism, The New School's literary readings cast light on the shadow of the American consciousness. Visiting guests include Carl Sandburg, e.e. cummings, Edith Sitwell, and William Carlos Williams.

Supreme Court Justice William O. Douglas delivers the commencement address for the class of 1952. In his speech, he encourages students 'to make common cause with the revolutionary struggles for independence and for equality that are now sweeping the world'.

CHINA, INDIA AND THE SOVIET UNION, 1942
PEARL BUCK

A presentation of the most pressing problems implicit in recent developments in these three countries, especially as they affect the United States.

MEDIA AND POLITICS OF PROPAGANDA, 2019
NINA KHRUSHCHEVA

This course examines political and cultural propaganda and its symbolism before, during, and after the Cold War. Significant focus will be placed on American ideology, or 'Americanism', which has been represented through various media such as: advertising, press, television, film, and now through the (still) relatively novel forum of social media. Concentrating on Donald Trump's presidency, his divisive cultural campaign 'Make America Great Again', and his twitter-agenda (governed by @realDonalTrump), we will survey the 2016 U.S. campaign election coverage and ask: is the Trump presidency a media creation? Comparing the U.S. elections with other campaigns from around the world, we will further investigate the role of social media and how it has enhanced political propaganda and public relation strategies. Ultimately, we will determine how new technologies are delivering political and ideological messages without the constraint of borders or time. Finally, we will broaden our scope to focus on the propaganda of the two former and current most prominent global rivals—the United States and the Soviet Union/Russia. We will reflect on how their respective propaganda strategies and tactics have been translated, transformed, and recycled in totalitarian North Korea, communist China, the Middle East, and some fundamentalist militant groups.

"What could have been my feeling when Orozco, the greatest mural painter of our time, proposed to contribute a mural. All I could say was, "God bless you. Paint me the picture. Paint as you must. I assure you freedom.""
↖ **ALVIN JOHNSON** First President and Founder

'To cooperate, we must understand each other, and to do that it is necessary to know what we ourselves are talking about.'
↗ **MARY HENLE** Faculty

'In every painting, as in any other work of art, there is always an *idea*, never a *story*. The idea is the point of departure, the first cause of the plastic construction, and it is always present all the time as energy creating matter. The stories and other literary associations exist only in the mind of the spectator, the painting acting as the stimulus.'
↗ **JOSÉ CLEMENTE OROZCO** Faculty and Site-Specific Artist

1952

IDEAS ARE HIGH EXPLOSIVES

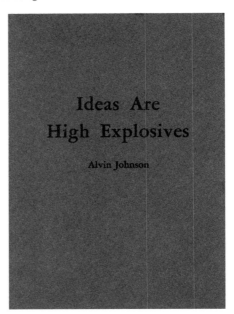

1962

'Never allow a person
to tell you no who doesn't
have the power to say yes.'
↗ **ELEANOR ROOSEVELT**
Advisory Committee Member
and Speaker

Alvin Johnson, the swashbuckling first President of
The New School, returns for his eighty-eighth birthday.

Johnson assumed the leadership of The New
School in 1922, as the result of a philosophical and
financial crisis that arrived with the seventh semester.
The model, as envisioned, was not sustainable. Johnson,
an insider / outsider — someone who had been party
to the internal formation of the school, but could also
see it externally — was enlisted to negotiate the
inescapable emendations.

As President, Johnson presided over The New School
through its years in Chelsea, at London Terrace, where
the arts were elevated to featured status; shepherded the
school to Greenwich Village, a neighborhood befitting
The New School's progressive and spirited identity;
commissioned and readied a new building, of international
stature, by Bauhaus-influenced architect and designer
Joseph Urban; fostered the introduction of 'workshop'
courses, which originated experiential, cooperative
learning in multiple subjects; ushered in the University
in Exile, bringing 181 fleeing European scholars through the
faculty roster of The New School; retained a core group
of University in Exile professors as full-time faculty in new
tracks in new departments; and initiated graduate degrees
in 1934, and undergraduate degrees in 1943.

In 1949, four years after he officially retired, Johnson
celebrated his seventy-fifth birthday on campus. In 1952,
he published his memoir, *Pioneer's Progress*, which was the
subject of conversation at his eightieth birthday, also held
at The New School, where he remained an influential figure.

For The New School celebration of his eighty-eighth
birthday, Johnson is presented with a limited-edition
monograph, eighty-eight-pages, collecting his post-
retirement editorials from *The New School Bulletin*, 1945–
61. The title, 'Ideas Are High Explosives', is drawn from
an October 1960 editorial which ponders the 'low brow'
and the 'high brow', the erosion of the distinction, and the
potential of an increasingly educated population: 'Ideas
are high explosives, and ... there is no adequate defense
against bad ideas except good ideas.'

The next year, 1963, Johnson wages one more
battle, leading the charge on a fundraising campaign that
rescues the school from a takeover by the lugubrious giant,
New York University.

'It seems safe to say that significant discovery, really
creative thinking, does not occur with regard to
problems about which the thinker is lukewarm.'
↗ **MARY HENLE** Faculty

'Although the college may send out young men
and women with minds well filled out and shapely,
they often arrive at the destination of maturity in
a terrible state of emaciation. "The world" they
pass through is intellectually drouthy.'
↗ **ALVIN JOHNSON** First President and Founder

Ideas Are High Explosives

Alvin Johnson

PUNK AND NOISE, 2019
EVAN RAPPORT

This course explores the aesthetics, techniques,
history, and elements of style in punk and noise
music, with an emphasis on American musicians,
audiences, and venues from the mid-1970s to the
early 1980s. Through analysis of musical style,
we explore historical and societal issues such as
changing ideas of race, shifting political pressures,
and exchanges between the U.S. and the U.K. The
course offers opportunities for performance, and
composition, and requires a commitment to
intensive training, but familiarity
but famil
need

PARSONS · SCHOOL · OF · DESIGN · 66 FIFTH AVENUE · NEW YORK · 10011 · MARCH 1990

'ANYTHING IS AN ART IF YOU DO IT AT THE LEVEL OF AN ART.'
↗ RICHARD AVEDON Student

'A whole literature of citations, eulogies, testimonials, of addresses, editorials and reviews has grown around the work and record of Alvin Johnson. How can one add anything without being repetitious? When he celebrated his seventy-fifth birthday his friends and admirers seemed to have made the "definitive" appraisal. Then he wrote his Pioneer's Progress and confounded those who thought they knew him well.'
↗ HANS SIMONS, TOASTING ALVIN JOHNSON AT EIGHTY Faculty

'ALL MY LIFE, MY HEART HAS YEARNED FOR A THING I CANNOT NAME.'
↗ ANDRÉ BRETON Faculty

Clockwise from top left:

Alvin Johnson, undated

'To the Living Spirit': promotional pamphlet describing the various programs at The New School for Social Research and addressing how the school was 'extending its programs as the times demand' during World War II, circa 1943

Parsonspaper, March, 1990

Alvin Saunders Johnson. Ideas are High Explosives, 1962

'THEATER IS A VERB BEFORE IT IS A NOUN, AN ACT BEFORE IT IS A PLACE.'

↗ **MARTHA GRAHAM** Faculty

DO WOMEN DARE?

'Far worse for me than all the real problems of those years was what is now referred to as McCarthyism, which from my point of view looked and felt like a reprise of the coming of fascism. ... Then began the time of betrayals, denunciations, the casting off of friendships and trust. Here is where my mind gets stuck – I remember it all and yet I recall nothing.'

↗ **GERDA LERNER** Faculty

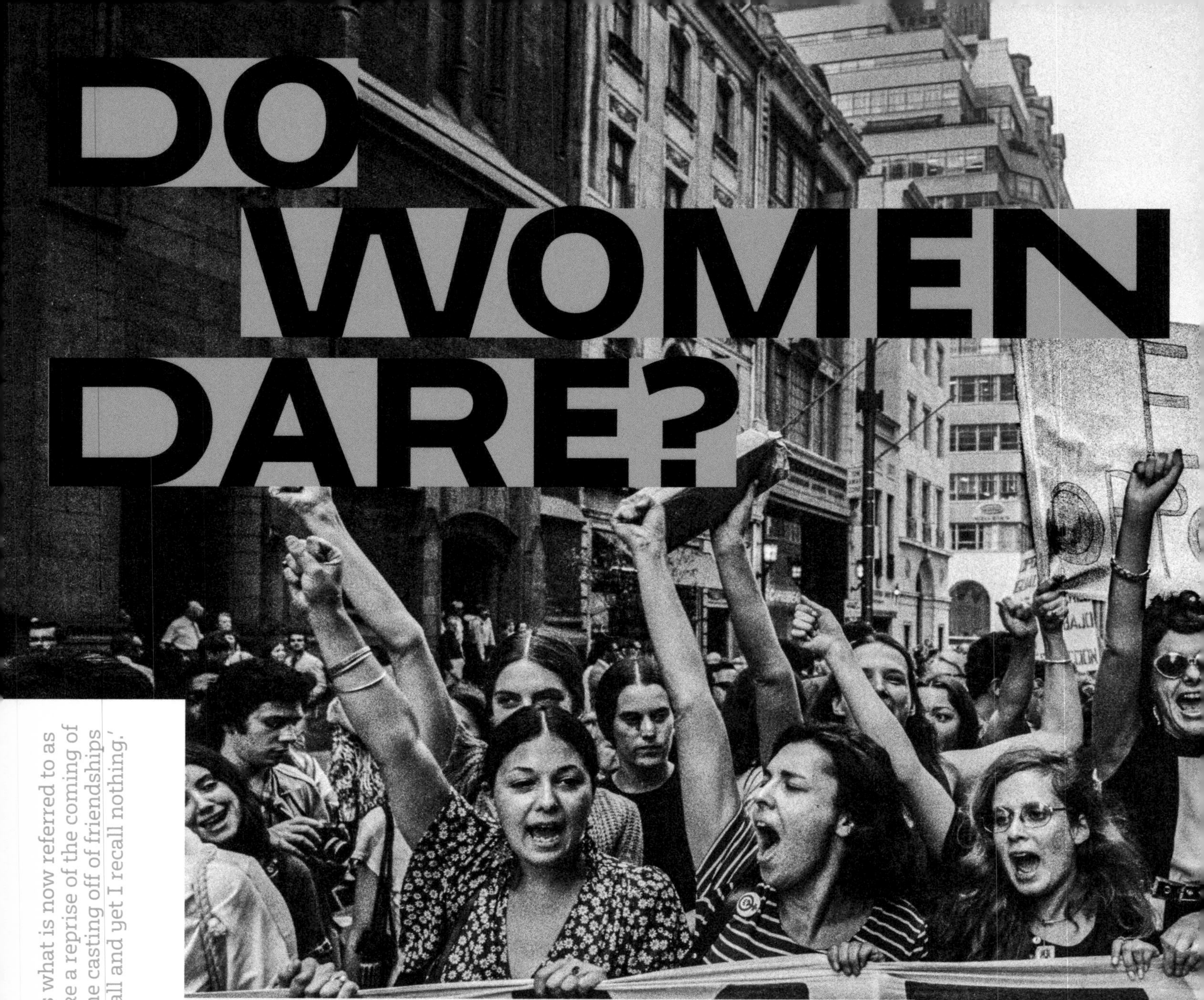

THE NEW SCHOOL FOR SOCIAL RESEARCH
66 West 12th Street, New York 11, N.Y.

for information:
Albert W. Landa, Director of Public
Information/Phone: ORegon 5-2700
Night: OR 5-2704/Home: DE 6-966

FOR IMMEDIATE RELEASE

AT LAST, AMERICAN WOMEN GET RIGHTFUL PLACE IN HISTORY

Few people are aware that non-violent resistance as practiced in the South today can be traced back past Mahatma Gandhi to America's own "abolitionist women."

This and other little-known facts about the nation's distaff population will be treated in a new course on "Great Women in American History," to be offered for the first time in the Fall semester, beginning September 24, at The New School for Social Research, 66 West 12th Street, Manhattan.

The course, to be conducted by author Gerda Lerner, will be held on Friday evenings, from 6:20 to 8:00 p.m. Registration is now open.

(more)

'KNOWING IS POWERFUL AND WE CAN BE MORE POWERFUL THAN WE HAVE EVER BEEN.'

↗ **GINA LURIA WALKER** Faculty

Alongside her husband, Carl Lerner, Gerda Lerner battles the Hollywood blacklist of the mid-twentieth century. As she would write in her 2001 memoir, *Fireweed*:

> *The witch-hunting and blacklisting system was built on old foundations … Like the medieval witch hunts, like fascism, it flourished by instilling fear and by letting the imagination of the victims work its self-destructive course. One did not need to imprison or kill large numbers of people — all one needed to do was to set an example with a few, and the fear this example created in other potential victims was sufficient to insure the falling in line of thousands of others.*

After nearly a decade, the Lerners return to New York City. Working theater and film professionals, they're looking for a new star — an escape from McCarthyism, as well as from a dogma of communism that had become constricted:

> *Ever since we had left Hollywood, our affiliation with the party was quite loose. Blacklisted people were dropped from participation in party activities; it was assumed they were being followed by the FBI and would therefore only endanger anyone with whom they were in contact. That distancing, at the time, suited us fine, for Carl and I had each in our own way experienced disillusionment, a slow eroding of trust. Had Cold War hysteria not taken such extreme forms we would have left the party years earlier than we did, for reasons of our own dissatisfaction.*

Recalibrating, Lerner turns from creative endeavors to cultural studies, and an academic career that begins with a Bachelor's program at The New School. Before she is awarded a degree, she develops the course that she found absent in the curriculum; her description for 'Great Women in American History' appears in The New School's Fall course catalogue of 1962. The course doesn't meet enrollment, but retitled 'The Role of Women in American Culture' runs in Spring 1963, with ten students. 'To my knowledge', Lerner would write in her 1979 work, *The Majority Finds its Past*, 'this was the first class on the subject since a short-lived attempt had been made to teach such a class at Radcliffe in the 1930s.'

THE ROLE OF WOMEN IN AMERICAN CULTURE, 1963
GERDA LERNER

The seldom-told story of women's crucial role in the development of America is particularly meaningful today. Since the status and problem of modern women are directly connected with American history, understanding the past can serve as an invaluable aid in making proper use of the opportunities and challenges of the present. This course presents the lives and personalities of outstanding American women, their contributions, their organizations, their struggles, in order to illuminate the position of women in today's world of rapidly shifting values. Topics will include: women in the colonies; women and education; reform for the slave, the child, the handicapped; the civil and legal rights of women; the growth of organizations; working women and their problems; social welfare as a central concern of women; old myths die slowly; women's status and role today.

WOMEN'S LEGACY AT THE NEW SCHOOL, 2018
GINA WALKER

Women's Legacy at The New School extends the contemporary global project of feminist discovery and recovery of historical women to the understudied female intellectuals, academics, performers, artists, activists, and others who contributed to the founding and evolution of the university and its programs. Our emphasis will be on project-based inquiry, supervised primary research, and production of original 'female biographies' that more accurately establish women's historical legacy. In preparation for the 100th anniversary of the school's founding in 2019, students will disseminate their new findings through print, social, and digital media, and a curated space on The New School History Website. Distinguished Guest Faculty from around the university will offer lectures on specific disciplines, individuals, and historical contexts. This is part of an ongoing effort to reclaim and celebrate the university's women.

'A sense of deep strain between women and men has been permeating our species' life as far back into time as the study of myth and ritual permits us to trace human feeling.'
↗ **DOROTHY DINNERSTEIN** Student

'The chattel character of women both qualifies them as gifts for the gods and precludes them from ascetic habits inconsistent with the rights of their human proprietors.'
↗ **ELSIE CLEWS PARSONS (WRITING AS 'JOHN MAIN')** Faculty

1963

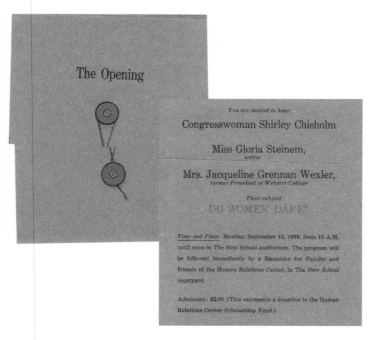

The Opening

You are invited to hear
Congresswoman Shirley Chisholm

Miss Gloria Steinem,
writer

Mrs. Jacqueline Grennan Wexler,
former President of Webster College

Their subject:
DO WOMEN DARE?

Time and Place: Monday, September 15, 1969, from 10 A.M. until noon in The New School auditorium. The program will be followed immediately by a Reception for Faculty and friends of the Human Relations Center, in The New School courtyard.

Admission: $2.00 (This represents a donation to the Human Relations Center Scholarship Fund.)

'In the world we live in, fear is an enormous tool of reaction. Fear is what's driving all this right-wing stuff in Europe, fear shut down feminist questioning. Because at the beginning of feminism in the '70s, believe me, fear was nowhere. There was excitement, sexual feeling, erotic thrill — you know, take back the night. There was a feeling that we would fear no more.'
↗ **ANN SNITOW** Faculty

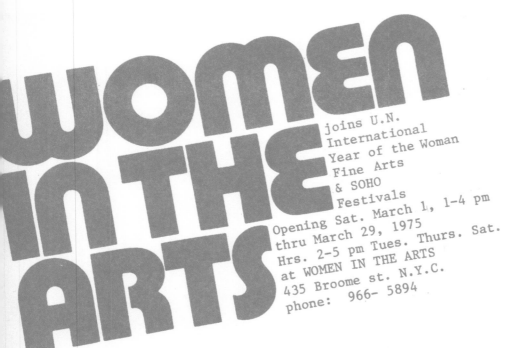

WOMEN IN THE ARTS

joins U.N. International Year of the Woman Fine Arts & SOHO Festivals
Opening Sat. March 1, 1–4 pm
thru March 29, 1975
Hrs. 2–5 pm Tues. Thurs. Sat.
at WOMEN IN THE ARTS
435 Broome st. N.Y.C.
phone: 966- 5894

'Tradition is what the past hands the future like any legacy, it changes according to the use we make of it, what we make of it, what we add to it or take away from it. We are heir to the quickening search for knowledge, the courage of spiritual adventure and planning, the conviction that the truth will make us free. But tradition is still in the making, now and forever, by students, faculty, administration, trustees.'
↗ **CLARA MAYER** Dean, Vice President and Trustee

Clockwise from top left:

▬▬▬ Invitation to the opening event for the Human Relations Center at The New School. The event featured Congresswoman Shirley Chisholm, Gloria Steinem, and Jacqueline Grennan Wexler speaking on the topic 'Do Women Dare?', 1969

▬▬▬ Shirley Chisholm, 1975

▬▬▬ First Women's Liberation march on Fifth Avenue. Bob Adelman, *circa* 1970

▬▬▬ Pamphlet announcing a new concentration in medical anthropology, *circa* 1979

▬▬▬ *Women in the Arts* exhibition announcement, 1975

Fall, 1969: the Human Relations Center hosts 'Do Women Dare', an event that headlines Congresswoman Shirley Chisholm, author and activist Gloria Steinem, and the President of Webster College, Jacqueline Grennan Wexler. Founded by Alice Rice Cook and with the support of New School Vice President and Dean Clara Mayer, since 1951, the Human Relations Center has been offering courses and programs that pursue issues of gender in a social, personal, and professional context. In the 1960s, under the leadership of Ruth Hendricks Van Doren, the program adds specialized courses that pertain to professions, for example, in health, education, and social services. The center reaches the apex of its popularity in the mid-1970s, with 3,000 students and seventy-five courses. In the mid-1980s, the center is designated the Vera List Center for Adult Studies.

In 1992, the Gender Studies and Feminist Theory program initiates what will become an interdisciplinary Master's degree. The track, beset by student and faculty protests, and interdepartmental conflict and criticism, is discontinued. As of 2019, The New School offers an undergraduate minor and a certificate in Gender Studies.

The Anthropology Committee of

The Graduate Faculty of The New School for Social Research

A New Concentration in Medical Anthropology

Leading to the Master of Arts Degree

GENDER AND ITS DISCONTENTS, 2019
RICARDO MONTEZ AND LISA RUBIN

This is the required core course for the university-wide graduate certificate in Gender and Sexuality Studies and it is open to all the graduate students who are interested in sexuality and gender studies. Our starting point is the acknowledgement that sex- and gender-based modes of social organization are pervasive and, further, that their prominence and persistence are reflected in sex- and gender-conscious research across the humanities, the arts, the social sciences, design, and studies dedicated to social policies and innovative strategies for social intervention. We will expand on this starting point through both an in-depth survey of influential theoretical approaches to sex and gender such as Marxist feminism, theories of sexual difference, queer studies, and postcolonial and decolonial feminism, and by paying attention to the significance of different approaches. Topics to be explored include, but are not limited to: equality and rights, exploitation and division of labor, the construction of gender, performativity, gender images, narrative and identity.

1953

Dated April 8, a memo from New School Publicity Director Agnes de Lima to New School President, Hans Simons, recounts a meeting with Alma Reed, an influential journalist with ties to the Mexican government who is committed to the work of José Clemente Orozco. As the result of political pressure on The New School, and an atmosphere of McCarthyism, several panels of Orozco murals have been covered by a yellow curtain; Reed has argued that the Mexico section should be uncovered, and suggests that Mexico might contribute to the restoration of the murals—Reed has also signaled a threat. 'As perhaps you remember', de Lima writes gently, 'Felipe Carrillo, the Mexican hero portrayed in the mural, was her betrothed so she feels particularly concerned aside from any injury the Mexican government might feel.'

De Lima goes on to make her recommendation: 'Perhaps it might be possible to uncover that part of the wall and let her know so that we don't have any repercussions from Mexico. She is in constant touch with people down there of course.'

De Lima, in pen, has added one word to the recommendation—the Mexico section of the wall should be uncovered 'promptly'. De Lima is delicate in her correspondence with the President; she has written numerous letters concerning Reed and the murals, and Reed had actually been quite angry, storming out of the room where the paintings were covered. As a result of de Lima's siege on the curtain, all but the Russian panel of the murals are uncovered.

De Lima, with Alvin Johnson, was one of the early editors at *The New Republic*. In the late teens and early twenties, she and Johnson, who was married at the time, had an extramarital relationship that resulted in a daughter, Sigrid de Lima, who would attend The New School and author five novels. (At least three of Sigrid de Lima's half-sisters, by her father, were also variously at The New School: Felicia Johnson Deyrup was a professor of economics at The New School for thirty-five years, beginning in 1949; Astrith Deyrup led a textile design art workshop through the 1960s and 1970s; Dorothy Deyrup, also an artist, exhibited at the school in 1934).

Clockwise from top left:

Flyer for an exhibition of paintings by Zola Marcus, 1952

Pamphlet for the exhibition *Sculptured Portraits of Distinguished American Negroes*, Ruth Brall, 1949

Agnes de Lima at the Peninsula School, Menlo Park, CA. 1930s

Flyer for an exhibition of work by Paul Terence Feeley, 1948

Memorandum from Agnes de Lima to Dr. Hans Simons regarding the covering of murals by José Clemente Orozco, April 8, 1953

EXHIBITION
of
SCULPTURED PORTRAITS
of
ISTINGUISHED AMERICAN NEGROES
by
RUTH BRALL

NEW SCHOOL FOR SOCIAL RESEARCH
66 West 12th Street, N. Y. C.

February 12th, thru Febru~~~

Daily 10 A. M. to 6 P. M. ~~~

RENCE FEELEY

PAINTINGS
ZOLA
MARCUS
GALLERY OF
THE NEW SCHOOL FOR SOCIAL RESEARCH
66 West 12th Street • New York, N. Y.

PREVIEW WEDNESDAY, JANUARY 23 • HOURS 4:30-7:30

THROUGH FEB. 6, 1952

16 - NOV. 30, 1948
OL FOR SOCIAL RESEARCH
T 12th STREET, NEW YORK

**CIVIL LIBERTY UNDER ATTACK:
THE FIGHT FOR AND AGAINST
FREEDOM, 1954
WILL MASLOW**

'THE INEVITABLE IS NO LESS A SHOCK JUST BECAUSE IT IS INEVITABLE.'
↗ JAMAICA KINCAID Student

NEW SCHOOL FOR SOCIAL RESEARCH
Inter-office Memorandum

To: Dr. Simons   Date: 4-8-53

From: AdeL   Re:

Alma Reed, a prominent friend of Orozco, has just returned from Mexico where she has written a book about him to be published in Spanish by the Mexican Government and by an American publisher in English.

She came in to tell us the great Mexican artist, Guitierez, an expert mural painter hes been very useful in Mexico in restoring damaged murals. He is coming East next fall following an exhibit of his work in San Francisco end Miss Reed hopes he can have a show here also. Miss Reed suggests that he might be very useful in restoring the Orozco murals and she hopes that it might be possible to get an appropriation from the Mexican government to help defray the expense.

She mentioned that she supposed the covering of the wall was for ideological reasons but expressed regret that the Mexican section was included. I told her that we expected to remove the curtain from that part of the wall. As perhaps you remember, Felipe Carrillo, the Mexican hero portrayed in the mural, was her be-trothed so she feels particularly concerned aside from any injury the Mexican government might feel.

Perhaps it might be possible to uncover that part of the wall and let her know promptly so that we don't have any repercussions from Mexico. She is in constant touch with people down there of course.

a.

Oh — I am all for this.
ab

RECEIVED
APR 3 1953
Office of the President

---

ures. An analysis of the
y problems of our day,
gal, and moral contexts
nd of the demands of
ortunity is provided for

of Civil Liberty.
, Hunter College.
: Their Uses
rmerly chief U.S.

es and Immunity.
cial prosecutor
k City; formerly
Board
oversy.
thedral

Programs:
. Harlan
eporter.
gitimate
rmerly
ns

e List: Political
, Professor

esponsibility.
wrence

Private
chairman,

the
Howe,

Agnes de Lima came to The New School in 1940 as a feminist, a prominent writer on education, and a progressive educator who was a formative contributor to the Little Red Schoolhouse, the Walden School, and the Elizabeth Irwin School. The archival record preserved by The New School of her relationship with Johnson, who retires in 1945, bespeaks a formal efficiency.

For two decades, de Lima is meticulously and personally invested in the exhibitions, outreach, and identity of the school; in the late 1940s, for example, she assists author William Styron, a former student of Hiram Haydn's New School writing workshop, in finding an inexpensive apartment in Brooklyn.

Alongside Clara Mayer, de Lima, with palpable disgust, navigates the U.S. Red Scare of the 1940s and 1950s. De Lima had prophesied the danger to progressive education in 1925 (the year of the Scopes Monkey Trial), in her nonfiction work *Our Enemy the Child*:

> The next heresy hunt will be directed against the rapidly growing number of people who believe in 'experimental' education. Some canny sleuth will discover that there is a direct connection between schools which set out deliberately to train children to think, and to develop creatively, and the radical movement. Not all progressive schools of course will be banned. ... The dangerous centers are those directed by people who have a vision of a new social order, and who believe that the way to prepare for it is to bring up a generation of free-thinking, self-directing young people whose spontaneity, originality, and native curiosity have not been stifled nor confined within narrow grooves of conformity.

In 1961, de Lima retires suddenly. The departure coincides with the appointment of New School President Henry David, who dismisses Clara Mayer; at the time, Mayer is unarguably the school's greatest ally. Within two years, David will nearly bankrupt the institution, and sell it for salvage to New York University.

'Breaking the rules, taking risks comes at a price, so does being critical of the past, but less so of the present or the future. Being silent may be the greatest mistake of all.'
↗ **SONDRA FARGANIS** Faculty

THEY, THE PEOPLE: POLITICAL JOURNALISM, PAST AND PRESENT, 2010 SAM TANENHAUS

Colonial era to the present, the most forceful political writers have also been prose masters who have struck a balance between argument and literary technique in their attempt to clarify the contradictions and tensions of American democracy. This course will examine how the best writers have done through close readings and discussion of selected works, past and present — including classics of political argument (the Federalist Papers, speeches by Lincoln, Martin Luther King Jr., Barack Obama), opinion columns (from Walter Lippmann and H.L. Mencken to David Brooks and Frank Rich) analytical essays and commentary (Richard Hofstadter, Edmund Wilson, Garry Wills), and narratives (James Baldwin, Joan Didion, Norman Mailer, David Remnick, Marjorie Williams).

aphic work by 55 artists including AFRO / P / RICHARD DIEBENKORN // LYONI MAIRE / RED GROOMS / JOHN HULTBERG / MICHAEL PONCE DE LEON / ROBERT F HMIDT / BEN SHAHN / ANDY WARHOL

day: 10 a.m.-5 p.m.
ngton's Birthday, Feb. 22)

Sculpture from the

ALBERT A. LIST FAMILY COLLECTION

75 works by 61 artists
including

Agostini / Arp / Bontecou / Calder / Di Suvero / Dubuffet Ernst / Giacometti / Hadzi / Kemeny / Lipchitz / Lipton Marisol / Moore / Nevelson / A. Pomodoro / Rosati / Segal Stankiewicz / Trova / Turnbull / Wines

October 5-November 4, 1965
Monday-Friday 1-8; Saturday 10-5

NEW SCHOOL ART CENTER
Director: PAUL MOCSANYI
66 West 12th Street

Admission Free   Please Post

'Persecution, whenever it occurs, establishes only the power and cunning of the persecutor, not the truth and worth of his belief.'
↗ **HORACE KALLEN** Founding Faculty

Clockwise from top left:

▮▮▮▮ Book cover for *Our Enemy The Child*, by educational reformer Agnes de Lima, 1925

▮▮▮▮ Exhibition poster for *Contemporary Urban Visions*, 1966

▮▮▮▮ Flyer for the exhibition *Sculpture from the Albert A. List Family Collection*, 1965

▮▮▮▮ Flyer for the exhibition *The Graphic Work of Minna Citron*, 1950

▮▮▮▮ Correspondence, The New School Publicity Office records, *circa* 1950

▮▮▮▮ Flyer for the exhibition *Mirta Cerra*, 1950

'THAT'S THE REAL REVENGE, THE MUSIC COULDN'T BE SHUT DOWN OR HIDDEN.'

↗ **BILAL OLIVER** Student

Following pages:

Lobby in front of the auditorium of the 66 West 12th Street building. 1990s

‘I'LL ALWAYS BE AN AMATEUR PHOTOGRAPHER.’

↗ **ELLIOTT ERWITT** Student

THE FIRST LADY WEARS RED

For the first inaugural ball of her husband, President Barack Obama, Michelle Obama wears an ivory, floor-length gown with rosette flourishes. The gown is designed by Parsons graduate Jason Wu, and marks the beginning of her term as the nation's foremost influencer: not since Jacqueline Kennedy has a first lady been so dedicated to arts and culture, and so true to a personal style. 'Jason's ... gown is a masterpiece,' she says. 'It is simple, it's elegant, and it comes from this brilliant young mind, someone who is living the American Dream.'

Through the course of eight years, 'Lady O' will wear the designs of dozens of Parsons graduates, emphasizing an international and environmental outlook through fashion. In 2011, she pairs long white gloves with a cross-strapped silk-georgette gown to a state dinner at Buckingham Palace hosted by Queen Elizabeth II. The Tom Ford ensemble underlines not only the transatlantic vision of an American Parsons designer, but a designer committed to conscientious, environmental fashion. Later that year, hosting South Korean President Lee Myung-bak and his wife Kim Yoon-ok at a White House State Dinner, the first lady wears a single-strap purple gown by Korean-American Parsons graduate Doo-Ri Chung. Lady O looks to Parsons not only for grand occasions, but for spirited chic by Chris Benz and J. Crew's Jenna Lyons, for example, and tailored dignitary by Marc Jacobs and Narciso Rodriguez. For President Obama's second inauguration, she returns to Jason Wu, becoming the first wife of a U.S. president to wear red to an inaugural ball in over a century.

In 2014, Lady O invites a delegation of Parsons representatives to the first White House Fashion Education Workshop. The group includes thirty-one students, associated faculty, and ten alumni — Lyons, Rodriguez, and Wu among them. Over the course of two weeks, Parsons students fabricate installations from repurposed materials that will transform the historic East Room of the White House.

'Fashion is really about passion and creativity, just like music or dance or poetry,' said the first lady. 'It is a calling.'

Clockwise from top left:

The Obamas arrive at the Inaugural Ball, 2009

Parsons alumnus Jason Wu attends the Parsons Spring Benefit, 2014

MY APPROACH IS TO IMAGINE MY WORLD.'

↗ **JASON WU** Student

'WHAT'LL HAPPEN WHEN INTELLIGENCE IS RECOGNIZED AS A GLOBAL RESOURCE?'

↗ **BUCKMINSTER FULLER** Associate

'When your father graduated ... he received two scholarship offers. One was to The New School, here in New York. The other one was to Harvard. The New School agreed to pay for everything – room and board, a job on campus, enough to support all three of us. Harvard just agreed to pay tuition. But Barack [Obama Sr.] was such a stubborn bastard, he had to go to Harvard.'

↗ **ANN DUNHAM TO HER SON BARACK OBAMA** Mother of President Barack Obama

The course is intended for students and professional artists interested in poster, layout, typography, fashion illustration, newspaper and magazine make-up, book design, package and product design, display, interior decoration, styling, art directing. The program is adapted to fit the experience and natural gifts of the student. The aim of the course is to help the student discover his individuality, crystalize his taste, develop his feeling for the contemporary trend by stimulating his sense of invention and perfecting his technical ability. The course is conducted as an (a) experimental laboratory, inspired by the ever changing tempo of our life; discovery of new techniques, new materials, new fields of operation; (b) practical workshop in close contact with current problems of leading magazines, department stores, advertising agencies, and manufacturers. Professional problems are analyzed in class. Aspects of the work include:

→ Nature as a source of inspiration: illustration, fashion illustration, design.
→ Composition: related to layout, typography, poster, photography, design.
→ Evolution of taste: habits, trends, text, slogan, Symbols, atmosphere. Fashion. Styling. Art directing.
→ Techniques with reference to reproduction: pen, wash, crayon, airbrush, photogram, watercolor, tempera, pastel, oil; new tools, new museums, new materials.
→ Work in three dimensions: Related to package and product design, exhibition and window display, outdoor signs.

'I usually stalk fans because I think they're really funny on Twitter. They don't know it, but I'll just go through their timelines, and if something is happening in the media, I always read fan accounts instead of the news because they have all the info and make the funniest jokes about it, so that's how I get my gossip — by stalking fans.'
↖ **GIGI HADID** Student

For the 2018 NYC Media Lab 100: The Demo Expo, the Parsons Study Collection in Virtual Reality is chosen to represent Parsons. Parsons students render a 1920s evening coat in virtual reality; an immersive experience of the coat provides historical and creative context for the garment. The Demo Expo is one of the largest cross-collegiate showcases for emerging media and technology in New York City. The event is held in The New School's newest building on Fifth Avenue, the site of three installation-specific artworks, a distinctive architectural approach, and green technology.

'Beauty is one of the marginalized and denigrated qualities that interests me. Most people think that 'the beautiful' is synonymous with beauty, and part of the continuing criticism of abstract painting is whether or not it's just decorative. The popular consensus is that beauty can't be on the exterior and true beauty is always inner or hidden, because of its incredible "power". Why can't we accept it for what it is?'
↗ **SHIRLEY KANEDA** Student

'I do struggle because I'm attracted to beautiful things, yet at the same time I am actually very aware, in some sense, of their lack of value and that the most important things in life are your connections to other people.'
↗ **TOM FORD** Student

'What fuels me is the process but what fuels the business is the product. And when you find a customer that is a kindred spirit who understands it's not just a product but something more, in that it alters them, the way they feel ... the way they move, that's wonderful. That's what I would like to achieve.'
↗ DOO-RI CHUNG Student

FASHION DESIGN, 1956 (CURRICULUM OFFERING) PARSONS SCHOOL OF DESIGN

Designers of today have developed fashions which are distinctively American in character, and the prestige of these original creations is recognized and exerts an important influence throughout the world. ... The courses of this department are planned to prepare students for careers as professional designers in the fashion world, which includes the wholesale and retail trades, stage, screen, and television, as well as custom work. In the beginning, students are given instruction in drawing from both life and the costumed model, color theory, the fundamentals of draping and dress construction. Lectures in the history of fashion, research work at museums, libraries, galleries, and shops help make the students fashion conscious and able to observe critically the current modes and trends.

HUMAN RIGHTS IN GLOBAL FASHION, 2019 A FREE COURSE AT THE NEW SCHOOL SAKIKO FUKUDA-PARR AND MARY WATSON

Fashion has long been home to some of the most glaring inequalities and injustices on an increasingly globalized scale, linking consumers and workers in distant places. Since the nineteenth century, the clothing sector has also been a site of social contestation that has been marked by struggles for worker rights, the rise of social movements, the exercise of corporate power, and the fallibility of national governments. It has also been a source of innovation in public policy, corporate accountability, monitoring—processes that have led to new twenty-first-century designs of the industry itself. This course provides an introductory overview of the key obstacles and opportunities, actors, rules, and methods for crafting innovative solutions in social mobilization, legal intervention, and design, with the aim of creating a more socially sustainable and economically inclusive fashion—a fashion that fulfills the human rights of workers in the supply chain. The course achieves this aim by analyzing (I) actors, power, and finance in the global value chain in the fashion industry; (II) international and local standards and institutions—including workers' human rights and corporate obligations and accountability; (III) social movements and international networks mobilizing worker power; (IV) monitoring and labeling schemes mobilizing consumer power; (V) and finding design solutions and technological systems that fulfill worker rights amidst new conceptions of industry design. The course introduces students to conceptual and theoretical frameworks for analyzing these processes, drawing on the human rights and the political economics of development.

Clockwise from top left: ▬▬▬ Classroom fitting, 1955

▬▬▬ Parsons School of Design students fitting mannequins and models, 1950s

If Art Is Politics
Vera List Center Forum 2018

Jane Lombard Prize
for Art and Social Justice

THE NEW SCHOOL

WALK DOWN THESE CROWDED STREETS

'WORDS ARE NEVER 'ONLY WORDS'; THEY MATTER BECAUSE THEY DEFINE THE CONTOURS OF WHAT WE CAN DO

SLAVOJ ŽIŽEK Faculty

The New School, with its historic academic offerings in architecture, urban planning, and political awareness, proposes the first academic and research center in the United States that considers a single area:

No institution of higher education has addressed itself directly to the task of education about the city for adults. Such a program may become a point of return for professionals in various urban fields — for the planners, architects, government executives, and business leaders in finance, real estate, and in labor, social work, and areas such as race and health. The New School may become the clearing house for ideas in the urban dimension. It may serve through criticism and the exchange of opinion among those holding leadership responsibility, as a catalyst for its city.

Mayor Robert F. Wagner, Mayor David Dinkins, State Attorney General Louis Lefkowitz, and many other city officials, planners, activists, and developers will visit and give their blessings to the new program. Inaugural offerings are announced in the Spring 1965 course catalogue:

In establishing the Center for New York City Affairs, The New School continues its exploration into one of the most vital and complex areas — metropolitan New York — offering a forum for education, discussion, and research on contemporary problems in the city's life.

Henry Cohen, a former New York City official in the Wagner and Lindsay administrations, and the founder and first Director of the Center, builds the school, according to *The New York Times*, 'into one of the foremost teaching centers of its kind in the country'.

In 1996, the center is renamed for New School trustee and supporter Robert J. Milano. As of 2019, the Milano School of Policy, Management, and Environment offers five degrees, and three certificates, and oversees the Center for New York City Affairs, the Community Development Finance Lab, Equity for Children, the Institute for Retired Professionals, the Observatory on Latin America, the Social Innovation Initiative, and the Vera List Center for Art and Politics.

'After people play these Sim games, it tends to change their perception of the world around them, so they see their city, house or family in a slightly different way.'
WILL WRIGHT Student

Clockwise from top left:

Parsons Environmental Design students and faculty on NBC to discuss institutional and prison design, October 21, 1971

The inaugural Vera List Center Forum, an international, annual convening of key participants in the field of art and politics, 2018

Open letter to Mayor Lindsay regarding the Women's House of Detention, *circa* 1970

face. Be thankful you get to walk so close to other humans. It's a privilege. Don't let
en than you are now, don't assume that exclusive always and everywhere means bet
he few: the private schools, private plans, private islands, private life. They are trying
h other's shelter and correction, the antidote to solipsism, and so many windows on

'Cities now have the most strategic opportunity for master planning since the opening of the frontier. The emergency approach to housing does not solve the housing problem at its roots.'

↗ **CHARLES ABRAMS** Faculty

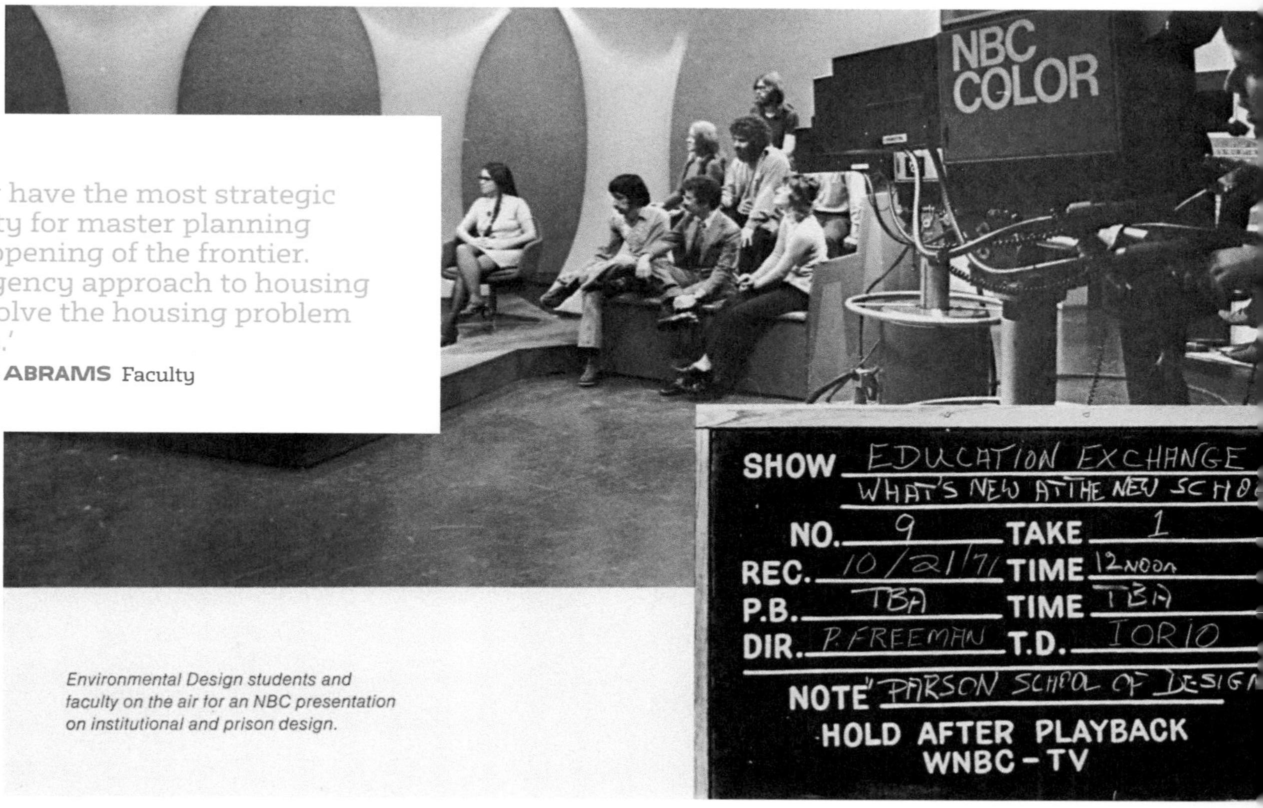
NBC COLOR
SHOW EDUCATION EXCHANGE
WHAT'S NEW AT THE NEW SCHO
NO. 9 TAKE 1
REC. 10/21/71 TIME 12 NOON
P.B. TBA TIME TBA
DIR. P. FREEMAN T.D. IORIO
NOTE PARSON SCHOOL OF DESIGN
HOLD AFTER PLAYBACK
WNBC-TV

Environmental Design students and faculty on the air for an NBC presentation on institutional and prison design.

'DESIGN IS SO SIMPLE, THAT'S WHY IT IS SO COMPLICATED.'

↗ **PAUL RAND** Student

1964

October, 1971, representing Parsons Environmental Design program, students and faculty go on the air for an NBC presentation on rethinking institutional prison design.

In 2010, Milano introduces a Master of Science degree in Environmental Policy and Sustainability Management.

In 2018, with the announcement of a ten-year plan to close New York City's notorious Rikers Island detention center, The New School hosts a panel of city government and justice officials, as well as leading influencers, to discuss lessons learned from Rikers' eighty-five-year history. The panel considers how Rikers particularly failed female, transgender, and non-binary prisoners. Panelists ideate systems that better support prisoners and communities.

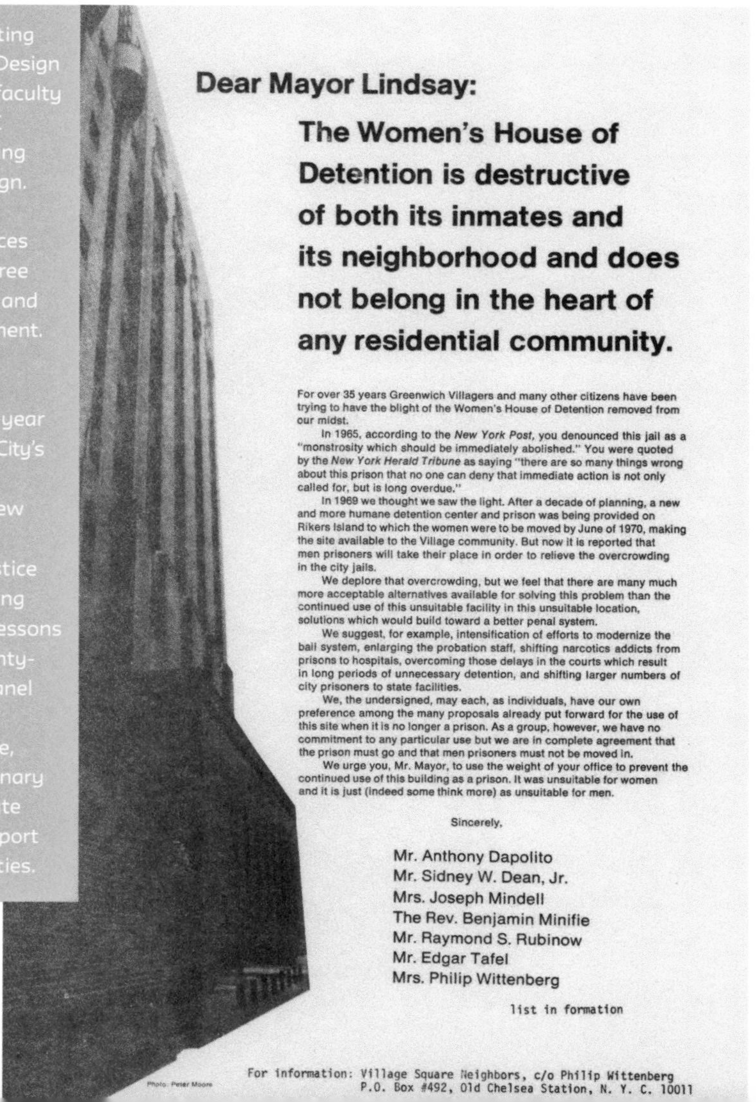

Dear Mayor Lindsay:

The Women's House of Detention is destructive of both its inmates and its neighborhood and does not belong in the heart of any residential community.

For over 35 years Greenwich Villagers and many other citizens have been trying to have the blight of the Women's House of Detention removed from our midst.

In 1965, according to the *New York Post*, you denounced this jail as a "monstrosity which should be immediately abolished." You were quoted by the *New York Herald Tribune* as saying "there are so many things wrong about this prison that no one can deny that immediate action is not only called for, but is long overdue."

In 1969 we thought we saw the light. After a decade of planning, a new and more humane detention center and prison was being provided on Rikers Island to which the women were to be moved by June of 1970, making the site available to the Village community. But now it is reported that men prisoners will take their place in order to relieve the overcrowding in the city jails.

We deplore that overcrowding, but we feel that there are many much more acceptable alternatives available for solving this problem than the continued use of this unsuitable facility in this unsuitable location, solutions which would build toward a better penal system.

We suggest, for example, intensification of efforts to modernize the bail system, enlarging the probation staff, shifting narcotics addicts from prisons to hospitals, overcoming those delays in the courts which result in long periods of unnecessary detention, and shifting larger numbers of city prisoners to state facilities.

We, the undersigned, may each, as individuals, have our own preference among the many proposals already put forward for the use of this site when it is no longer a prison. As a group, however, we have no commitment to any particular use but we are in complete agreement that the prison must go and that men prisoners must not be moved in.

We urge you, Mr. Mayor, to use the weight of your office to prevent the continued use of this building as a prison. It was unsuitable for women and it is just (indeed some think more) as unsuitable for men.

Sincerely,

Mr. Anthony Dapolito
Mr. Sidney W. Dean, Jr.
Mrs. Joseph Mindell
The Rev. Benjamin Minifie
Mr. Raymond S. Rubinow
Mr. Edgar Tafel
Mrs. Philip Wittenberg

list in formation

Photo: Peter Moore

For information: Village Square Neighbors, c/o Philip Wittenberg
P.O. Box #492, Old Chelsea Station, N. Y. C. 10011

THESE UNITED STATES, 1939
EDWIN SEAVER, CHAIRMAN

The aim of this course is to acquaint students residing in New York with what the American people are thinking and doing in various parts of the country, the cultural pattern of their lives, their social, political, and economic perspectives. New York, it has been said, is not America, and the course is designed to help explore the cross currents of American life with authoritative observers as guides. A guest lecturer speaks at each session.

Dorothy Canfield Fisher—Vermont
William Allen White—Kansas
Jonathan Daniels—the South
Thomas Hart Benton—the Middle West
Ruth McKenney—the 'industrial valley'
Robert P. Tristram Coffin—Maine
Merle Colby—Alaska
Other lecturers to be announced

HOW NEW YORK CITY IS GOVERNED, 1965
JEROME LIBLIT

A study of the government system of the City. The Office of the Mayor, the Board of Estimate and the Council, the operating departments, boards, and bureaus. The City's relationship with the State and Federal Government. Problems of metropolitan regional government. The budgetary and taxing systems. Examination of major City problems. Consideration of latest proposals for improvement of City Government. The political life of the City and the role of special interest groups.

USING ELECTRONIC COMMUNICATION

'The New School is pleased to announce a new way to complete courses toward a Bachelor of Arts degree. Using electronic communication, you will be able to come to The New School by turning on your computer at home or at work.'

In 1993, DIAL — Distance Institution for Adult Learning — commences with three courses, led by three different professors in three different areas of study: 'Identity: The Modular Construction of Personality', Sondra Farganis, social and political theory; 'The Making of Americans', Robert Polito, writing; 'Philosophical Dilemmas of Technological Society', Mark Schulman, media studies. The pilot program, the first like it attempted for credit, is underwritten by a grant from the U.S. Department of Education. In its third semester, Summer 1994, DIAL offers the first online for-credit writing workshops, with a poetry workshop led by Robert Polito and a fiction workshop led by Robert Dunn. By 1996, 114 courses are available online; topics range from 'English Country Houses' and 'Gardens and Decorative Arts' to 'Hypertext Poetry'. As of 2019, The New School offers six degree programs and twelve certificates online.

Do not fear that as the globe gets utility organized your daily life will not remain (or become as the case may be) disorganized, characterized by chaos, illuminated anarchically. You'll have nothing to do; so what will you do? A lifelong university (Fuller)?

↗ **JOHN CAGE** Student and Faculty

'DESIGN IS A CONSTANT CHALLENGE TO BALANCE COMFORT WITH LUXE, THE PRACTICAL WITH THE DESIRABLE.'

↗ **DONNA KARAN** Student and Visiting Critic

Clockwise from top left:

Apple computer monitor displaying Connect Ed information. Bob Adelman, 1980s

Poster for *Hans Jonas: Technology and Ethics*, 1981

The New School Bulletin, 1985 Fall, Vol. 43, No. 1

The Center for Understanding Media/Antioch College Master of Arts in Media Studies, course catalog 1974–5

'SOCIETY WILL DECIDE AFTER THE TECHNOLOGY IS CREATED WHAT WE WILL AND WON'T ACCEPT.'

↗ JESSE EISENBERG Student

'I'm not an expert in instruments, beat programming, or electronics. For some people it's all about doing it themselves. But for me, it's all about finding the people that can help make my vision come true.'
↗ MATISYAHU Student

In the Spring of 2018, The New School offers a large lecture course to students on-campus and online — the first of its kind. In the University Lecture Course (ULEC) 'Work, Love, Learn, Play: Our Lives on the Internet', Claire Potter, a Professor of History at The New School, integrates asynchronous and synchronous learning; lectures that would have been delivered in a lecture hall are offered via broadcast-produced video lectures and interviews. The mixed-delivery modality expands the range of options for student course selection and approaches to learning.

'When the starry sky, a vista of open seas, or a stained-glass window shedding purple beams fascinate me, there is a cluster of meaning, of colors, of words, of caresses, there are light touches, scents, sighs, cadences that arise, shroud me, carry me away, and sweep me beyond the things I see, hear, or think.'
↗ JULIA KRISTEVA Guest Speaker

MOVEMENT OF JAH PEOPLE: REGGAE, MEDIA, AND REPRESENTATION, 2019 ONLINE COURSE
JEAN OLIVER-CRETARA

Reggae originated on the island nation of Jamaica, but it is one of the most popular musical forms in the world and is heard in a multitude of derivative forms in every corner of the planet. Reggae's revolutionary spirit has stood as a potent symbol of independence and social critique and has informed notions of selfhood, nationhood, race, ethnicity, religion, and politics. The course begins with a history of reggae that considers the genre in its various forms (ska, rocksteady, dub, roots rock, DJs, toasting) and its influence on popular music worldwide. We explore the ways in which people around the world have adopted the genre's gestures, attitudes, and icons as their own and discuss the role of media in the international spread, adaptation, and enjoyment of reggae. Reading the critical and historical literature about reggae music and studying the reggae texts themselves (songs, films, videos, and images), we track its influence and responsiveness to music and cultures from the Caribbean to Britain, the United States, Latin America, Japan, Australia, and western, southern, and eastern Africa.

HYBRID PROJECTS, 2019
JESS IRISH AND LAURA THOMPSON

How can writers and image-makers deepen their practices by exchange, collaboration, and exploration? Students will come together to view and read

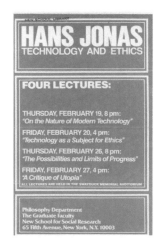

NEW SCHOOL LIBRARY

HANS JONAS
TECHNOLOGY AND ETHICS

FOUR LECTURES:

THURSDAY, FEBRUARY 19, 8 pm:
"On the Nature of Modern Technology"

FRIDAY, FEBRUARY 20, 4 pm:
"Technology as a Subject for Ethics"

THURSDAY, FEBRUARY 26, 8 pm:
"The Possibilities and Limits of Progress"

FRIDAY, FEBRUARY 27, 4 pm:
"A Critique of Utopia"
ALL LECTURES ARE HELD IN THE SWAYDUCK MEMORIAL AUDITORIUM

Philosophy Department
The Graduate Faculty
New School for Social Research
65 Fifth Avenue, New York, N.Y. 10003

The Center for Understanding Media/Antioch College

Master of Arts in Media Studies 1974-75

TO BE FRAGILE

On October 28, 2012, the Statue of Liberty, after a year of renovations, reopens. The same day, New York State Governor Andrew Cuomo declares a state of emergency. A megastorm, Hurricane Sandy, has been dubbed 'Frankenstorm' by the National Weather Service. The Statue of Liberty closes on October 29, and remains closed for the rest of the year.

On Tuesday, October 30, at 1pm, Hurricane Sandy floods the basement of The New School's William Street residence; the location is downtown, in the financial district, which is the lowest elevation of Manhattan. Power in the area is already out, and the building is evacuated. Manhattan is largely cut off from surrounding areas; bridges, tunnels, roads, and subways are flooded. Con Ed reports that 900,000 customers have lost power, and 100,000 power lines are down.

Many William Street students seek refuge at nearby Pace University, not knowing The New School's Arnold Hall, at 13th Street and farther uptown at a higher elevation, is open to them. Pace opens its doors, but New School students will later charge, as is reported by *The New School Free Press*, that bedding, food, and wifi was reserved for Pace students; Pace, which also evacuated a residence hall, will later deny the claim. Linda Reimer, The New School's Senior Vice President for Student Services, had secured shelter for New School students at the Pace facility, but the storm's effects last much longer than projected. The city, which originally opened seventy-six shelters, reduces the locations to sixteen. Shelters throughout impacted areas are filled to capacity. Downtown, grocery shelves are swept bare, and some neighborhood stores and chains, such as Duane Reade, have doubled the price of water. Universities, such as NYU, are closing off assistance to all but their own communities.

As of Monday night, when the power first went out, approximately 100 students, from Yeshiva University's Benjamin N. Cardozo School of Law and The New School, are camped out at Arnold Hall, which is running on generator power. Culinary services is prepared to serve food for a week. The Theresa Lang Center, a large room on the second floor, has been outfitted with bedding. New School President David Van Zandt, who led the preparedness for the hurricane, has also lost power in his 11th Street brownstone; he waits out the outage with The New School community — charging his devices and taking respite in occasional puzzles and board games with students at Arnold Hall. 'Hurricane Sandy', he will remember in 2019, 'was a very serious situation for New Yorkers. But New Schoolers responded with their characteristic orientation to finding collaborative solutions, acting with compassion, and modeling resilience. I was extraordinarily proud of our campus community.'

As mass transit schedules are resumed, two more New School buildings open to students. A week after the storm, New York City schools, colleges, and universities begin to reopen; classes are set back by transit delays and overcrowding; some schools remain unheated. Thousands of New Yorkers are homeless. The city has sustained approximately $19 billion in damage; the state, upwards of $30 billion; as many as 8 million people have lost power. In 2018, New York City will initiate a lawsuit against big oil; Mayor Bill De Blasio demands restitution.

Following Sandy, President Van Zandt takes steps to expand The New School's emergency contact list; with dorms in the new University Center, in 2013, The New School disbands the William Street residence.

'A city is a place where there is no need to wait for next week to get the answer to a question, to taste the food of any country, to find new voices to listen to and familiar ones to listen to again.'
↗ **MARGARET MEAD** Faculty

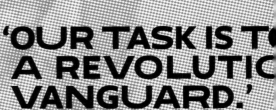

'OUR TASK IS TO A REVOLUTIO VANGUARD.'
↗ WILLY BRANDT Honorary Degree Recipient

POWER PREPAREDNESS & PRECARITY, 2019
SAMANTHA FOX

We have learned to expect the end of the world as we know it: sea levels are rising, carbon fuel reserves are diminishing, global migration patterns are shifting. This course asks how new imaginations of the built and natural environments are emerging in response to climate change and the specter of future crises. How can we can orient ourselves— socially, materially, politically, and morally—towards a future that must involve radical change if it is to entail our survival as a species? Drawing primarily on anthropology, sociology, and urban studies, this course will be arranged around three themes: power, preparedness, and precarity. We will begin the semester by thinking about the built environment as an instrument of power and governmentality. We will then examine conceptions of crisis and disaster preparedness, drawing on case studies such as the European migrant 'crisis' and Hurricane Sandy. We will end the semester by thinking about the Anthropocene, conceptions of the natural, and potential futures, post-human and otherwise.

ENVIRONMENTAL HISTORY, RACE & RESOURCE MANAGEMENT, 2019
MIA WHITE

In Spring, 2012, The New School establishes New Challenge, an annual competition of innovative approaches to social and environmental challenges. New Challenge projects will be put into action in New York City, Eastern Europe, Liberia, Cambodia, Colombia, and Honduras. Th New Challenge is furthered by The New School's Impact Entrepreneurship Initiative (IEI) and Parsons Entrepreneurial Lab (ELab).

In October, 2015, for the thir anniversary of Hurricane Sandy, The New School host 'Hurricane Sandy +3: Buildin Resilient Neighborhoods'. Moderated by John Rudolph, the panel discussion—with Onleilove Alston, Hugh Hogan, Klaus Jacob, and Daniel Zarrilli—follows up on Sandy and looks to the future.

'There's a recognized need for sustainability, especially if you're a large business. We're at a point where there's nowhere to hide. You can't make excuses like "It's not within my control," or "I didn't know about it."'
↗ **BURAK CAKMAK** Parsons Fashion Dean

The New School

Volume 51 Number 4 December 1993

Bulletin

January 2019, the [Ti]shman Environment and [D]esign Center at The New [S]chool mounts the exhibit [E]nvironmental Rights as [H]uman Rights. 'Climate [c]hange means that the [c]ommunities who are least [r]esponsible for the climate [c]risis will feel its impacts the [w]orst and first around the [w]orld. Small island nations [li]ke Antigua and Barbuda [a]re really the example of this [cl]imate injustice,' explains [An]a Baptista, Chair of TNS [Environ]mental Policy & [Sustaina]bility Management [Program and Associ]ate [Director at the Tish]man [C]enter. 'In order to address [cl]imate injustice we must [h]old developed countries like [th]e United States to account [fo]r the damages that have [al]ready begun to be felt [a]nd that will continue to [im]pact the most vulnerable [pl]aces around the world'. [Th]e Tishman Center, with [ov]er forty associated faculty [m]embers, works across [th]e university, in whatever [su]bject or department, to [su]pport research, initiatives, [e]vents, and curricular [d]evelopment dedicated to [is]sues of environmental [ju]stice.

'ALWAYS BE LEARNING.'
↗ CHARLES NIX Faculty

'When you approach the second half of your life, you start to unconsciously consider what you're passing on. As a writer, that's obviously part of what you're doing. And as a teacher, that's another way of passing on information, history, or whatever you have.'
↗ **MARY GAITSKILL** Faculty

URBAN RESILIENCE, 2019
TIMON MCPHEARSON

Urbanization and climate change are on a collision course. With increasing frequency, intensity, and impacts of extreme events in cities, building resilience is fast becoming one of the most important issues for cities globally. The aim of this course is to examine the past, present, and future relations between cities, urbanization, and ecological infrastructure; to introduce students to urban systems science, including biophysical and social science and planning as lenses for exploring resilience of complex urban systems; and to encourage empirical, normative, and imaginative reflection on the possibilities (and potential pathologies) that lie behind discourse of 'urban sustainability' and 'resilience'. The central objective of this course is to explore historical and current scientific perspectives on human-dominated ecosystems and resilience; future prospects of the study of cities through a critical systems theory lens and how they can be resilient to rising urban pressures including climate change and development. We will explore key terms, concepts frameworks, and models in urban ecology and the development of urban systems science. We will use recent extreme events in the Americas from Hurricane Sandy, Harvey, and Maria to heat waves and other climae-change-related extreme events as a backdrop for examining what practices currently exist in planning and policy to adapt and build resilience to the rising social, ecological, and technological infrastructure impacts. This course will expose students to on-the-ground resilience challenges and opportunities in New York City through a series of field visits, place-based explorations and analyses, and guest speakers. Together, we will cover such key questions as: What are complex adaptive social-ecological-technological systems? What is resilience and how are cities vulnerable to disturbances, disasters, and changing climate regimes? Can cities be designed as sustainable and resilient systems?

2012

In December, 2018, in time with the sixth anniversary of Hurricane Sandy, the Anna-Maria and Stephen Kellen Gallery, Sheila C. Johnson Design Center present 'The Earth Manual Project—This Could Save Your Life'. The interdisciplinary exhibit puts forth a poetic response to ecological disaster. Curated by Parsons faculty Jim Osman and Andrew Cornell Robinson, the Earth Manual Project features work by artists Fanny Allié, Ina Archer, Andrew Bachatif, Anney Bonney, Eddie Chu, Greg Climer, Blane De St. Croix, Brenda Garand, Scherezade Garcia-Vazquez, Julien Gardair, Edward Heins, Whitney Hess, Frank Holliday, Wendy Letven, Roxanne Jackson, Carter Kustera, John Masterson, Jennifer O'Connor, Jim Osman, Megan Pope, Timo Rissanen, Andrew Cornell Robinson, Christopher Robinson, David Brooke Robinson, Elise Siegel, Diana Shpungin, Harvey Stein, Kate Teale, Eva Perez de Vega, C. Emily Waters, and Etty Yaniv.

'MAYBE BEING POWERFUL MEANS TO BE FRAGILE.'
↗ **AI WEIWEI** Student and Guest Speaker

This page:

TIDES WORLD

In 1958, The New School offers the first course on 'Computers and Automation' for non-engineers/computer/data specialists. The course, hosting guest lecturers from IBM, is led by Rudolf Hirsch, a 'mathematician-programmer' who was 'formerly with Central Intelligence Agency'.

DEVELOPMENT OF ART IN CHINA, 1951 HUANG WEN-SHAN

This course is devoted to a study of the arts in China from prehistoric times to the twentieth century. Emphasis is on the style of each important stage in China's art development; and in different periods, on bronze, pottery, porcelain, painting, literature, architecture, textiles as the quintessence of Chinese culture for that period. Due attention is paid to foreign influences, e.g. Buddhism and Westernism, as well as to native cultural movements such as Confucianism, Taoism, Neo-Confucianism. Illustrated with photographs, slides, and specimens.

GLOBAL URBAN STUDIO: HONG KONG, 2019 MIODRAG MITRASINOVIC

Global Urban Studio Intensive: Hong Kong, Macau, Shenzhen includes travel to the Pearl River Delta between January 9 and 19, 2019. Given the global patterns of migrant mobilities, and the precarious context of political uncertainties in South-East Asia, our task is to study practices and processes of production and appropriation of public space in Hong Kong, and to develop scenarios and design strategies for its production and use. During the design workshop at the Hong Kong Polytechnic University (January 13–18, 2018), The New School students will work together with graduate students from the HK Polytechnic School of Design, and with students from Shenzhen University. In addition to the intensive workshop in Hong Kong, expert-led field trips to Macau and Shenzhen are also organized. Upon return, this class will meet four additional times between January and May 2019 in order to finalize proposals created during the January workshop. Students must cover the cost of airfare, accommodation, and food.

'IF YOU SEE THE MAGIC IN A FAIRY TALE, YOU CAN FACE THE FUTURE'
↗ DANIELLE STEEL Student

'The importance of art is in the process of doing it, in the learning experience where the artist interacts with whatever is being made.'
↗ ROY LICHTENSTEIN Associate

'Though inherently dramatic, performative democracy — formed in the process of speaking and listening to others — is a joyous and affirmative dimension of the political. It releases a robust civic creativity, and helps bowed backs to straighten up. It is truly transformative for those engaged, as it launches a process of learning, forming opinions, reasoning, and speaking. And this brings about change. It is clearly an alternative to tanks and bullets, and it creates conditions for recovering the lost dignity of people.'
↗ ELZBIETA MATYNIA Faculty

In 1908, twenty-two-year-old Jiang Menglin of Yuyao, Ningbo, Zhejiang Province, China, arrives at the University of California, Berkeley, to pursue advanced study in agriculture. His interests shift, and in 1912 he is awarded his PhD in Education from Columbia University, where he studies with John Dewey. As Jiang will write in his 1947 memoir, *Tides from the West*:

> *In New York I was impressed by the skyscrapers, the rapid circulation of subways and elevated trains, the dazzling lights of moving advertisements on the tops of tall buildings; the theaters, night clubs, hotels, and restaurants; fashionable Fifth Avenue, Greenwich Village, the East Side Slums. ... America alone is capable of producing such a great, highly industrialized city and vast melting pot.*

In 1919, taking a sabbatical from Columbia University, John Dewey teaches in the first semester of courses at The New School. Method in Social Sciences is a lecture course; the duty is light in comparison to his customary schedule at Columbia, and Dewey is able to concentrate on his upcoming trip to Japan, which soon includes a visit to China. Dewey's former student, Jiang Menglin, now the President of Peking University, is among the Chinese scholars and educational administrators who invite Dewey to tour China. As Dewey will write in a letter to his son:

> *My former Chinese students seem to be making as elaborate plans for our reception as we have enjoyed here. The only trouble is that I shall have to lecture all the time to help even up. I don't know the program exactly, but I know it calls for lectures in Shanghai, Nanking, and Peking, and I assume other places. You look up your geography and you will see how far apart the places are.*

Upon his arrival in China, Dewey is so excited he manages to extend his sabbatical to two years. His time in China will profoundly influence his thinking on education and the broader cultural integration of education. As Dewey will note in his December 1919 essay, 'Chinese National Sentiment':

> *What the Chinese abundantly possess is community of life, a sense of unity of civilization, of immemorial continuity of customs and ideals. The consciousness of a unity of pattern woven through the whole fabric of their existences never leaves them. To be ... Chinese is not to be of a certain race nor to yield to allegiance to a certain national state. It is to share with countless millions of others in certain ways of feeling and thinking, fraught with innumerable memories and expectations because of long-established modes of adjustment and intercourse.*

In his 1934 collection of essays, *Art as Experience*, Dewey will explore an ideation of democratic principles as art in life and art in action. It is during his stay in China that Dewey begins to make the shift—seeing democracy as a cultural pursuit rather than a governmental one. Confucianism and Dewey's social and moral democracy align. (In the twenty-first century, the ideas will find common intellectual terrain in 'Confucian Democracy'.) Community and personal growth, through education and experience, are simultaneously outcomes and preconditions to healthy democratic systems. In 1939, on the occasion of his eightieth birthday, Dewey will write:

> *Democracy as a way of life is controlled by personal faith in personal day-to-day working together with others. Democracy is the belief that even when needs and ends of consequences are different for each individual, the habit of amicable cooperation— which many include, as in sports, rivalry and competition—is itself a priceless addition to life. ... To cooperate by giving differences a chance to show themselves because of the belief that the expression of difference is not only a right of other persons, but is a means of enriching one's own life-experience, is inherent in the democratic personal way of life. ... Democracy is the faith that the process of experience is more important than any special result attained, so that special results achieved are of ultimate value only as they are used to enrich and order the ongoing process. Since the process of experience is capable of being educative, faith in democracy is all one with faith in experience and education. All ends and values that are cut off from the ongoing process become arrests, fixations. They strive to fixate what has been gained instead of using it to open the road and point the way to new and better experiences.*

Clockwise from top left:

Lilian Wu (front row, left) standing next to her sister, Vivien Wu. Back row from left: Wen-hui Wu (Lilian's father), Zeng-gu Tao (Lilian's grandmother), Jiang Menglin (Lilian's grandfather), Betty C. Wu (Lilian's mother). Taipei, Taiwan, 1956.

Shenzhen City, China, 2017

In a 2019 interview, Lilian Shiao-Yen Wu remembers her grandfather, Jiang Menglin:

We were living in New Zealand, and one summer we went to Taiwan to visit my grandfather. I had a very strong New Zealand accent and his English was American. I would say things like tahmato. And he would yell at me and say: tomato tomato tomato. And then at some point my father wanted me to learn what it meant to be Chinese. It was thought that it would be good for me to go to junior high school in Taiwan. I thought that was terrible. But my grandfather was an educator and he felt it could be done gently. At the same time he was worried that I was going to lose my ability to speak English. So he decided he would take a very practical approach. He would give me a penny a day, if I spoke to him in English.

At a dinner party in the 1990s, Wu, then working at IBM with advanced technologies in higher education, meets Jonathan Fanton, the President of The New School. Intrigued by The New School philosophy, and dedicated to principles of education, she joins The New School's Board of Trustees in 1998.

I was surprised by how open minded the school was. Everyone I talked to had an attitude of 'let's try it'. The instinct comes from saying that to students: 'You're interested in this topic, you know what you want to do, let's see what happens.' One thing I tried to do was bring in quantitative reasoning. In the early days, when there were very few quantitative courses, I would explain that the subject wasn't math, it was more like learning a new language. For example, if you were interested in environmental questions, a good project would be to go around the campus and with a simple, inexpensive device, measure temperature at specific locations and map major heat losses in a building. So the numbers themselves could make for a very different expression of a project proposal for, let's say, the Tishman Environment and Design Center.

In the 1990s, Parsons School of Design begins to see a significant increase in students from Asia, specifically from South Korea, and by the mid-2000s, from China. In 2016, Parsons is invited to explore the possibility of a branch campus in the booming technologies city of Shenzhen. In 1980, Shenzhen became the first special economic zone in China, which allowed for market capitalism to coexist within the Chinese political state. The population of the city exploded from 30,000 in 1980 to over 20 million in the metropolitan area in 2019. Just fifteen minutes from Hong Kong by high-speed rail and only a short flight from other regional hubs of design and innovation, Shenzhen is situated in China's newly designated Greater Bay Area, which is a geographic and economic conglomeration that includes Hong Kong, Macau, Shenzhen, Guangzhou, and Zhuhai. The innovation emphasis in Shenzhen's industries and the strategic direction of the Greater Bay Area are enticing circumstances for a possible Parsons graduate-level branch campus.

In a 2019 interview, Mike Fu, from the Office of Global Partnerships at Parsons School of Design, explains the opportunity:

China's middle class is increasingly globalized, with a huge number of young people benefiting from travel and study abroad. One of the most appealing things about Shenzhen is the potential to offer Parsons' pedagogy and our commitment to sustainability and social justice to a whole new demographic: students who don't have the means to come to New York or Paris, or those who might be enticed by an English-language graduate curriculum in China for other reasons. The addition of a Shenzhen campus would further internationalize our institution and broaden opportunities for New School students and faculty worldwide.

Carol Kim, The New School's Senior Vice President for Global Partnerships, gave an update in May 2019 as to the potential Shenzhen campus:

Among our Board of Trustees in New York City, as well as our partners in Shenzhen, there is a palpable excitement, sometimes guarded and other times exhilarated. The challenges are significant, but so are the possibilities: for The New School, for Shenzhen, and — pardon my informed optimism — for the world. We in our Global office proceed with full awareness of the issues in maneuvering and strategizing and dealing with a single-party government, but we remain committed to sharing the institutional culture and educational practices of Parsons while keeping The New School's century-long dedication to social justice. Previously, I lived in Beijing for two years, also working in education, and I know that to build a school, you need to persevere until you can swing open your doors in triumph and welcome the students and their families, the faculty, the staff, and the community. I also know that in China there is a hunger for educational opportunities, particularly from families with burgeoning daughters and sons who want to pursue their dreams, including dreams of becoming fashion designers or architects or industrial designers. And one thing lacking in the country of 1.4 billion people is a top design school — and we're trying to change that by creating Parsons Shenzhen.

'Time passes faster and faster, but with every project I always want to find the next challenge and the next challenge is just as exciting as the previous one.'
↗ **ALEXANDER WANG** Student

IIO W.75 St
May 29, I950

Dr.Saul K.Padover
The New School
N.Y.II,N.Y.

Dear Dean Padover:

Last year,when I was President of the Provincial College of Law and Commerce of Kwangtung and concurrently Professor of Anthropology and Sociology of the National Sun Yat Sen University at China,I wrote President Bryn J.Hovde of my plans to establish a school at Canton patterned after the New School,the aims and organization of which seem admirable to me. I was greatly encouraged by the kind reply. Unfortunately the Chinese Republic has since been faced with the greatest challenge in its history. My hopes and plans are suspended.

The present course of events has brought me to this country,to continue my studies,and I trust,to do some teaching in my field. As I expressed my desire to Dr. Hans Staudinger,he did advise me to approach you directly in his letter dating Feb.5. Recently Dr.Carl Mayer informed me that he has given you one of my letters. I should welcome the opportunity of a talk with you, about my work in the general field of Culturology and especially Chinese Cultural History,and the possibility of courses at the New School in the field.

As an old student of the New School I shall be happy to visit you at your convenience.

Cordially yours,

Huang Wen Shan
Huang Wen Shan

This page:

Letter from Huang Wen Shan
to Saul Padover, May 29, 1950

'I'M NOT PLAYING A ROLE.
I'M BEING MYSELF, WHATEVER THE HELL THAT IS.'

↗ **BEA ARTHUR** Student

FUNCTION IN THE PRESENT AND FORECAST THE FUTURE

Parsons Design for Social Innovation and Sustainability Lab (DESIS Lab) is instituted in 2009 as a research, action, and academic superstructure that imagines, investigates, tests, and applies design-driven social innovation. In 2009, with support from the Rockefeller Foundation, the DESIS initiative 'Amplifying Creative Communities' explores models of community-based sustainable living in urban areas; in 2011, also with Rockefeller support, DESIS' 'Public and Collaborative' investigates design assistance in the dialogue between people and government. In 2014, DESIS joins the New York City Mayor's office, and Citi Community Development in Designing for Financial Empowerment, which strives to facilitate the efficacy of public-sector financial services.

Previous pages:

Parsons School of Design students at Museum of Modern Art, 1950s

Clockwise from top left:

Detail of the auditorium of the 66 West 12th Street building of The New School, after 1930

Construction of the auditorium of the 66 West 12th Street building, designed by Joseph Urban, *circa* 1930

In 1930, having lost its lease at Chelsea's London Terrace building, The New School acquires three buildings on West 12th Street. Alvin Johnson, who assumed the directorship of the school in 1922, has negotiated a cut rate from New School benefactor Daniel Cranford Smith; in exchange for the discounted sale, 'Uncle Dan', it is agreed, will be provided a penthouse atop the new building. There, Johnson argues, the higher elevation will surely increase longevity.

Under the leadership of Johnson, Joseph Urban is secured to design and architect the new building. Urban, a twenty-year New Yorker originally from Vienna, is associated with the Metropolitan Opera and Florenz Ziegfeld of the Ziegfeld Follies; he's beaten out Frank Lloyd Wright for the commission. Johnson asks Urban for a building that will encourage interdisciplinary study and collaboration, and 'function in the present and ... forecast the future'. The completed building, employing an unusual theatrical facade which will become iconic of The New School and a century of the events held in the first-floor auditorium, is New York's first example of the International Style of architecture, an incarnation of Modernism. The building is Urban's crowning achievement; he dies of a heart attack in his apartment at the St. Regis Hotel in 1933.

In 1992, the auditorium, not significantly altered but badly in need of renovation, is restored to the original specifications. Among the many notable features is an innovative ceiling structure that refines the acoustics of the rounded interior. The same principle is employed in Radio City Music Hall, completed in 1932, one year after The New School building. The auditorium is designated as a New York City Landmark in 1997.

'There is no such thing as an empty space or an empty time. There is always something to see, something to hear. In fact, try as we may to make a silence, we cannot.'
↗ **JOHN CAGE** Student and Faculty

ART IN THE SOCIAL ORDER, 1935
EDGAR JOHNSON

Art, like many other activities today, has lost its certainties. It sails erratically in all directions under a multiplicity of pilots. It shares the confusion in other realms—revisions of thought in philosophy, economics, politics, industry—that makes the period in which we live one of transition. These revisions proceed not merely from what we believe to be additional knowledge, but also from a new way of looking at our knowledge. For even more than to enlarge the scope of human activity, our endeavor is to discover a new attitude toward that activity. The ultimate goal transcends the reorientation of those fields individually: it is their reintegration in a new synthesis. For any synthesis to be complete, our conception of the function and value of art in modern society must be clearly defined. The question is not the academic one of what role art has played or should have played in the past, nor even what it is playing at present, but what role, in the light of its potentialities and of the revisions in other fields of thought, it may play in the immediate future.

UTOPIAS AND POLITICAL SCIENCE, 1939
LEO STRAUSS

Surveying the most outstanding Utopia of both ancient and modern times, the following problems are discussed: Utopias and prognosticating science; Utopias and the Golden Age; Utopias and eschatology; Utopias and natural man; Utopias and satire; Utopias and genuine political science.

1992

'ARCHITECTURE SHOULD BE AS MUCH A PART OF THE TIME AND OF THE PLACE AS THE CURRENT NEWS.'
↗ **JOSEPH URBAN** Architect of 12th Street Building

'Pageantry's whole point lies in the fact that it is not, and cannot be, the work of a single individual.'
↗ **MARY PORTER BEEGLE URBAN** Trustee

Clockwise from top left:

━━━ The historic Tishman Auditorium

━━━ Detail of the auditorium of the 66 West 12th Street building of The New School, after 1930

━━━ Auditorium of the 66 West 12th Street building with unidentified stage set, after 1940

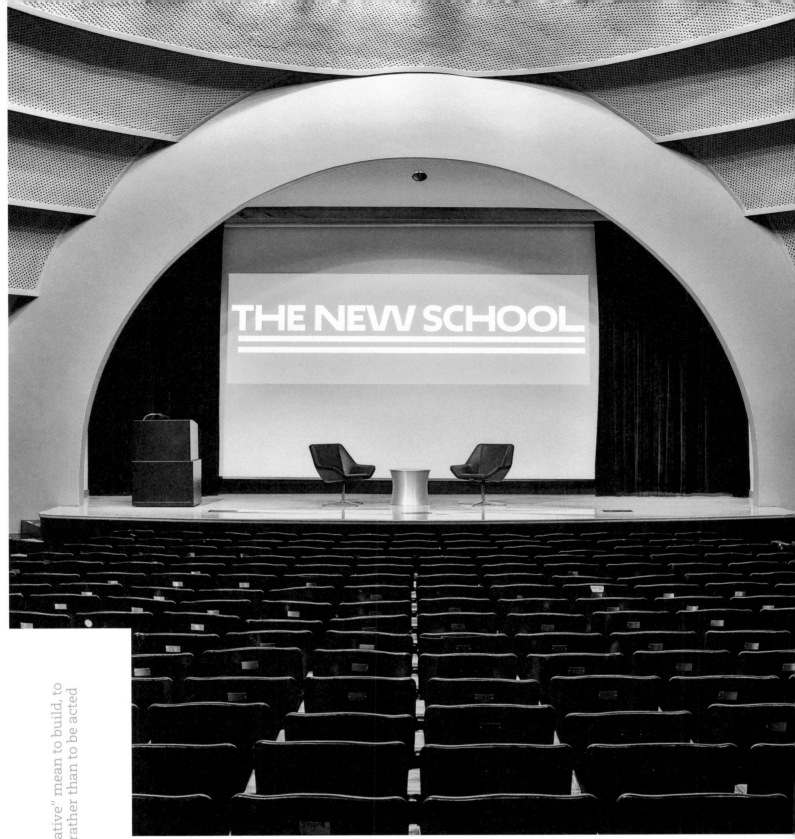

'Does not the very word "creative" mean to build, to initiate, to give out, to act — rather than to be acted upon, to be subjective?'
↗ **BERENICE ABBOTT** Faculty

'THERE'S SUCH A FEELING OF SATISFACTION WHEN SOMETHING YOU IMAGINED TURNED INTO SOMETHING REA

↗ PRABAL GURUNG Student and Faculty

SILHOUETTE AND STEREOTYPE

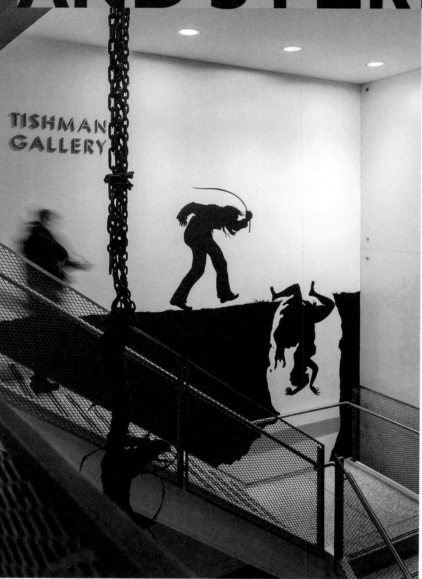

Commissioned in 2003 and completed in 2005, Kara Walker's *Event Horizon* is the first site-specific work at The New School by a woman. The mural of black silhouettes on a white ground coils a floor-through stairwell at Arnhold Hall. Walker's engagement with stereotype, race, and the history of American art is all at once nightmarish, agitating, beautiful, and breathtaking. The work is intended to draw a reaction that is generated not just by the artist, but by the viewer. As Walker told *Index* magazine in 1996: 'The silhouette says a lot with very little information, but that's also what the stereotype does. So I saw the silhouette and the stereotype as linked.'

In 2015, The New School's Mannes College of Music moves to Arnhold Hall; students from the college debate the appropriateness of *Event Horizon* in the context of a conservatory. The New School's *Free Press* assigns coverage, quoting students on both sides of the discussion. Jean Taylor, New School Drama faculty, brings her class to the mural and the conversation. 'It's provocative,' she tells the *Free Press*, 'but it's in a place and in a school that wants to talk about those issues.'

2005

'When I was born, I was colored. Soon after, I became a Negro. Not long after that, I was black. Most recently I was African American. It seems we're on a roll here . . . But I am, first and foremost, in search of freedom.'
↗ **HARRY BELAFONTE** Student

Clockwise from top left:

Kara Walker, *Event Horizon* (detail), 2005. Latex paint on wall, 432 in. x 719 in. New York, The New School Art Collection

At the memorial after Martin Luther King's assassination, mourners gather downtown. Memphis, TN. Bob Adelman, 1968

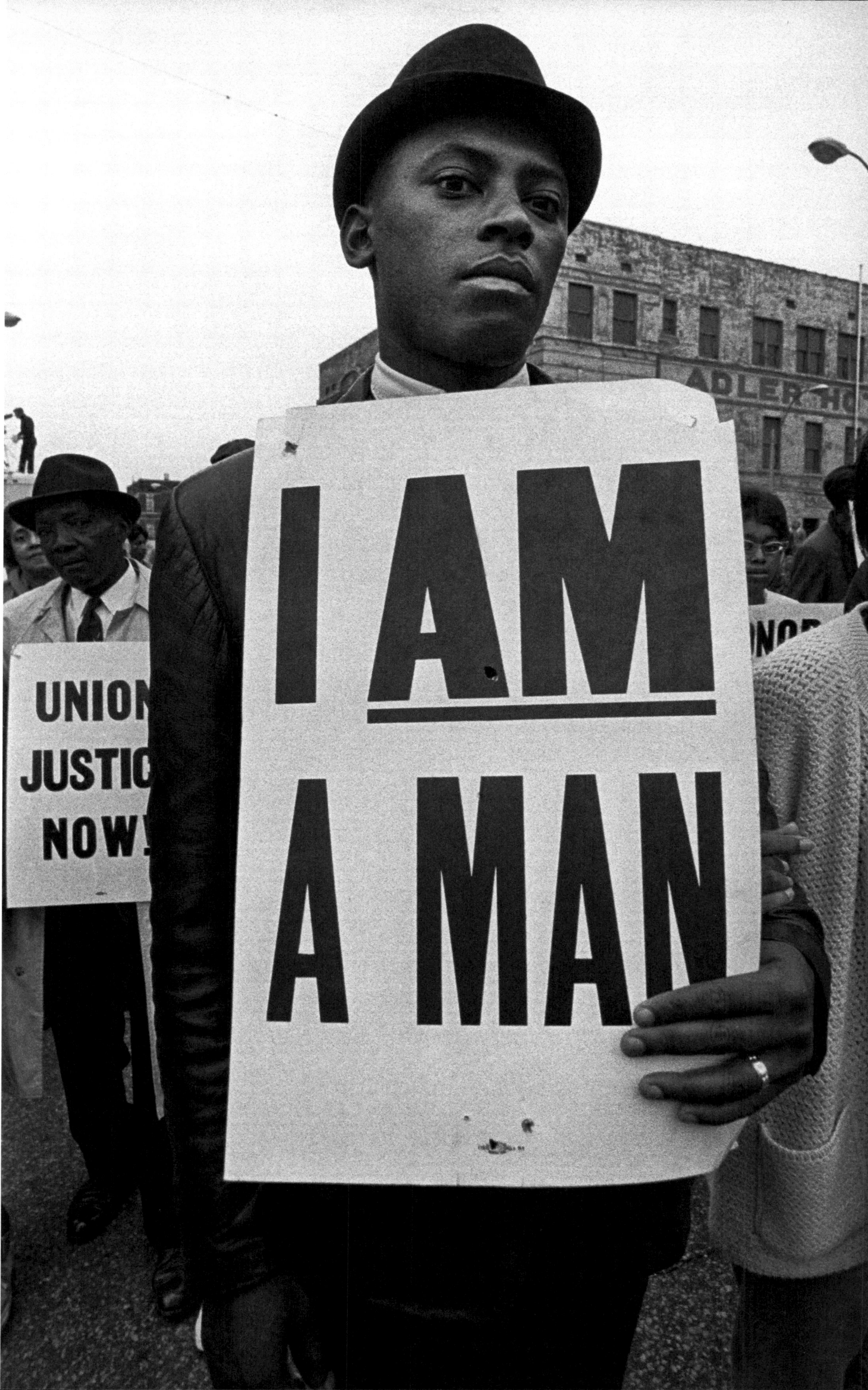
I AM
A MAN
UNION
JUSTIC
NOW!
ADLER HO

In 1931, to celebrate the opening of The New School's Greenwich Village building, the Société Anonyme, an organization journalists deem 'the last word on modern art', initiates the exhibition schedule of art at The New School. *International Exhibition Illustrating the Most Recent Development in Abstract Art* shows work never before seen in America. In 1920, with Marcel Duchamp and Man Ray, Katherine Dreier founded the Société as America's first 'experimental museum'. Dreier exhibits work in The New School installation, and curates inclusions by, among others, Heinrich Campendonk, Leon Carroll, Max Ernst, Wassily Kandinsky, Paul Klee, Yasuo Kuniyoshi, Fernand Léger, Johannes Molzahn, Piet Mondrian, Amédée Ozenfant, Man Ray, Kurt Schwitters, Joseph Stella, Max Weber, and Marguerite Zorach. Dreier's nephew, Theodore, will be one of the founders of Black Mountain College, which overlaps with The New School in the Bauhaus and anti-Nazi faculty who flee Europe in the 1930s, and U.S. faculty and associations such as Josef Albers, John Cage, Allen Ginsberg, and Charles Seeger, who also serves as faculty at the Mannes School of Music. Fluxus emerges simultaneously at Black Mountain College and The New School; John Cage is central to the formation of Fluxus, and many Fluxus practitioners have attended Cage's popular New School course, 'Experimental Composition'. To cite just a few of Cage's former 'Experimental Composition' students who contributed to the Fluxus movement: George Brecht, Jim Dine, Al Hansen, Dick Higgins, Toshi Ichiyanagi, Allan Kaprow, Jackson Mac Low, Richard Maxfield, Yoko Ono, Larry Poons, George Segal, and La Monte Young.

'There are two still points in the physical life: the motionless body, in which thousands of adjustments for keeping it erect are invisible, and the horizontal, the last stillness. Life and dance exists between these two points and therefore form the arc between two deaths.'
↗ **DORIS HUMPHREY** Faculty

'Style is, above all, a system of forms with a quality and meaningful expression through which the personality of the artist and the overall outlook of a group are visible. It is also a vehicle of expression within the group, communicating and fixing certain values of religious, social, and moral life through the emotional suggestiveness of forms.'
↗ **MEYER SCHAPIRO** Faculty

NEW YORK CITY SUN
JANUARY 31, 1931

Explorative Art on View

New School of Social Research Shows Group of Modern Paintings.

All those who are interested in the explorative art of the day should make a point of inspecting the art collection in the galleries of the New School of Social Research. It has been arranged by Katherine Dreier, who has had the aid, in Paris, of Marcel Duchamp, who has many friends in New York. At the same time, and on the same floors of the new building, the mural decorations of Thomas Benton and Mr. Orozco can be studied.

For what I have called the "explorative art" of the day, people ought to be especially generous, but I don't find, as a rule, that they are. Geographical and scientific explorers of course, are greatly honored and most people are ready to believe in advance that what the scientists discover is worth while, but toward the arts, strangely enough, there is a contrary attitude. In the arts the term "conservative" is almost synonymous with "adamantine" and "wooden." The conservatives look on innovations with horror and condemn them on sight.

go straight to the "picture" by Man Ray. There they will get what they want. Mr. Ray has obtained a metallic background and on it has scribbled lines that would make the late Mr. Ruskin turn over in his grave. There is also one of the new, geometrical pictures by Mondrian that could create trouble, and works that are interesting in various ways, by Jacques Villon, Ozenfant, John Graham, M. Zorach, Viollier and Max Ernst. H. M'B.

GENERAL ADMISSION 483
NEW SCHOOL SUMMER ARTS FESTIVAL COURTYARD
(in the event of rain, AUDITORIUM)
66 WEST 12th ST., NEW YORK
SATURDAY EVE., JUNE 22, 1963 at 7:45
THELONIOUS MONK QUARTET
Established Price $3.00

New School Summer Arts Festival
INTERNATIONAL TICKET CO., NEWARK, N.J.
GEN. ADMISSION $3.00

Good Only SAT. EVE. JUNE 22 1963
483

Clockwise from top left:

▬▬▬▬ Newspaper clipping, *New York City Sun*, January 31, 1931

▬▬▬▬ Brochure for the Summer Arts Festival, May 16, 1963

▬▬▬▬ Ticket for Thelonius Monk Quartet's performance in The New School's courtyard as part of the New School Summer Arts Festival, June 22, 1963

▬▬▬▬ Art Farmer Quartet performing in The New School's courtyard as part of The New School Summer Arts Festival, 1963

'TELL ME WHOM YOU HAUNT AND I'LL TELL YOU WHO YOU ARE.'

↗ ANDRÉ BRETON Faculty

Through the summer of 1963, The New School hosts 'Jazz IS Music', a musical series in the courtyard between 12th and 11th Street. Music and jazz instructors from The New School give performances and explanations. In a rare public appearance, Thelonious Monk speaks and plays for the series. Events at the school cross-section creative, intellectual, and popular culture, and Monk's visit is contemporaneous with campus events welcoming Alexander Calder, Judith Crist, e.e. cummings, Max Ernst, Martin Luther King, Sonny Rollins, Carl Sandburg, Rudolf Serkin, Anita Sheer, Barbara Tuchman, William Carlos Williams, and Edith Sitwell.

In 1991, The New School is the first institution to challenge the NEA anti-obscenity clause. Fueled by the political fervor of this legal battle (and subsequent win), two years later, the Vera List Center opens to promote and support practice, research, and exhibition at the intersection of art and politics. The New School, in tandem, initiates a two-year program titled 'Art and Politics', which consists of lectures, seminars, and special events.

in the new school cou...

FOLK MUSIC
OSCAR BRAND

Saturday, June 15
JAZZ IS MUSIC
HORACE SILVER QUINTET

Sunday, June 16
POETRY READING
JOSEPH CERAVOLO, FRANK L...
AND DAVID SHAPIRO

Friday, June 21
FOLK MUSIC
BROCK PETERS

Saturday, June 22
JAZZ IS MUSIC
THELONIOUS MONK QUARTE...

Sunday, June 23
POETRY READING
GREGORY CORSO
MICHAEL BENEDIKT

Friday, June 28
FOLK MUSIC
ANITA SHEER (Flamenco)

Saturday, June 29
JAZZ IS MUSIC
SONNY ROLLINS & COMPANY

Sunday, June 30
PREVIEW '64:
THE OFF-BROADWAY THEATER

Excerpts from three new works; discu...
producers Caroline Swann and Clai...
and playwrights Jay Thompson and...
Mitchell, moderated by Allan Lewis...

Friday, July 12
FOLK MUSIC
ODETTA

Sunday, July 14
PREVIEW '64:
NEW WAVE MOVIE MAKERS

Excerpts from films in progress; dis...
director Frank Perry (David and Li...
film makers Bob Ross and Bert Brow...
moderated by Richard Griffith, Cu...
the Film Library, Museum of Mode...

Friday, July 19
FOLK MUSIC
JEAN REDPATH (Scottish)

Sunday, July 21
PREVIEW '64:
THE BROADWAY THEATER

Excerpts from the forthcoming mus...
productions: Golden Boy, The Roth...
and Golden Spur. Discussion by H...
Elkins, producer (Bye Bye Birdie),
Lee Adams and Charles Strauss, c...
moderated by Norman Nadel.

Jazz concerts will begin at 7:4...
all other events at 8:30 P.M.
Admission to the jazz concerts ...
$3.00 per person; to all other e...
$2.50 per person.

Changes may be made in the...
scheduling of events listed abo...
In case of rain, events will be...
the auditorium. For ticket info...
and reservations, OR 5-2700.

Piano for jazz concerts courtesy of...
Yamaha Piano.

...ole F. Schwartz, Director

CHOOL

...MER

...RTS

...TIVAL

...EET, IN THE VILLAGE

MOVING PARTS

Endowed by Louise and Leonard Riggio (of Barnes & Noble), the Writing and Democracy Program at The New School merges creative writing, close reading, and civic, societal, and cultural engagement. The Riggio Honors Program: Writing and Democracy, is the first academic program to treat writing, equality, and justice as a single subject, and to implement its philosophy in its internal structure. The program mints a new undergraduate curriculum, an ongoing event series in the Writer's Life Colloquium, seven new teaching-assistant positions for graduate students, and thirty-six undergraduate scholarships.

'Louise and I have always believed that skillful writing provides the centering for all political movements,' says Leonard Riggio. 'With respect to democratic institutions, their ability to function and remain relevant in a rapidly changing world can be seen as a function of the many nuances of the language which is their lifeblood. Our interest, then, is to encourage more participation in the "programming" of our democracy by an ever wider circle of informed people.'

Overseen by The New School's MFA in Creative Writing, the thirty-two-credit program curates a three-year sequence of workshops, seminars, and colloquia led by distinguished writers and thinkers. Faculty in the first year of the program includes Patricia Carlin, Sam Haselby, Deborah Landau, Suzannah Lessard, Sigrid Nunez, Francine Prose, Helen Schulman, Prageeta Sharma, Rene Steinke, and Lynne Tillman.

In 1944, students of The New School establish the *12th Street Journal*. A 'prospectus' lays out the intentions and role of the publication:

Every new publication needs a raison d'être, particularly in these times. Our plan is to publish, four times a year, the work of students and alumni of The New School and the Graduate Faculty of Political and Social Science. The fields we hope to cover will in general correspond to the curriculum of The New School: the social sciences, philosophy, and psychology, and the arts; there will also be some creative writing.

The quarterly, published and edited by students, remains in production until 1950. In 2008, students of the Riggio Honors Program resume publication of 12th Street, with an award-winning integration of writing and design.

'One of the great things about feminist theory and intellectuals is the way they keep redefining the nature of our problem.'
↗ **ANN SNITOW** Faculty

'WHO WE ARE WHEN WE ARE NOT LOVE HAS ALWAYS CAUSED US SHAME.'
↗ **AKILAH OLIVER** Faculty

'When I started out, I used photography as a way of measuring my country and the life I was born into, a New Jersey boy only ten badges short of Eagle Scout. I worked as a photojournalist for twenty-five years. The kinds of stories I chose to do I later realized were mostly about American myths. I photographed small towns, immigrants, the barrio in New York, and then the enormous changes that came with the 1960s. But maybe I had a sell-by time, an expiration date for being a witness. In the early 1970s, I started questioning this reportage for myself. A host of manipulators had so corrupted and warped public events, I could no longer trust the authenticity of what I was seeing.'
↗ **CHARLES HARBUTT** Faculty

Clockwise from top left:

The New School University Center

Seventh-floor library, The New School University Center

WRITING THE SHORT STORY, 1960
RICHARD YATES

A workshop course in which students' stories as well as those by established authors are read, discussed, and evaluated in group criticism. Emphasis is on the craft and art of the short story as a serious fictional form, rather than on its commercial possibilities. The student writer, through classroom discussion and individual conferences on work in progress, is encouraged to develop his own critical standards to find his own literary voice.

BEGINNING FICTION WRITING, 1975
GILBERT SORRENTINO

This course is for the beginning writer and is designed to develop the basic skills needed to compose fiction. Students are encouraged to look at their work not as a homogenous unit, but as the end result of many 'moving parts' — words, syntax, grammar, often punctuation and paragraphing. There are exercises in the function of adjectives and verbs and nouns, and in the invention of stories and highlights circumscribed as to language by the form. Because many words readers may casually accept, asked to write from a point of view diametrically opposed to their own, and 'accident' in writing is explored. Various writings of established authors are read and discussed in class to assist students with their writing problems, and as models of technique. Students are also asked to keep a daily journal from which a fictitious narrative may be developed. Emphasis in this course is on the fact that good fiction is the result of endless choices and alternatives, not magical 'inspiration'.

TGIRLS, 2015
TIPHANIE YANIQUE

Historically, the girl child in literature has often been a stand-in for innocence and / or the violent removal of innocence. Modern feminist literature has sought to redefine what the girl might be capable of and what the girl might represent by asking questions such as: Do girls have adventure? Do girls have subjectivity? What voice do girls have in our modern culture? How do male and female writers use the girl's voice to create narrative and character? What are girls' bodies doing in our literature? In this class we will explore these questions but also ask: What are girls up to in your writing?

> ## 'I ALWAYS FELT I NEEDED TO TEACH TO SURVIVE.'
> ↗ **LEONARD BASKIN**
> Honorary Degree Recipient and Student

> ## 'THE UNIVERSE IS A CONTINUOUS WEB. TOUCH IT AT ANY POINT AND THE WHOLE WEB QUIVERS.'
> ↖ STANLEY KUNITZ, Guest Speaker

In 2010, as part of the Parsons' School of Design Strategies, the Master of Fine Arts in Transdisciplinary Design, led by founding Director Jamer Hunt, initiates a first-like-it program in socially responsible, innovative, and big-picture design. International in scope, the project-based curriculum approaches complex problems through comprehensive design, spanning teaching and research, social action, and entrepreneurship and commerce. 'Designing for services considers first and foremost the situation, the context of the lived experience and then introduces the designed artifacts,' explains Associate Professor and Program Director Lara Penin, in an interview concurrent with the 2018 release of her book, *An Introduction to Service Design: Designing the Invisible*. 'The future of service design should be more mission driven and focused on socially meaningful projects. We need more radical experiments of service design to be developed in different sectors, to help us reinvent social, cultural, and environmental mindsets,' On campus, the MFA in Transdisciplinary Design is proximate to Design and Urban Ecologies, Strategic Design and Management, and Theories of Urban Practice.

April, 2011: 'The New School Presents Noir' explores Noir across creative disciplines, and initiates an 'Arts Festival' series of programs. 'The Arts Festival reflects the range of artistic and intellectual activity at The New School,' explains President David E. Van Zandt, who points to Noir's imprint on culture. The week-long event is curated by Robert LuPone, Director of the School of Drama, James Miller, Chair of Liberal Studies, and Robert Polito, Director of the MFA in Creative Writing. Among the

A NONVIOLENT ARMY HAS A MAGNIFICENT UNIVERSAL QUALITY

In a radical, even dangerous act, The New School initiates a for-credit lecture series: The American Race Crisis Lecture Series. The school invites sixteen leaders of the American Civil Rights Movement, just one year before the passage of the Civil Rights Act of 1965, to offer thought and dialogue on the issues of social justice, racial integration, and equal access to education.

In the run-up to the event, President John F. Kennedy is shot in Dallas. Nine days after his death, while the nation mourns, Malcolm X—among the speakers invited to participate in the Race Crisis series—comments on the assassination in the context of violence against blacks: 'Being an old farm boy myself, chickens coming home to roost never did make me sad; they've always made me glad.' Alvin Johnson, President Emeritus of The New School, along with most of white America, is enraged by the controversial analogy, and sets in motion Malcolm X's disinvitation from the engagement. Johnson's requital is gratuitous; Malcolm X's scheduled lecture falls within a ninety-day term of silence imposed on him by the Nation of Islam for his inopportuneness.

On February 6, 1964, Dr. Martin Luther King leads the series with a speech from the stage of the iconic Tishman Auditorium of Joseph Urban's 66 West 12th Street building.

Fifty years later, The New School enters a joint partnership with the Schomburg Center for Research in Black Culture to commemorate the lecture series and reflect upon the ongoing Civil Rights Movement; *Voices of Crisis*, an exhibition and event series mounted at The New School's Arnold and Sheila Aronson Galleries, presents transcripts, documentation, and photographs of the 1964 program, and features original audio of Dr. King's address. The research builds on Senior Thesis findings of recent Eugene Lang College alumnus Miles Kohrman; in connection to his research in 2011, the King recordings were discovered in a storage room.

1964

Clockwise from top left:

David Hammons, *African-American Flag*, 1989. Dyed cotton. 96 in. x 60 in. The New School Art Collection

Martin Luther King Jr. speaking at the 'American Race Crisis' lecture series at The New School, February 6, 1964

'For 100 years since Emancipation Negroes had searched for the illusive path to freedom. They knew that they had to fashion a body of tactics suitable for their unique and special condition. The words of the Constitution had declared them free. But life had told them they were a twice-burdened people. They lived in the lowest stratum of society. And within it they were additionally imprisoned by a cast of color.'
↗ **MARTIN LUTHER KING** February 6, 1964, at The New School

'The argument that nonviolence is a coward's refuge, lost its force as its heroic and often perilous acts uttere wordless but convincing rebuttal in Montgomery in the sit-ins, on the freedom rides, and finally in Birming There is a powerful motivation when a suppressed people enlist in an army that marches under the banner nonviolence. A nonviolent army has a magnificent universal quality. To join an army that trains its adheren methods of violence you must be of a certain age. But in Birmingham some of the most valued foot soldiers young — youngsters ranging from elementary to teenage high school and college students.'
↗ **MARTIN LUTHER KING** February 6, 1964, at The New School

During the "Red Summer" of 1919, anti-black riots break out in dozens of American cities. With the northward post-war migration of African Americans, economic competition for jobs results in racial violence. Woodrow Wilson argues "the American Negro returning from abroad would be our greatest medium in conveying Bolshevism to America"; W.E.B. Du Bois issues a plea to African American WW1 Veterans, "We are cowards and jackasses if now that the war is over, we do not marshal every ounce of our brain and brawn to fight a sterner, longer, more unbending battle against the forces of hell in our own land." The New School for Social Research, in its first two course catalogues, Spring and Fall of 1919, makes no reference to contemporary issues of race.

'I must honestly say that I never intend to adjust myself to segregation and discrimination. I never intend to become adjusted to religious bigotry. I never intend to adjust myself to the madness of militarism, and the self-defeating effects of physical violence. For in a day when sputniks and explorers are dashing through outer space, and guided ballistic missiles are carving highways of death in the stratosphere, no nation can win a war. It is no longer the choice between ... violence and nonviolence, but it is now — nonviolence and/or nonexistence. And the alternative to disarmament, the alternative to suspension of nuclear tests, the alternative to strengthening the United Nations, and thereby disarming the whole world, may well be a civilization plunged into the abyss of annihilation.'
↗ **MARTIN LUTHER KING** February 6, 1964, at The New School

December 5, 1963

Minister Malcolm X
153 Lenox Avenue
New York, N. Y. 10026

Dear Mr. Malcolm X:

In letters sent to you October 18 and 30, 1963, and through subsequent conversations with you, Faculty Member Daniel Anthony invited you to speak at The New School during the Spring Semester, 1964, as a part of the program, "The American Race Crisis."

In view of utterances made by you, as reported in the press of December 2, concerning the recent murder of the President of the United States, and the actions taken by Elijah Muhammad regarding your conduct as reported in the press this date, we hereby withdraw and rescind this invitation. Your personal conduct has not been in keeping with the traditions and decencies honored at The New School. You are now not invited to speak at The New School during the Spring Semester 1964 or at any other time. The use of your name in connection with this Program will be immediately discontinued.

Sincerely yours,

William Birenbaum
Dean

WMB:meb

cc: **Mr. Daniel Anthony**
ccb: **Dr. MacIver**
Mr. Landa

Clockwise from top left:

■■■■■ Poster for 'The American Race Crisis' lecture series, February, 6, 1964

■■■■■ Flyer for 'Race in the U.S.', a free public course responding to issues of race in the contemporary U.S., 2017

■■■■■ Letter from William Birenbaum disinviting Malcolm X to The New School, December 5, 1963

■■■■■ Poster for the 2014 exhibition and event 'Voices of Crisis' that explored 'The American Race Crisis Lectures' held at the New School in 1964

THE AMERICAN RACE CRISIS

15 LECTURES BEGINNING FEBRUARY 6, 1964
THURSDAYS 8:30-10:10 P. M. *

*Except the Robert C. Weaver lecture on February 27, which will begin at 6:20 p.m.

SERIES $40.00; SINGLE ADMISSION $3.25; REGISTRATION OPENS JAN. 6; DANIEL S. ANTHONY, COORDINATOR

Persons who wish to take this course for 2 points of undergraduate credit, should consult the
Office of Educational Advising regarding requirements and fees prior to January 30, 1964

REV. MARTIN LUTHER KING, JR. FEB 6
President, Southern Christian Leadership Conference

JOSEPH MONSERRAT FEB 13
Director, Migration Division, Dept. of Labor, Commonwealth of Puerto Rico

DAN W.
Director, Center for Human Relations

DODSON FEB 20
and Community Studies, New York University

ROBERT C. WEAVER
Administrator, Federal Housing and Home Finance Agency

FEB 27   JOHN O. KILLENS MAR 12
Author; Chairman, Harlem Writers Guild Workshop

MELVIN TUMIN MAR 19
Professor of Anthropology and Sociology, Princeton University

CHARLES ABRAMS
Urban Planner; Former Chairman, N.Y. Commission Against Discrimination in Housing

MAR 26   ALGERNON D. BLACK APR 2
A Leader of the American Ethical Movement; Chairman of the Board, Natl. Committee Against Discrimination in Housing

LOUIS E. LOMAX APR 9
Social critic; Author of The Negro Revolt

WHITNEY
Executive Director, National Urban League

M. YOUNG JR. APR 16
OSSIE DAVIS
Author of the play, Purlie Victorious

APR 23   JAMES FARMER MAY 21
National Director, Congress of Racial Equality

ALSO: JAMES BALDWIN   DICK GREGORY

REV. MILTON A. GALAMISON
CHAIRMAN, CITY WIDE COMMITTEE
FOR SCHOOL INTEGRATION,
MARCH 5

THE NEW SCHOOL
66 WEST 12TH STREET, NEW YORK CITY; PHONE OREGON 5-2700

PLEASE POST

December, 2017: in response to the 2016 U.S. election and its fallout, The New School hosts 'Race in the U.S.A'. Over the course of weekly events and lectures that span three months, the free-to-the-public course responds 'in real time' to issues of race in the United States. Guest speakers include New School Professors Michelle DePass, Darrick Hamilton, and Michael Omi, as well as New School Senior Vice President for Social Justice, Maya Wiley, New Yorker writer Lawrence Weschler, Black Lives Matter Director of Communications Shanelle Matthews, and Women's March organizer Linda Sarsour.

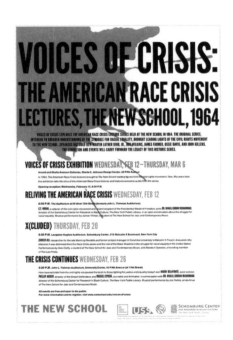

'By 1963, most of America's working population had forgotten the Great Depression, or had never known it. The slow and steady growth of unemployment had touched some of the white working force, but the proportion was still not more than one in twenty. And this was not true for the Negro. There were two and a half times as many jobless Negroes as white, in 1963. Many white Americans of goodwill have never connected bigotry with economic exploitation. They have deplored prejudice, but tolerated or ignored economic injustice. But the Negro knows that these two evils have a malignant kinship.'

↗ **MARTIN LUTHER KING** February 6, 1964, at The New School

'WHATEVER YOU'VE BEEN GIVEN IT'S TO GIVE BACK.'

↗ **DONNA KARAN** Student and Visiting Critic

ASTONISH

Bob Adelman, a photographer who chronicled the Civil Rights era, returns to his alma mater, The New School, to document a class in session. The students are engaged with the academic subject, their teacher, and one another. As if a shadow of their group focus and dedication, the figures of Thomas Hart Benton's ten-panel mural, *America Today*, background their foreground. The students, and the figures of the mural, are quintessentially American—strong and full of the future.

Adelman's energetic captures of campus life in the 1970s and early 1980s, and the seamless integration of photojournalism and innovation that he brings to the courses he teaches, help to define The New School's image of the day. His aesthetic—passionate and documentarian— hearken to the vigor of Benton's mural, which he would have first encountered as a student while attending Alexey Brodovitch's 'Design Laboratory' at The New School (Brodovitch also taught at the New York School of Fine and Applied Art, later known as Parsons). Professor Brodovitch, ten years younger than Benton and a Russian immigrant, offered a foundation of European Modernism similar to what Benton had once offered his students at the Art Students League. (Jackson Pollock, Benton's student, appears in *America Today* as a model.) The Art Director at *Harper's Bazaar* from 1934 to 1958, Brodovitch was as at ease in photography as he was in layout. The course description for the 'Design Laboratory' elaborated:

Previous pages:

Parsons alumna Donna Karan fitting a model, circa 1980

Clockwise from top left:

New School class in the room with Thomas Hart Benton murals. Bob Adelman, *circa* 1979

New School class in the room with Thomas Hart Benton murals. Bob Adelman, *circa* 1979

Harper's Bazaar cover, designed by Alexey Brodovitch, October 1947

Harper's Bazaar cover, designed by Alexey Brodovitch, September 1958

'PHOTOGRAPHY HELPS PEOPLE TO SEE.'

↗ BERENICE ABBOTT Faculty

'LIBERAL EDUCATION IS LIBERATION FROM VULGARITY.'

↗ LEO STRAUSS Faculty

Harper's BAZAAR

HARPER'S BAZAAR

INCORPORATING JUNIOR BAZAAR

NEWS FROM PARIS & THE USA: A FULL FASHION REPORT

SEPTEMBER 1958

60 CENTS

The aim of the course is to help the student to discover his individuality, crystallize his taste, and develop his feeling for the contemporary trend by stimulating his sense of invention and perfecting his technical ability. The course is conducted as an experimental laboratory, inspired by the ever-changing tempo of life, discovery of new techniques, new fields of operation in close contact with current problems of leading magazines, department stores, advertising agencies, and manufacturers. Subjects include design, layout, type, poster, reportage, illustration, magazine make-up, package and product design, display, styling, art directing.

The laboratory was wildly popular, with up to sixty registered students at a time. In addition to Adelman, and among others, there was Diane Arbus, Eve Arnold, David Attie, Richard Avedon, Harvey Lloyd, Hiro, Lisette Model, Garry Winogrand, and Tony Ray-Jones. The Brodovitch credo, 'Astonish me', references Sergei Diaghilev's direction, 'Étonne-moi', to poet Jean Cocteau in conceiving a ballet scenario. (The result was *Parade*, 1917, which benefited from additional collaborators Pablo Picasso, who was affiliated with The New School's Atelier 17, Léonide Massine, who performed at The New School in the 1930s, and Erik Satie, whose work inspired modern dance performances that debuted at The New School, also in the 1930s.)

The Benton room, once a boardroom (Alvin Johnson appears as a figure speaking to Benton in a lower corner of the work), will soon see a major renovation, as will the entire building at 66 West 12th Street. *America Today*, original to the location and the Joseph Urban architecture of the building, will move to upper walls in the lobby of the Equitable Life Tower on Lower Broadway, and from there to a permanent site, which will precisely duplicate the proportions of the Urban room, at the Metropolitan Museum. The decision to sell the Benton will be prompted by much-needed maintenance to the building, the principle of a dynamic art collection, and, possibly, a trend against Benton's representational style, regionalism, and outdated ideology. Benton had been paid for the mural in only the egg yolks he required for his tempera, and The New School will predicate the sale of the work upon two exacting conditions: that the panels not be separated, or sold to be exhibited outside the United States.

WORKSHOP IN PHOTOGRAPHY, 1934 BERENICE ABBOTT

This course will present a general outline theory and practice of elementary photog It will emphasize practical workshop expe in connection with the theory of the photo process, including the understanding of le cameras lighting, exposure, printing, deve enlarging, etc. It will also include discussi the functions of modern photography as independent medium, divorced from the p pictorial school which associated photogr with painting and drawing, and deriving it approach rather from the social, psycholo aesthetic, and commercial values of the m individual expression.

ERIK SATIE: THE EVOLUTION OF A COMPOSER, 1957 JOHN CAGE

All of Satie's works are discussed and as as possible performed, live or by recording chronological order, the purpose of the co to recreate the experience the composer h had in his music writing.

THIS IS NOT A PIPE: ART AND THE SURREAL, 2019 NANCY GROVE

When Surrealism was officially defined in poet André Breton as 'pure psychic autom the visual arts were not considered to be appropriate means for expressing the unc However, within a few years, painters, scu photographers, and filmmakers — includin Salvador Dalí, Alberto Giacometti, Man Ro Luis Buñuel — were established as importa members of the group, and artworks such *Persistence of Memory* became Surrealist Although the group no longer exists, invocation of the surreal through paradoxical juxtapo and playful improvisation has continued t important strategy of contemporary visua as witnessed in recent exhibitions such as *Surrealism*. This class explores the poetry, artists' writings, films, photography, paint sculpture of Dada and Surrealist artists of as well as the works of present artists inv with the surreal. Readings, discussions, cla presentations, slides, videos, and field trip further knowledge and understanding.

In January 1956, Alistair Cooke visits The New School to lecture on the nature of 'Mass Media and Minority Culture'. Cooke is one of the many celebrity media guests to visit Arno Huth's longstanding, popular course, 'Mass Media and International Relations'. The visit is preceded by a reception.

'I always wanted to be a filmmaker when I was younger, not an actor. I was an eight-year-old who dreamed of being a writer on *The Simpsons*, which was a weird dream to have. But I started taking acting classes as a way to learn how to direct actors and I sort of fell in love with it.'
↗ JONAH HILL Student

'IF YOU COULD SAY IT IN WORDS THERE WOULD BE NO REASON TO PAINT.'

↗ **EDWARD HOPPER** Student

'Home was the place where I was forced to conform to someone else's image of who and what I should be. School was the place where I could forget that self and, through ideas, reinvent myself.'

↗ **BELL HOOKS** Scholar-in-Residence

Clockwise from top left:

▬▬▬ Thomas Hart Benton restoring his *America Today* mural. Peter Moore, 1968

▬▬▬ Thomas Hart Benton with paints as he restores his *America Today* mural. Peter Moore, 1968

▬▬▬ Lisette Model, undated

NO LONGER IN EXILE

The Parsons Kellen Archives, which collects and maintains documentation and materials about Parsons dating back to the school's 1896 origin, draws the curatorial interest of Alexandra Anderson and P.J. Carlino, Master's students at Parsons. With the assistance of Archive Director Wendy Scheir and Kellen Archivist Jenny Swadosh, the concept takes form with *Inspiring Women: Selected Designers from Parsons' Anna-Maria and Stephen Kellen Archives*. At the invitation of Ann Snitow, a Professor of Literature and Gender Studies in New School's Eugene Lang College, the show opens in conjunction with the forty-speaker conference, 'No Longer in Exile: The Legacy and Future of Gender Studies at The New School'.

The exhibition showcases: Margaret McKay Tee '10; Dorothy Haon '24; Mildred Orrick (Boykin) '28; Claire McCardell '28; Joset Walker '28; Elizabeth Hoopes '30 (faculty); Mildred Irby '30 (faculty); Lea Hoyt '33; Eleanor Horst '36; Margaret Hodge '45; Andrée Golbin '43; Adri '58; Bea Feitler '59; Tracy Reese '84; Cipe Pineles (faculty); Lorraine Fox (faculty); Esta Nesbitt (faculty); and Edith d'Errecalde (designer and critic).

'Women — if you would dominate your husband, your home, your social circle, or your country; decide which of these spheres you want to conquer, and then go to it with a vengeance.'
↗ **FRANK ALVAH PARSONS**
Director of the New York School
of Fine and Applied Art and Parsons

The curatorial direction of *Inspiring Women* begins with two precepts: the subjects must be women and must have something to do with Parsons. While the curation is intended not as a final word but as an invigoration of the extraordinary New School archive, the show presents a cohesive vision of Parsons' influence. From the outset, Parsons has seen mentorship as fundamental, and the maturation of the designers featured in the show is an illuminating cross-hatch of students, faculty members, peers, and coworkers. Frank Alvah Parsons, in developing a curriculum, was prescient enough to see the history and future of women in design, which was evolving from a 'whim to a professional art industry'. The show tracks multiple firsts for women in the creative field, and segues into a more familiar, contemporary Parsons (with Donna Karan's lineage as a student, for example). Through the curation of archival works, ranging from magazine spreads to student notebooks, the Parsons impact is apparent in fashion, film, and stage costume, as well as design, illustration, and media.

'There is nothing new under the fashion sun,' said the outspoken Joset Walker, for example, talking to *The New York Times* in 1996. 'Clothes I designed 30 years ago are as new as today. You could put them on and be right in style.' The works, on display at The New School from March through May, 2010, are as impactful as the biographies and personalities of the featured artists, professional power player to rediscovered virtuoso.

Opposite:

Richard Avedon. *Bea Feitler and Ruth Ansel*, (contact sheet), 1965

'I LOVE WARM COLORS, AND I HAVE DARED TO USE THEM.'

↗ **JOSET WALKER** Student

'Clothes have to function today – whether it's your sports life, your daily life, your office life, or even when you go out.'
↗ **EDITH D'ERRECALDE** Visiting Critic and Guest Speaker

Clockwise from top left:

▬▬▬ Andrée Golbin at work
in Oregon Studio, 1988

▬▬▬ Margaret McKay
Tee painting, 1920s

▬▬▬ Adri, 1971

▬▬▬ Donna Karan

▬▬▬ Dorothy Haon, *circa* 1935

ANTHROPOLOGY IN THE MODERN WORLD, 1950
MARGARET MEAD

The application of anthropological methods to contemporary problems:

→ Cross-national communication, with special references to World War II experience with Japan, Germany, and Great Britain;

→ Changes in living habits, with special references to nutrition;

→ Dependent peoples and underdeveloped areas, and the cultural problems raised by Point Four;

→ Communication within a democratic society versus totalitarian society; problems of manipulation, control, and the preservation of areas of freedom;

→ The method of anthropology, what's meant by a pattern of culture;

→ Anthropology and the problem of social invention.

PHILOSOPHICAL ASPECTS OF BIOGRAPHY: THE NATURE AND STUDY OF LIVES, 1975
SARA RUDDICK

In this course we will exa[...]
techniques, dangers, and [...]
the ability to work, the re[...]
sexual roles, sexuality, [...]
process, the impulse to p[...]
of age and the meaning [...]
encouraged to select a p[...]
write an autobiographic[...]
their own lives.

'Clothes have to function today — whether it's your sports life, your daily life, your office life, or even when you go out.'
↗ **EDITH D'ERRECALDE** Visiting Critic and Guest Speaker

'IN A BOOK PROJECT, I'M NOT SO INTERESTED IN DESIGNING BOOKS. I WANT TO GIVE THEM A SOUL.'
↗ **BEA FEITLER** Student

Clockwise from top left:

Women Dancing, fashion editorial directed by Bea Feitler

Cipe Pineles Golden. _Parsons School of Design: Our Campus Is the Art Center of the World: New York City_, after 1971

Cipe Pineles Golden. _Have You Got It In You?_, after 1971

'The Stocking, Modern, Magnificent', designed by Edith d'Errecalde, 1960s

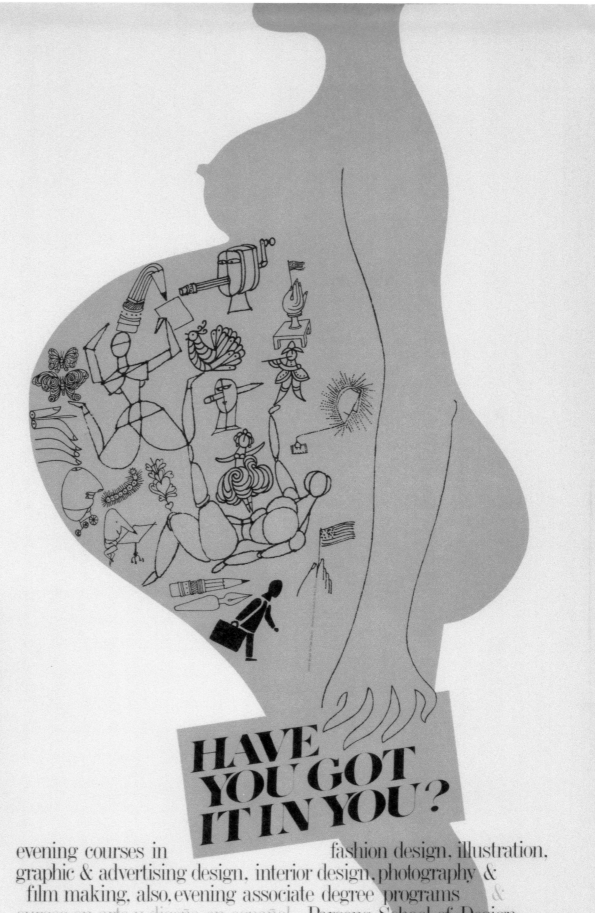

HAVE YOU GOT IT IN YOU?

evening courses in   fashion design, illustration,
graphic & advertising design, interior design, photography &
film making, also, evening associate degree programs   &
cursos en arte y diseño en español. Parsons School of Design,
affiliated with the New School, 66 fifth ave. ny. ny. 10011, 741 8933

Lorraine Fox. *Second Thoughts
from a Former First Lady*.
Advertisement for Lady Bird
Johnson interview, after 1972

Ms. magazine cover, *Peace on
Earth Good Will Toward All People*,
designed by Bea Feitler, 1971

UNFETTERED, INFORMED

The 1994 *New School Bulletins*, Spring, Summer, and Fall, which list General Catalogue courses for The New School, compile 667 pages of offerings. The year marks the seventy-fifth anniversary of The New School. A pamphlet commemorates the occasion:

> *The New School may well be the only university to be born not out of the educational needs of a geographical area or of a faith or profession, nor out of the civic commitment or generosity of an affluent family. Instead, it is the institutional expression of a democratic idea passionately embraced by our founders — one that cuts across the boundaries of regions, religion, class, or academic discipline — which is that only through the unfettered study of human thought and behavior, and only through the creation of an informed public, can democracy realize its great potential for political freedom and betterment of its citizens. Seventy-five years ago, a small, bold group of American scholars made that idea the founding premise of a new kind of educational institution in New York City. Concerned about the curtailment of free inquiry at their own universities, they decided to create a school in which unfettered inquiry in research and the arts would contribute to the development of an informed public.*

KAMAU BRATHWAITE AND ALLEN GINSBERG

The New School Writing Program has been a vital forum for writers in New York City ever since Gorman Munson, a member of the Stieglitz circle, 'on impulse' offered our first writing workshop. This seventy-fifth-anniversary reading is co-sponsored by the Academy of American Poets.

THE W.E.B. DU BOIS LECTURE
LANI GUINIER

CONVERSATIONS ABOUT WOMEN: WRITING A WOMAN'S LIFE
GINA LURIA WALKER

Reversal of Fortune: Artworld Rules for the Nineties Moderator: Stuart Horodner, Director, Horodner Romley Gallery Panelists: Saul Ostrow, artist, critic, curator; J. Robert Orton, Jr., collector, advisor, author. Elizabeth Hess, Village *Voice* critic; Barbara Pollack, artist, publicist. Respondents: Charlie Finch, WBAI Radio talk show host, editor of *Coagula* magazine; Sue Scott, critic, curator or Orlando Museum of Art.

JOSEPH BEUYS BEHIND THE MASK: HIS TRAVELS IN AMERICA
RONALD FELDMAN

APPROACHING THE MILLENNIUM: CULTURE AT THE EDGE
MARSHALL BLONSKY

THE ACTORS STUDIO SEMINARS: THE CRAFT OF THEATER

Participants: Alec Baldwin, Anne Bancroft, Ellen Burstyn, Robert De Niro, Olympia Dukakis, Sally Field, John Goodman, Julie Harris, Dennis Hopper, Harvey Keitel, Martin Landau, Norman Mailer, Paul Newman, Al Pacino, Estelle Parsons, Arthur Penn, Sydney Pollack, Frank Rich, Eric Roberts, Mark Rydell, Martin Scorsese, Neil Simon, Stephen Sondheim, Christopher Walken, Gene Wilder, Shelley Winters.

UNCONSCIOUS GENDER POLITICS
ANDREW SAMUELS

SHOULD MARIJUANA BE LEGALIZED?
JEROME D. LEVIN

TABLOID TELEVISION OR INVESTIGATIVE JOURNALISM
LINDA SHUB

THE 1920S: THE EMERGENCE OF MODERN AMERICA
HERBERT M. GREENHUT

TTHE LEAN YEARS: LIFE IN THE EARLY THIRTIES
CARLA STEVENS

LOVE AND DEATH: THE POLITICS OF PASSION
JEAN MARC COICAUD

THE CHANGING NATURE OF EUROPEAN POLITICS
WILLIAM J. BUCKLEY

BIO-PSYCHOLOGY OF LOVE AND LUST
ROCHELLE SILFEN

THE CONTEMPORARY AUTHORITARIAN PERSONALITY
GERDA LEDERER

THE TEN COMMANDMENTS OF TASTE
JERRY SALTZ

WHAT MADE HARLEM FAMOUS?
KAREN F. TABORN

DRACULA: FACT, FOLKLORE, FICTION AND FILM
ARTHUR LIEBMAN

THE CULTURE OF CAFFEINE
IRENE FIZER

PASSIONATE PAIRINGS: FAMOUS COUPLES WHO REVOLUTIONIZED 20TH-CENTURY ART
HARRIET LEBISH

DADA AND SURREALISM: A WORKSHOP
LYNNE SHAPIRO

MURDER INK AT THE NEW SCHOOL IN COOPERATION WITH MURDER INK BOOK SHOP OF NEW YORK CITY

An ongoing series of readings and discussions by distinguished writers of mystery and crime fiction.

EXPLODED TEXT: POETRY IN PERFORMANCE WORKSHOP
BOB HOLMAN

AFRICA AND THE AFRICAN FILMMAKER
KABU OKAI-DAVIES

FROM THE AZTECS TO BAHIA: MUSIC OF LATIN AMERICA
JEANNINE WAGAR

MAKE A JOYFUL NOISE: MUSIC OF THE AFRICAN DIASPORA MADELEINE
YAYODELE NELSON

FROM BIRDLAND TO BROOKLYN: A MUSICAL HISTORY OF NEW YORK CITY
SUSAN E. RICHARDSON

A HISTORY OF BRAZILIAN JAZZ
PAMELA BLOOM

JAZZ HISTORY: FROM AFRICA TO ELLINGTON
JOAN STILES

THE BROADWAY PLAY
ZOE KAPLAN

MUSIC, THEATER, AND CABARET
WITH MARILYN SOKOL

INTERMEDIATE JUGGLING
MARC STOLZENBERG

PUPPETRY
SUSAN D. WHEDON

ABSURD, TWISTED
COMEDY WRITING
ELLIOT TIBER

ROLLER BLADING
LEZLY ZIERING

IN HONOR OF GAY / LESBIAN
PRIDE MONTH
QUEER ART TODAY

Moderator Robert Atkins, *Village Voice* columnist,
author of *ArtSpeak: A Guide to Contemporary
Ideas, Movements and Buzzwords* and the
forthcoming *Gay and Lesbian Looker: Queer Art
Since Stonewall*, and curator of *From Media
to Metaphor: Art about AIDS*.

OUT-TAKES
LAURA KAMINSKY,
COORDINATOR

FILMMAKERS ON FILMMAKING
WITH RICHARD BROWN
SUMMER SOUNDTRACK

Over the quarter-century this course has been
offered, we have previewed just about all of
the important motion pictures, beginning with
Butch Cassidy and the Sundance Kid, and through
today's masterpieces like *Schindler's List*. ... The
final guest list is always keyed to the movies
we see and who is in New York in any given
week. This year's guests include: Ron Howard
(*The Paper*), Mia Farrow (*Widow's Peak*), Emma
Thompson (*Remains of the Day*), Charles Grodin
(*Clifford*), Michael J. Fox (*Greedy*), and Shirley
MacLaine (*Guarding Tess*).

CULTS
CHARLES G. CASE

MALCOLM X:
THE EVOLUTION
OF A REVOLUTIONARY
WILLIAM R. DORSEY

JOURNEY TO THE INTERIOR:
ELIZABETH BISHOP AND
SYLVIA PLATH
PEARL LONDON

CONTEMPORARY
CULTURE IN HARLEM
KAREN F. TABORN

WATCHING TELEVISION:
THE HISTORY AND
AESTHETICS OF THE MEDIUM
ALAN SONDHEIM

DOO WOP OF THE '50S AND '60S
BOBBY JAY

BREAKING INTO
THE WOMAN'S MAGAZINE
SUSAN SHAPIRO

THE CLINTON ADMINISTRATION
AND THE WORLD:
A CONVERSATION WITH
GEORGE STEPHANOPOULOS

GOING TO GALLERIES:
ART IN THE TRENCHES
JERRY SALTZ

THE SPOKEN WORD SCENE:
NEW POETRY, NEW YORK
BOB HOLMAN

POETRY: WORKS IN PROGRESS
PEARL LONDON

EXPERIMENTS IN POETRY
BERNADETTE MAYER

CONTEMPORARY STYLES OF
POETRY: WHERE DO YOU FIT IN?
ELAINE EQUI

MASTERCLASS IN POETRY
WITH DAVID TRINIDAD
DAVID TRINIDAD

FICTION WRITING
SIDNEY OFFIT

MASTERCLASS IN FICTION:
THE SHORT STORY
ED VEGA

FINDING YOUR
VOICE IN NONFICTION
CANDY SCHULMAN

THE RECYCLED OBJECT
LINDA LEE

HOW TO OPEN A COFFEE BAR
GARY A. GOLDBERG

HIGH RISK BOOKS

Amy Scholder, Ira Silverberg, editors of High Risk
Books, with June Jordan, Gary Indiana,
John Giorno, Pagan Kennedy, and Sapphire.

ALTERNATIVE RADIO:
VIN SCELSA'S IDIOT'S DELIGHT
VIN SCELSA

THE PARIS REVIEW
YOUNGER WRITERS' NIGHT
CO-SPONSORED BY THE
ACADEMY OF AMERICAN POETS

George Plimpton, Richard Howard, with
Bernardine Connelly, Tony Sanders,
Robyn Selman, and Joanna Scott.

THE CULTURE WARS
JAMES DAVISON HUNTER

CONVERSATIONS ABOUT
WOMEN CHANGING HISTORY:
WOMEN'S HEALTH IN
OBSERVANCE OF WOMEN'S
HISTORY MONTH
GINA LURIA WALKER

J.M. KAPLAN CENTER FOR NEW YORK CITY AFFAIRS: WOMEN WHO BUILD BUILDINGS ETHEL SHEFFER

MIND TO LIFE: THINKING ABOUT WOMEN THROUGH TIME GINA LURIA WALKER

THE CREATIVE MIND CARLA STEVENS

AFRO-BRAZILIAN PERFORMANCE AND SEXUALITY ZECA LIGIÉRO

CONTEMPORARY ART / CONTEMPORARY SOCIETY KENNETH A. SCHACHTER

UNDERSTANDING CONTEMPORARY ART JONATHAN SANTLOFER

THE ACADEMY OF AMERICAN POETS AT THE NEW SCHOOL

→ The Best American Poetry 1994: James Cummins, James McManus, Angela Shaw, and Alicia Stallings; introductions by A.R. Ammons and David Lehman.
→ Carolyn Forché and Jane Miller; introduction by Cyrus Cassells.
→ New Voices: Rafael Campo, Suzanne Gardinier, and Carl Phillips; introduction by Marilyn Hacker.
→ A Tribute to John Berryman: Michael Dennis Browne, Joel Conarroe, Jane Cooper, Robert Giroux, Jorie Graham, Philip Levine, Paul Mariani, W.S. Merwin, and Charles Wright.
→ James Fenton and Andrew Motion; introduction by Lawrence Joseph.
→ W.S. Di Piero and Thom Gunn; introduction by Mark Rudman.
→ John Ashbery and Kenneth Koch.
→ Cynthia Macdonald and Tom Sleigh.
→ Fiftieth-Anniversary Celebration of the Quarterly Review of Literature: Reading and discussion with editors Theodore and Renée Weiss and friends.
→ Ciaran Carson and Nuala Ní Dhomhnaill: An evening with two prominent Irish poets.

GREAT CHEFS AT THE NEW SCHOOL

In these special cooking classes, highly acclaimed chefs and pastry chefs prepare menus which feature their favorite recipes and illustrate their distinctive styles of cooking and baking.
→ Stefano Battistini
→ Anne Rosenzweig: Arcadia
→ Michael Romano: The Union Square Cafe
→ David Bouley: Culinary Scholarship Benefit
→ Great Pastry Chefs: Sarabeth Levine of Sarabeth's
→ Great Pastry Chefs: William Yosses of Restaurant Bouley

BEHIND THE SCENES AT THE GREAT RESTAURANTS OF NEW YORK

In each two-hour class ... participants meet the chef or owner of one of New York's finest restaurants, are given a private cooking demonstration and tour of the facility, and savor a special, selected tasting — truly a memorable experience.
→ Petrossian
→ The Russian Tea Room
→ The 21 Club
→ Zoë
→ Le Chantilly
→ Rosa Mexicano
→ The Regency Hotel
→ TriBeCa Grill
→ Tatou
→ One Fifth Avenue
→ China Grill
→ Lespinasse at the St. Regis
→ Palio
→ Petrossian
→ Capsouto Frères
→ Becco
→ Cascabel
→ Campagna
→ The Hudson River Club

FILMMAKERS ON FILMMAKING WITH RICHARD BROWN FALL 1994: A BLOCKBUSTER SCHEDULE

Enjoy as many as twenty new films and guests including many of the following: *The Browning Version*, Albert Finney, Matthew Modine; *Dead Giveaway*, Sally Field, Jon Voight; *A Good Man in Africa*, Sean Connery, Lou Gossett, Jr.; *Interview with the Vampire*, Tom Cruise, Christian Slater; *It Happened in Paradise*, Nicolas Cage; *Junior*, Arnold Schwarzenegger, Danny DeVito, Emma Thompson; *Just in Time*, Marisa Tomei, Robert Downey, Jr.; *Legends of the Fall*, Anthony Hopkins, Aidan Quinn; *Little Women*, Winona Ryder, Susan Sarandon; *Love Affair*, Warren Beatty, Annette Bening; *Frankenstein*, Robert De Niro, Kenneth Branagh, Tom Hulce, Aidan Quinn; *Miracle on 34th Street*, Richard Attenborough; *Prêt-à-Porter*, Lauren Bacall, Julia Roberts; *Quiz Show*, John Turturro, Rob Morrow; *The Road to Wellville*, Anthony Hopkins, Bridget Fonda, John Cusack, Matthew Broderick, Robin Williams; *The Shawshank Redemption*, Tim Robbins, Morgan Freeman; *Stargate*, Kurt Russell, James Spader; *Tom and Viv*, Willem Dafoe, Miranda Richardson; *The War*, Kevin Costner, Mare Winningham.

THERE IS NO CONSERVATORY OF MUSIC IN THIS COUNTRY

'I always reach a point with a piece where I want to throw it out the window. I think it's a total disaster and I want to kill myself. And then it's a matter of trying to rescue it. That's where the struggle is.'
↗ **PETER DE SÈVE** Student

'STYLE IS PRIMARILY A MATTER OF INSTINCT.'
↗ ...

**DANCE FORMS AND THEIR DEVELOPMENT, 1931
JOHN MARTIN, IN COOPERATION WITH MARTHA GRAHAM AND DORIS HUMPHREY**

The object of this course is to trace the essence of the dance form [in] its earliest manifestations down to the present, laying emphasis not on the historical aspects of the case but on the constant development of one central idea through a maze of differing forms. The program will include folk and ritual dance; theatrical dance including classic ballet; classic Italian Ballet; Noverre and ... ... François Delsarte; Loïe Fuller ... ... ance period; Isadora Duncan, the reform of ...

'You have to give people a sense that they have courage and they have the ability to do much more than they think they do.'
↗ **ELIZABETH AARON** February 6, 1964, at The New School

Clockwise from top left:

Martha Graham and ensemble in *Appalachian Spring*

Martha Graham in *Appalachian Spring*

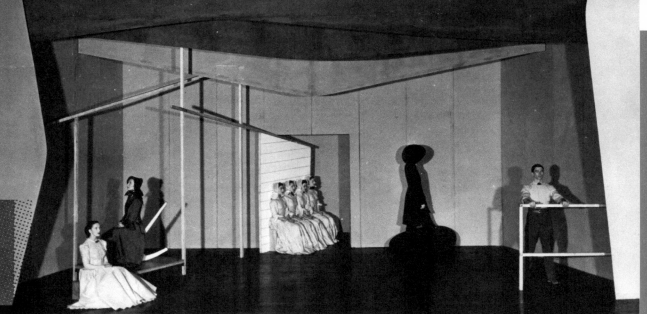

McGraw Hill releases *What to Listen For in Music* by Aaron Copland; the book demystifies music appreciation with thorough yet accessible concepts and language. Based on Copland's lectures, offered at The New School from 1927 to 1939, *What to Listen for in Music* will remain core reading through the century and beyond. As H. Howard Taubman writes in *The New York Times* (April 9, 1939):

> Being articulate in the language of words as well as in that of music, Mr. Copland has written his book with conciseness and simplicity. He does not waste time on side issues, but plunges into the heart of his subject. His book is devoted largely to discussions of the elements of music: rhythm, melody, harmony, and tone color, and to the fundamental forms: sectional, variation, fugal, sonata, and free. He employs a minimum of musical examples — these are as simple as possible — and relies on illuminating comparisons. ... He brushes away the misconceptions that have made the composer a man of mystery.

As a composer, Copland's lauded works incorporate an American heritage of jazz and folk, in compositions simultaneously innovative and traditional. His emergence as a national icon defies a presumption that U.S. classical music is second tier to the greater achievements of European composers. In the pages of *Trend* magazine, 1934, U.S. composer and educator Harrison Kerr describes The New School of the 1920s and 1930s as a 'laboratory' singular in its fostering of an American idiom in music:

> It is a rather appalling feature of the case that there is no conservatory of music in this country making any valuable attempt to build up an American school of composition or even to recruit an audience for such music as our native composers may write. ... To the best of my belief the only intelligent effort along these lines is the one being made at The New School for Social Research in New York under the leadership of Henry Cowell. ... It is interesting to note that, of seventy-two courses offered for 1933–4, thirty-five have to do with the fine arts and that twenty-six of these are concerned partially, or altogether, with today's expression.

'As much as you want something, the actual career side of it should not be the only end result. It comes down to how much do you love to do that thing that you are doing.'
↗ **MYUNG-WHUN CHUNG** Student

> This hospitality to a sphere of study not usually so considerately treated, is extended to the inclusion of thirteen courses in music, most of them concerned with contemporaneous effort. Many public musical programs are presented and are designed to be part of the various musical courses. These are attended by the students, of course, but are frequented as well by a musical public that finds there music that can be heard nowhere else.

In 1941, Copland follows up with a second book based on his New School lectures, titled *Our New Music*. In 1944, Copland is awarded the Pulitzer Prize in composition for his accompanying score to *Appalachian Spring*, a ballet by Martha Graham, also former New School faculty.

'Life was meant to be lived, and curiosity must be kept alive. One must never, for whatever reason, turn his back on life.'
↗ **ELEANOR ROOSEVELT**
Advisory Committee Member and Speaker

1939

#100YEARSNEW

Fall, 2017, eighteen months before The New School's centennial birthday, the university convenes a cross-departmental working group to determine how best to inspirit the occasion. Provost Tim Marshall sends an all-call to faculty for ideas. A 'Festival of the New' takes form; the October 2019 celebration will host thought-leaders from around the globe, offer programming to the public, welcome returning alumni, and interrogate the conceptualization of 'the new'. In August, 2018, in a joint email addressed to the campus, Marshall and President David Van Zandt announce the week-long celebration:

> This series of lectures, symposia, performances, and exhibitions will together celebrate, and critique, the idea of 'the new' with inquiry into what it means today, what it has meant historically, and what we believe it will mean in the future. Envisioned as an academic extension for our students as well as an invitation to the greater New York City community, this festival will allow students, faculty, staff, alumni, and the public to attend programs from across the university while we disrupt regular classes.

As of the summer of 2019, hundreds of talks, workshops, events, and performances are scheduled and in the planning stages, with two books slated to launch. 'It's a whirlwind of activity,' said Ashley Bruni, Director of Brand, toasting the crowd at an April centennial reception held at President Van Zandt's campus townhouse on 11th Street. 'We want you, our community, our neighbors, our partners, to join us in celebrating this momentous occasion and in envisioning The New School into our second century'.

After a preliminary Spring semester, The New School for Social Research formally opens on October 1, 1919, with an expanded roster of courses, and a succession of newspaper announcements. Opening at Parsons' Kellen Gallery in July 2019, *In the Historical Present* will exhibit artist responses to the mercurial experience of history. The curators, Anna Harsanyi '08 and Macushla Robinson '16, articulate their query in the exhibition statement:

It begins with the audacity of a name: The New School. Not a new school, The New School. The New School's centennial presents a paradox—the bold hope that one will never grow old. When does something stop being 'new'? What does it mean for an institution to carry this moniker forward in time? Will the word 'new' cease to define the moment in which we perpetually live, just as 'modern' has lost its capacity to denote an ever present?

During the centennial celebration week, October 1–6, 2019, 100 years since the first 'full program' of courses at The New School, alumni representing decades of education will return to campus to share their stories: Jillian Hervey '11 of Lion Babe is set to headline a concert in Union Square; Anna Sui '72 will discuss her time and experiences 'At the Parsons Table'; Dr. Ruth Westheimer '59 will screen her new film, *Ask Dr. Ruth* in conversation with Esther Perel. The New School, with support from former President Jonathan Fanton, will re-confer an honorary doctorate to Adam Michnik, who, in 1983, was unable to accept his degree in person due to his imprisonment in Poland. Initiated in the 1980s to support an ongoing discussion of global democracy, The Democracy Seminars was progenitor to numerous New School programs, including today's Public Seminar, an online 'intellectual commons for analysis, critique and debate'; at a daily lunch series, student performers will dramatize excerpts from the journal. At other centennial events, original members of The Democracy Seminars will parley with a new guard of activists, scholars, and academics who continue to give voice to dissident scholars.

2019

The New School for Social Research

will open October first for the study of current economic and governmental problems. The work will be conducted by a group of well known writers and teachers among whom are

Graham Wallas of London, Thorstein Veblen, James Harvey Robinson, Wesley Clair Mitchell, John Dewey, Dean Roscoe Pound, Thomas S. Adams, Harold J. Laski, Moissaye Olgin, Charles A. Beard and Members of the Bureau of Municipal Research, Robert Bruère and Members of the Bureau of Industrial Research.

Courses will include lectures on Economic Factors in Civilization, The Development of the United States into a World Power, The Historic Background of the Great War, Modern Industrialism, Social Inheritance, Recent Tendencies in Political Thought, Problems of American Government, etc.

There will be late afternoon and evening lectures and conferences to permit the attendance of those engaged in regular professions. No academic degrees will be required but the standard of postgraduate work will be maintained. There will be general lectures and discussion for larger groups and small conferences for those equipped for special research.

Registration will begin September twenty-second.

Announcement will be sent upon application to the school at

465-9 West Twenty-Third St., New York

THE FESTIVAL OF NEW

SAVE THE DATE OCTOBER 1-6, 2019 NYC

The New School has always been a community of changemakers. For our Centennial, we are opening the university doors with performances, talks, and exhibitions that explore the 'new'—what it has meant, means today, and might mean in the future.

#100yearsnew
newschool.edu/100

THE NEW SCHOOL

Clockwise from top left:

Daniel Bejar, *Rec-elections (Don't say you don't remember)*. Sketch for poster, 2019

Lion Babe, with alumna Jillian Hervey

Newspaper clipping, *The Independent*, August 16, 1919

Toasting the New School's centennial, 2019

Musician and New Schooler Ani DiFranco in conversation with former President of Planned Parenthood, Cecile Richards, The New School, 2019

Poster for *The Festival of New*, designed by John Lepak, 2019

During *The Festival of New* campus will be astir with activity: Faculty members James Miller, Shelley Fox, Simon Critchley, and Paul Goldberer will host a cross-disciplinary public conversation on "the tradition of the new". Wollman Hall, overlooking Greenwich Village, will host morning wellness programming with yoga, dance, and meditation open to the community. From sunset to sunrise— John Cage Musicircus to morning ragas in the Vera List Courtyard— A Night of Philosophy will occupy the Joseph Urban building with talks, performances, and happenings. Author and activist Shaun King will work with students on promoting social justice initiatives via social media. A zine-making workshop will take place on-site at the University Archives. The Moth will host a story slam with the theme of 'The New'. The College of Performing Arts will stage an [Un]Silent film with a live score. Families of current students are invited to join the students on campus for Family Weekend, with many planning to attend the 'New American Narrative on Immigration', organized by Alex Aleinikoff and featuring performer Aasif Mandvi, at the closing ceremony on Ellis Island.

Don't say you don't remember.

'A century ago, The New School's founders were among the first to recognize that contemporary higher education must have a global perspective. Our academic vision is more vital and relevant than ever in the twenty-first century, where political, economic, and cultural discourse take place on a global scale. ... As we mark the university's centennial, we have much to be proud of and much to build on. The New School is an extraordinary university, a community ready for any challenge, because of the people who choose to learn, teach, and work here.'
↗ **DAVID VAN ZANDT** President of The New School

'LIFE LIVED ONLY FOR ONESELF DOES NOT TRULY SATISFY MEN OR WOMEN. THERE IS A HUNGER IN AMERICANS TODAY FOR LARGER PURPOSES BEYOND THE SELF.'
↗ BETTY FRIEDAN Faculty

AND, SCÉNE

In 1926, The New School offers the first course on film studies. While a trade course on film, 'Photoplay Composition', had previously been offered in an extension program of Columbia University, 'The Motion Picture' is the first comprehensive consideration of the maturing art of cinema. The course is led by Terry Ramsaye, a writer, editor, and producer who had worked on early comedies by Charlie Chaplin.

Six years prior to 'The Motion Picture', circa 1920, James R. Quirk, editor-in-chief of *Photoplay Magazine*, had the editorial realization that the birth of cinema was yet to be surveyed in a cogent, synoptic manner; Quirk enlisted Ramsaye to pen a twelve-part series, *The Romantic History of the Motion Picture*. The series was extended to a thirty-six-part series, which in turn was collected in Ramsaye's 1926 book, *A Million and One Nights: A History of the Motion Picture through 1926*. The subject of film, tainted by new technology and a Jewish association, is contemptible to the discussion of contemporary art, literature, and theater, and the publisher secures an endorsement from Thomas Edison:

> *This is, I believe, the first endeavor to set down the whole and true story of the motion picture. I have been in contact with the author's researches through his years of preparation and I am aware of an unrelenting effort at exact fact. A high degree of detailed accuracy has been attained. Ramsaye's theories, opinions, and deductions are his own.*

Released in 1926, to coincide with Ramsaye's course at The New School, *A Million and One Nights* is grudgingly recognized in an anti-Semitic review by *The Saturday Review of Literature* as 'The first complete source book on the motion picture', and Ramsay is sniffily named 'the first authentic film historian'.

The twelve sessions of 'The Motion Picture' cover: pre-history; invention; development; market; actors, 'stars', and salaries; syntax; the public and the studio system; text, titles, press; propaganda and politics; education; ethics and censorship; and the screen of tomorrow.

'Photography is a reality high. It comes from that impulse which makes one turn and say: "Hey, did you see that?"'
↗ **CHARLES HARBUTT** Faculty

'You thought the stage, you thought Broadway: that was the pot at the end of the rainbow. The idea of being in Hollywood was like going to the Moon or Mars.'
↗ **PETER FALK** Student

ART APPRECIATION: COMPARISONS, SIMILARITIES AND CONTRASTS, 1933 J.B. NEUMANN

This course will relate only to works of art which can be seen in New York collections, or which will be shown in original during the lectures.

→ The Origin of Art
Forms of art in nature. Primitives old and new. Cave paintings. New drawings of children.

→ Pre-Christian Religious Art
The life of Buddha. The religious art of China. Decoration of temples. Egypt — gods, gods and other gods.

→ Greek and African Artistic Influences
What did Greece do to the past generations? What has Africa done to us. Greek Ideal vs. Negro sculpture. Cultural self-expression in applied art.

→ Christian Art
The Christian spirit. Cathedrals. Fresco. Mosiac. Illustrations and the early woodcut. Illustration of the first books printed. Art for the glory of God.

→ The Birth of Modernism
Easel painting. The six pioneers — Giotto, Hieronymus Bosch, Piero della Francesca, Grünewald, El Greco, Rembrandt.

→ Smile and Laughter
A new discovery. Newspaper cartoons and

Clockwise from top left:

— New School students in the filmmaking studio. Bob Adelman, *circa 1979*

— Eadweard James Muybridge, *Time-lapse photographs of a man riding a galloping horse*, 1887

— Newspaper clipping from The New School publicity scrapbook, *circa 1930*

'Film is something for people to feel. It's not a class that people should understand perfectly. ... Forget about strong words or strong scenes, I just want to present with fewer and fewer words, and facial expressions.'
↗ **YANG YONG-HI** Student

'I feel a closeness to writers, poets, and painters, much more than to traditional film directors. For one thing, we ciné experimenters are not bound by the plot-driven mechanics of cause and effect that, for me, often bring the transcendent experience of watching a movie to a grinding halt.'
↗ **LYNNE SACHS** Faculty

FILM WORKSHOP, 1940
THE DRAMATIC WORKSHOP
LEWIS JACOBS

Scheduled subject to Mr. Jacobs not being called to Hollywood.

The aim of this course is to provide technical training in the fundamentals of movie making, and to study the values of the film as a separate medium from the stage or literature. Technical instruction in continuity, camera work, directing, and editing will be stressed through actual production. Film classics will be projected for discussion and analysis. Motion picture equipment will be provided for group use. At least one short film will be made each semester as a collective venture. In addition, projects will be undertaken in conjunction with other Dramatic Workshop groups for use in their theatrical productions.

THE NEW YORK AVANT-GARDE
FILM SCENE, 1973
JONAS MEKAS

A survey of the last ten years of avant-garde film activity in New York. Introduction into the techniques, styles, genres, and content of the avant-garde film. Discussion of the leading figures of the movement with some examples of their work screened. Some of the filmmakers will be present to answer students' questions.

THE AMERICAN
MUSICAL FILM, 1981
JERRY DELAMATER

A study of the Hollywood musical confronts a number of issues that belie its popularly accepted position as a film genre of questionable seriousness; those issues are the focus of this course. The Hollywood cinema was predominantly a genre cinema, and musicals were an important genre, dependent — perhaps even more strongly than the other genres

'Hollywood was a bore. Everybody was trying to impress everybody else. Besides, it was too far from Paris.'
↗ **JOSET WALKER** Student

MICROCINEMAS AND
ALTERNATIVE MEDIA, 2013
LYNNE SACHS

Engage actively with the programs, audiences, and organizational models of small, non-commercial NewYork City sites for exhibition, education, and community-building around alternative media arts. What is the place of underground, niche, repertory, and other cinema spaces in our culture? Programmers from local microcinemas talk about their visions and the day-to-day challenges. Students make case studies and a curatorial and/or educational outreach program proposal.

Circa 1954–6, the Cinema 16 Film Center, an influential New York City film society founded and directed by Amos Vogel, is hosted by The New School.

July, 1963: The New School series 'New Wave Movie Makers' previews and considers a movement of New Wave cinema with screenings and discussions. Richard Griffith, Curator of The Museum of Modern Art Film Library, leads the exploration of a burgeoning underground movement.

In 2013, a three-event screening and conversation series hosted by the School of Media Studies refreshes the forty-seven-year association between The New School and the Millennium Film Workshop, which provides media resources, education, and context in a community arts model. 'New From Old: Practices of Appropriation' features Martha Colburn, Bradley Eros, and Colleen Fitzgibbon; 'Exuberant Emulsions' features Jennifer Reeves; 'Intimate Projections: Experimental Diary Films' features Barbara Hammer, Peter Hutton, and Amie Siegel.

'So we got there at 6 a.m. We'd be shooting by 6:45. We wouldn't break for lunch, we'd just pass food around all day. And we would just rock and roll till 4, then Matty Libatique, our great cinematographer, would say, "Outta light, guys," and that was it.'
↗ **JOEL SCHUMACHER** Student

NOT JUST A PRETTY PICTURE

INSTRUCTORS

CAMILO EGAS, *Art Director*

1938-1939

BERENICE ABBOTT
Photography

PEGGY BACON
Black and White Pastel

WILL BARNET
Lithography and Etching

JOSÉ DE CREEFT
Sculpture in Stone
and Wood

CAMILO EGAS
Painting, Drawing,
Murals, Frescoes

FRITZ EICHENBERG
Illustration

ELIOT ELISOFON
Photo Reportage

YASUO KUNIYOSHI
Painting and Drawing

HARRY STERNBERG
Etching and Lithography

MARGUERITE ZORACH
Watercolor

WILLIAM ZORACH
Sculpture

NEW SCHOOL FOR SOCIAL RESEARCH
66 WEST 12th STREET   NEW YORK

Photo by Irving Lerner

EW SCHOOL FOR SOCIAL RESEARCH

ART CLASSES

938   1939

Berenice Abbott, who has studied photography and art in Berlin and Paris, and worked as an assistant to Man Ray, indefinitely prolongs a short visit to New York to more thoroughly photograph the cityscapes. She remains in New York's Greenwich Village, and in 1934, at The New School, leads one of the first university-level courses in photography; she will teach at The New School until 1958. In 1959, Abbott's work will be shown at The New School in an exhibition that is meticulously planned with then Vice President of the School, Clara Mayer. In one of her many letters to Abbott, Mayer passes along the praise of science educator Dr. Elbert P. Little, with whom Abbott shares scientific interests: 'I am happy that the exhibit has been such a success — but what else should we have expected! We are all grateful to Berenice Abbott, for her talent and for her infinite patience in achieving perfection.' With her three books — *Changing New York* (1939), *Greenwich Village Today and Yesterday* (1949), and *A Portrait of Maine* (1968) — Abbott gains increasing financial freedom and recognition, and exhibits internationally; in 1970, twenty years before her death, the Museum of Modern Art mounts a major retrospective of her work.

Throughout her career, Abbott is gracious in advocating for peers and predecessors. She finds kinship in the writings of Lewis Mumford, who taught at The New School from 1923 to 1935, offering the first courses in urban planning and architecture. Abbott is dedicated to the posthumous recognition of Eugène Atget, a Parisian photographer she met with Man Ray in 1925. In 1951, she arranges a show of Atget's photography at The New School. During the discovery process for the show, a currently unidentified interviewer thanks Abbott for her generosity:

> I want to thank you in the name of The New School and more through you I should like to thank all those other countless artists, writers ... and professionals ... who contribute toward making The New School what it is, a kind of rallying point for the world's talents and especially for those who find in their work and being able to share it with others a principal pleasure in living.

Clockwise from top left:

Berenice Abbott,
date unknown

*New School for Social Research,
Art Classes 1938–1939.*
List of Instructors, *circa* 1938

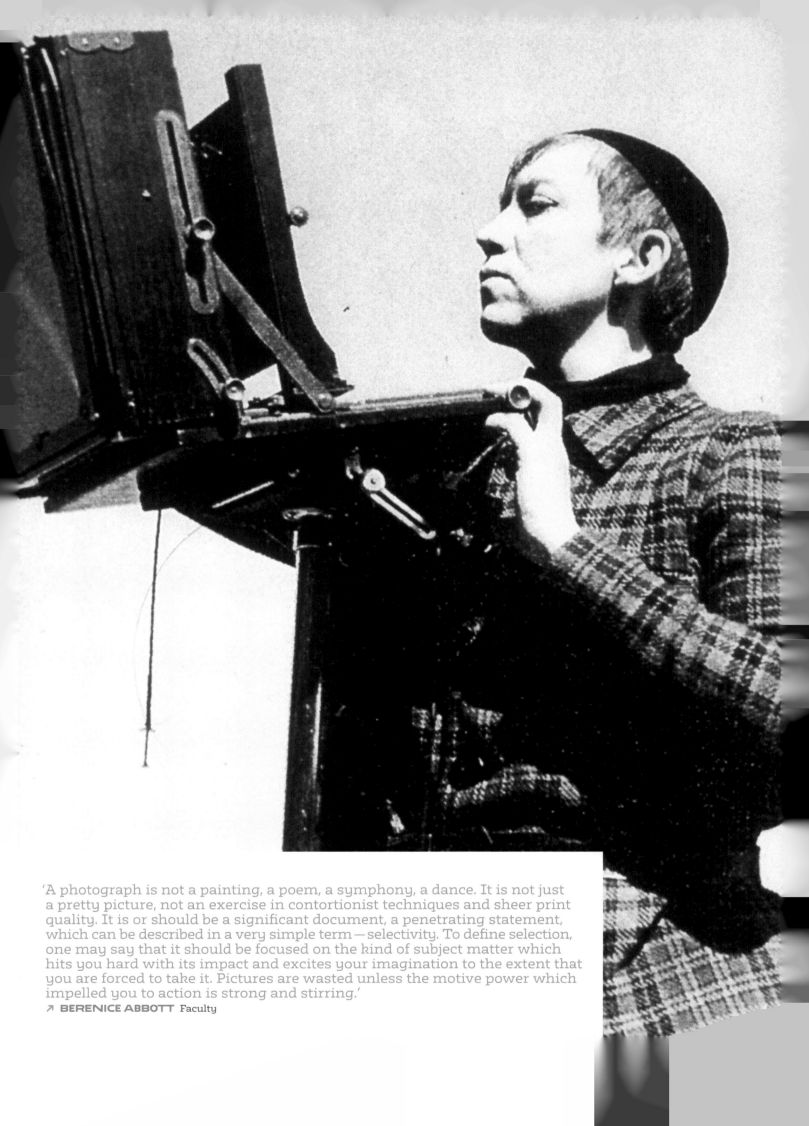

'A photograph is not a painting, a poem, a symphony, a dance. It is not just a pretty picture, not an exercise in contortionist techniques and sheer print quality. It is or should be a significant document, a penetrating statement, which can be described in a very simple term — selectivity. To define selection, one may say that it should be focused on the kind of subject matter which hits you hard with its impact and excites your imagination to the extent that you are forced to take it. Pictures are wasted unless the motive power which impelled you to action is strong and stirring.'
↗ **BERENICE ABBOTT** Faculty

'One particular thing has to do with the upright bass. I've been living in New York City for about twelve years, as an upright bassist, doing a lot of sessions and gigs around town, and trying to produce the biggest sound you can get. To a degree, some of that is compensating for being a woman. People will assume a woman is smaller in sound. I wanted to have a big, loud sound. Everyone wants to have presence. That was very important to me, having a full sound, having a good *humph* to the beat. One thing that has changed is the notion of having to pull so hard to get that sound. At this point in my life, there's something to having presence and sound without having to pull so hard.'

↗ **LINDA MAY HAN OH** Faculty

CORNELL CAPA
DUANE MICHALS
ARNOLD NEWMA
ELLIOT ERWITT
GARY WINOGRAND
BARBARA MORGAN
BERENICE ABB
RAY METZKE
ON PHOTOGRAPHY
HORST P. HORST
FREDERICK SOMMER
BURK UZZLE
AARON SISKIND

BARBARALEE DIAMONSTEIN

visions & imag

PARSONS SCHOOL OF DESIGN

'In general it can be said that a nation's art is greatest when it most reflects the character of its people.'

↗ **EDWARD HOPPER** Student

A 2019 exhibition at David Zwirner Gallery in New York assembles representations of James Baldwin in *God Made My Face: A Collective Portrait of James Baldwin*. Curated by former Master of Fine Arts in Creative Writing faculty member Hilton Als, the show regards creative interconnectivity, including Baldwin's friendship with Richard Avedon, and Baldwin and Avedon's shared interest in the photography of Eugène Atget.

'THE SEQUEL TO THIS VOLUME LIES IN THE MINDS OF ITS READERS.'
↗ MARY HENLE Faculty

'I am a passionate lover of the snapshot, because of all photographic images it comes closest to truth.'
↗ LISETTE MODEL Faculty

Clockwise from top left:

Poster for *Visions & Images*. Designed by Cipe Pineles Golden, 1980

José Clemente Orozco. Berenice Abbott, 1936

Berenice Abbott leads a photography class at The New School, *circa* 1939

Berenice Abbott in Paris. Photographer unknown, 1927

Isamu Noguchi. Berenice Abbott, 1927

A RESTLESS VISION

This book tells the rambunctious, fragmented, and inspired story of The New School. Looking backward we can see these histories as various tributaries flowing together and joining into an ever-expanding institution; but of course, that is not how it was experienced or anticipated — it is only in retrospect that it becomes a story. Things started, stopped, attached themselves, merged, emerged, and receded in a restless, contingent, contextual, opportunistic, and dynamic flow marked by a grand vision and the pragmatics of financing this vision. So much of this fascinating history can only be understood as people seizing opportunities, responding to a situation, or pursuing a vision — and, typically, all three in combinations.

The cavalier, rebellious, and contingent nature of the 1919 vision for The New School for Social Research was almost perverse in its optimism; it would work out despite no obvious source of long-term financial support. Dorothy Straight's generosity in the first years notwithstanding, this vision was, and remains, inspiring. When most of the academic world was looking for ever greater security and insulation from the world, the founders of The New School agreed: no endowment, no degrees, no tenure, no government support. They denied themselves the standard ways of creating the security that was deemed necessary to undertake serious research. The founders challenged the core logic of the academy by saying: 'We are going to do serious social research and survive on our ability to make it relevant to the people for whom the traditional academy was largely inaccessible.'

Over the years, The New School has been integrating the creative and the critical in education and research initiatives; this vision connects the ability to understand a situation, context, or history, with the capacity to act, to propose, and to intervene. These two impulses are often kept at arm's length in higher education, but the capacity to act decisively and effectively with regard to contemporary problems and issues necessitates this ability to move from critical insight to propositional and creative interventions.

The considerable effort it takes to reconcile, as best as possible, these incommensurate ambitions has resulted in cycles of waxing and waning. It is this that makes The New School's history so consistently fleeting, so compelling, and so beguiling. This book is an attempt to capture a certain quality of who-we-are-now by providing insights into the people who made this university what it is today — why and how it came to be. John Reed has done a superb job in capturing the energy and importance of this story. It should also be noted that New School faculty members, Professors Julia Foulkes and Mark Larrimore, have developed a wealth of material over a number of years regarding the history of The New School, which they have delivered in lectures, in a class they regularly run entitled 'New School Histories', and the oft-updated website, www.newschoolhistories.org.

The New School for Social Research was established by a group of academics who left Columbia University as an act of protest against loyalty oaths associated with the politics of World War I. The New School is the product of three wars: founded during World War I, shaped by World War II, and consolidated in reaction to the Vietnam War. The University in Exile, Atelier 17, and École Libre established the clearest possible statement of the institution's courage, values, and commitment in response to the horrors of World War II, heralded our first formal degree (PhD), and initiated our first foray into undergraduate, for-credit education via the post-war GI Bill. The protests over the Vietnam War unified faculty and students from Parsons School of Design and The New School for Social Research in a common purpose.

As with most histories, there are traits and characteristics detectable in The New School now that have been there since the beginning. These include an effort to defy the unexamined institutional norms of higher education; a dedication to new ideas, relevance, and intellectual rigor; the willingness to design institutional forms to facilitate the marriage of high ambition and practical reality; an appreciation that creative and cultural practices are progressive forces as powerful as economics, politics, and philosophy, and even more so when they engage with each other.

The New School, at its best, has been very much 'in the moment', more intellectual and creative commons than ivory tower. Because of that, the various efforts to move toward normalization that mark the latter half of its history ultimately made little sense. This is arguably our greatest challenge: how to push and reshape the stubborn forms we inhabit and the regulations that govern us, to break the mold and yet, at the same time, face the harsh fiscal realities of the prohibitively high-cost structure of higher education in New York City. In a world of ever-expanding government compliance together with the inevitable conservatism that comes with high-cost education, we must ask: How can we live up to our legacy?

At their founding, both Parsons School of Design and The New School for Social Research, respectively, represented a dramatically new approach to education.

Opposite:

Course Titles from The New School's first century, typographic art by Ruedi Baur and the Intégral Paris Team. University Center, 2019

Following page:

Jack Kerouac, New York City, 1953

The New School for Social Research was one of the first institutions of higher learning established on a secular ideal, bound together by an egalitarian and humanistic philosophy of education. Parsons School of Design shared this secular position and developed its own distinctly cosmopolitan and urban approach to art and design education.

The New School also continues to be distinct in that its major outside support base is largely bound to the institution because The New School represents a compelling idea and ethos. The University in Exile was a proud expression of this ideal. But the school of 1919 represented a modernizing force — it was secular, global, and, as a result of having many female governors, funders, students, faculty, and academic administrators, women were central in the founding and ongoing innovation and success of the university. It is very rare indeed to have a university that stands as much for an attitude, an approach, and a worldview as for the quality of its education and research.

This legacy includes, and was in many ways made possible, by the fact that for much of our history we were the place where people came to do their most groundbreaking work while also participating in a broad network of intellectual institutions and creative practices. A quintessential instance that gives insight into how The New School for Social Research has served as both a network and a platform for radical movements is its role in the pre-history, foundation, and development of the Fluxus movement. The movement was founded by a group of designers, artists, composers, and performance artists, all of whom met and participated in New School courses, such as Richard Maxfield's class on electronic music and John Cage's class entitled 'Experimental Music Composition'. It quickly became a creative and intellectual movement that was radically interdisciplinary, emphasizing the street and process over high art; globally integrated, bringing together Japanese, American, and European artists; and a major art movement with a sizable membership of women artists.

Merging Parsons School of Design and Mannes School of Music into The New School in 1970 and 1989, respectively, made sense in this context, but there was a catch. As a melting pot of activities cutting across the creative and intellectual domains, The New School for Social Research was unconstrained by traditional departments and disciplines. When the traditional forms were incorporated into this dynamic structure — first a PhD program, then a liberal arts degree, a design school, a conservatorium, an accredited drama training program (the Actors Studio), and a traditionally conceived ('Swarthmore in the City') undergraduate college — an institutionally 'small c' conservative force was gradually brought to bear on this eclectic avant-garde melting pot. There was a drift toward an increasingly 'regular' university, of sorts — it was during this period that The New School became the birthplace of the New Museum and *The Village Voice*, after all!

Over the last twenty years, The New School has benefited from efforts to revive those early radical impulses. We have crossed and weakened academic boundaries, in order to make the academy—this academy—more relevant. We trusted in the original impulse of interdisciplinarity and now take it further. It is something to live up to while daring to take the institution in new directions. The key part of our legacy, I would argue, is not the form or the content of a particular period of time; rather, it lies in the preparedness to do the most relevant work. It also happens to be the most urgent work, as the massive and interrelated upheavals of climate change, new and pervasive technologies, and global migration, among other contemporary challenges, all raise the recurring question of how the deep but segmented knowledge and expertise of various disciplines and professional guilds can change in the messy, overlapping, and entangled realities of the real world.

Take a walk down the fire stairwell of 63 Fifth Avenue and read the names—written on the ceiling in a randomized pattern—of some of the courses that have been taught across the history of The New School. You will encounter 'N.Y.C.: A Look into the Future', taught by Jane Jacobs and Charles Abrams in 1958, next to 'Photographing New York and Its People', taught by Lisette Model in 1951, alongside 'Urban Anthropology', taught by Allen Austill in 1978. And as you descend the staircase, above your head: 'Desegregation Gradualism', Marshall Thurgood, 1954; 'Social Philosophy: Minority Group Relations', Alain Locke 1946; 'Bolshevism and Fascism: A Comparison', Maurice Parmelee, 1930; 'Art Applied to Graphic Journalism, War Propaganda, Advertising', Alexey Brodovitch, 1942;

'Interior Design', Philip Johnson, 1952; 'The Evolution of Modern Music', Aaron Copland, 1927; 'Instrumentation', George Szell, 1940; 'Old Weird America: Music', Greil Marcus, 2007 are all there with courses in Fashion Design by Christian Dior in 1953, Ralph Lauren in 1973, Donna Karan in 1982, Marc Jacobs in 1989. And of course you see 'Method in the Social Sciences', John Dewey, 1919, along with 'Anthropology and Modern Culture', Margret Mead, 1955; 'Social Problems of the Sexes', Olga Knopf, 1931; 'Biology and Its Social Implications', Otto Glaser, 1923; 'The Language and Technique of Poetry', W.H. Auden, 1940; 'Modern Poetry and Reality', Stephen Spender, 1948; 'Fine Arts', Kiki Smith, 1995; 'Costume Design and Illustration', Elsa Schiaparelli, 1946; and 'Metal Design', Mary Ann Scherr, 1986. And the history of advanced teaching is there in 'The Power of the Press', Silas Bent, 1927; 'Computer Programming', Rudolph Hirsh, 1962; and 'The Consumer and the Automobile', Ralph Nader, 1966.

Increasingly, the most interesting and challenging work is produced by faculty and students from across these areas working together, blurring who is the maker, who the performer, the writer, the scholar. They assume the blurring of the critical and the creative to a point where the distinctions (critical versus creative) are increasingly inconsequential. Our current environment, where students no longer see the opportunities of education demarcated in the way the academy has been structured historically—the liberal arts for the book smart, studio arts for the creative, business degrees for the pragmatic—is tremendously uplifting and optimistic.

The questions that have challenged the later history of The New School have been: Is it greater than the sum of its parts? Are the parts the point of our story and not the whole? Is this simply an ever-expanding box of parts to reconfigure? Is this something to celebrate or overcome? The shunning of an endowment during the early decades has led to the unintended consequence of The New School not being in a position to extend substantial scholarship places to a meaningful percentage of student applicants. This is a savage irony for a university founded on a specific effort to reach those excluded from higher learning. And that is the burning issue of our day: the price tag that comes with access to higher education, student debt, and the sheer expense of studying at a tuition-based university in the heart of Manhattan. This, of course, intersects with issues of race, class, stratification, and the various forms of systemic disadvantage that are part of our defining mission. The social justice values that we have inherited need to be reenergized and turned more explicitly toward these pressing questions. And this must be done not to affirm abstract principles but rather to continue to diversify our faculty and student body so as to include those who would never at this time think to join The New School.

As a U.S. institution we have to try to tackle these issues, while fully embracing our position as a global force. We have one of the highest percentages of international undergraduates in the United States of America, the first offshore campus (Parsons Paris) of a United States art and design school; The New School for Social Research is as well or better known in Europe, Latin America, and Australasia than it is in the United States of America; and Parsons and Mannes are extremely prominent in South-East Asia, China, India, and elsewhere. We have helped develop institutions around the world that have then transferred students from South Korea, Japan, India, and the Dominican Republic to New York, making our education at least somewhat more financially attainable for a wide range of international students. But we have never done this within the United States. How can we, now, use this global identity and the immersive urban experience that lies at the heart of our education while returning to the vision of 1919 so as to open wider the doors to our particular approach to education?

It is increasingly evident from our students' choices that the categories of accreditation and manner of organizing our curricula (BA, BFA, BBA, etc.) no longer align with their needs, interests, and aspirations and, not surprisingly, they do not reflect future trajectories of global or national economies. We should take courage from the 1919 impulse and continue to break away from constraining institutional forms. Our liberal arts students want to make, perform, and create, while our studio and performing arts students are some of the best students in philosophy, sociology, and so on. The most recently funded research centers, such as the Graduate Institute for Design, Ethnography, and Social Thought, the Digital Equity Laboratory, and the Integrative PhD program; transformational planning documents such as 'Mannes in a New Key' and 'Designing the Design School'; and new curricular directions such as the Journalism + Design open-source curriculum project are all exploiting the possibilities of this institution.

This book celebrates our centennial year and will be launched during the Centennial Festival. We are also embarking on something we are calling the 'Centennial Project', which will invite The New School community and friends to explore how we want to position ourselves within the sphere of higher education. We will be asking hard questions to address the issues of who gets the opportunity to participate on our campus, on what terms, and with what consequences with appropriate seriousness. Various constituents are invited to participate in co-designing the proposals for the way this university unfolds in the future, and to determine what we think will put us in the best possible position to succeed for the next generation of students, faculty, and staff.

We started trying to square the circle of access to higher education with fundamental research and creative practice. Performances of the works of American contemporary composers were staged at The New School for Social Research only months after it opened its doors. Is there a twenty-first-century gesture that would address the profound challenges of our time — democracy, technology, climate, migration, and economic and political exclusion? How can we deploy design processes, methods, and form-making to help integrate this research so that it reflects and can better act upon these challenges as they actually exist — enmeshed and deeply implicated in each other? In other words, how can one think about climate change without considering migration? How can one think about mass migration without considering how it will affect particular democratic processes? How can we think about stratification without addressing the fact that the poor and marginalized around the globe will disproportionately suffer due to climate change? The state is an inadequate entity for addressing such transnational issues. But how do we design our political and economic processes to apprehend these new realities?

The times we are living through and the legacy of our university demand that we think profoundly and openly about the future. We trust and anticipate that those who write the historical account for the bicentenary will judge positively the work we are undertaking!

TIM MARSHALL, MAY, 2019

Opposite:

Following pages:

Dancer, choreographer, and co-founder of The New School's Dramatic Workshop, Maria Ley-Piscator, 1921

Covers of Parsons course catalogues

ALUMNI

Summer 1965

**PARSONS
EVENING DIVISION
FALL 1974**

P A R S O N S

Continuing Education, Graphic Design, Illustration and more, including AAS degree and Certificate Programs **Spring 1996**

PARSONS
SCHOOL OF DESIGN

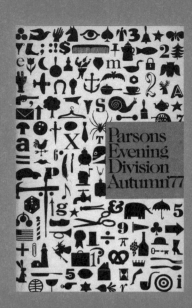

PARSONS
PORTFOLIO AND
CATALOG

PARSONS SCHOOL OF DESIGN

Parsons
Evening
Division
Autumn '77

PARSONS
School of Design

1948-1949

PARSONS
SCHOOL OF
DESIGN

evening division
fall 1975

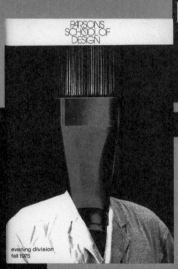

PARSONS
School of Design

1953-1954

Parsons School of Design
New School Bulletin,
Vol. 35, No. 3, Oct. 3, 1977

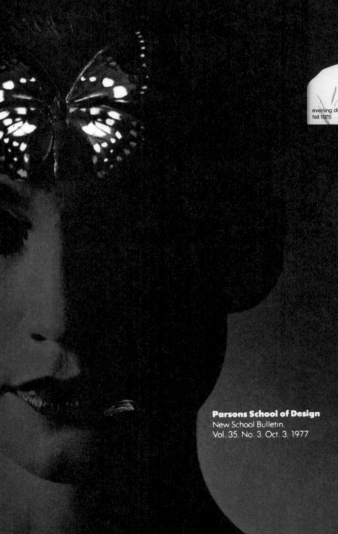

PARSONS SCHOOL OF DESIGN, NEW YORK

The Big Apple

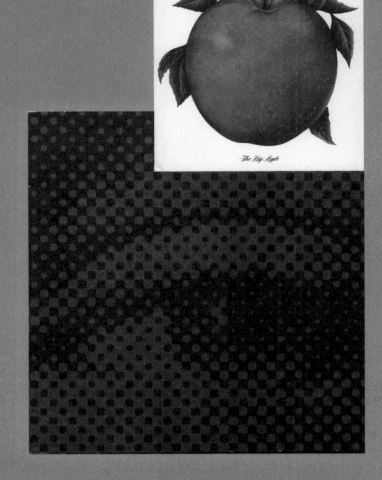

INDEX

PICTURE CREDITS

All images and original documents are sourced from The New School Archives, The New School, New York, unless otherwise specified.

Photograph Berenice Abbott: 20–21 (bottom right), 245; Bridgeman Images: 58, 61 (bottom); Getty Images: 22, 246 (bottom left and right). © Bob Adelman Estate: 20 (bottom left), 20–21 (top), 114–15, 186–87, 189 (right), 203 (top right), 213, 224 (left and right), 242–43 (bottom). David Attie/Getty Images: 87 (top right). Photograph Richard Avedon, © The Richard Avedon Foundation: 229. Photograph B. A. Bakalar: 168–69. Photograph Alfred J. Balcombe: 89, 90 (left and right), 91 (top). © Sophie Barkham: 98 (bottom). Artwork © Daniel Bejar: 241 (top center). Photograph Neal Boenzi, The New York Times. Redux: 62–63, 116. Photograph Gin Briggs: 67 (left), 80–81 (top). Photograph George Leroy Chinsee: 28–29. Photograph Joe Covello: 66 (left). Photograph Griffith J. Davis: 22–23. DoD photos by Tech. Sgt. Suzanne Day, U.S. Air Force/Alamy: 197. Photo by Atelier Eberth/ullstein bild via Getty Images: 259. Photograph Carly Erikson/BFA NYC: 196–97. Courtesy Paul Feeley Estate / Artists Rights Society (ARS), New York: 191 (top right). Photograph Benedict J. Fernandez: 36–37. Copyright Ben Ferrari: 98–99, 211, 241 (top right). Courtesy Francis J. Geck: 271. © Bonnie Geller-Geld: 25. Photo Alexandre Georges: 108 (top), 108–109 (bottom). Photo by © Allen Ginsberg / CORBIS / Corbis via Getty Images: 254–55. Photograph Jonathan Grassi: 41, 200. Photograph Tore Hanssen Grimstad: 40–41. Keith Haring artwork © Keith Haring Foundation: 147. Courtesy Hearst Magazines: 225 (left and right). Artwork © Alfredo Jaar: 71–73. Photo by JHU Sheridan Libraries/ Gado/Getty Images: 144 (top). © Peter A. Juley & Son Collection, Smithsonian American Art Museum: 9, 128–29. © Clemens Kalischer: 206–07. Photo by Keystone-France/Gamma-Rapho via Getty Images: 247. Photograph Fernanda Kock: 212. © Copyright Spencer Kohn: 175 (bottom right). Photograph Marvin Koner: 132–33. © Jeff Koons: 52 (bottom right). Image courtesy Library of Congress: 51 (top left), 76, 144 (bottom), 145; Music Division: 238 (base and overlay), 239. Image courtesy Joan Liftin: 34 (left). © Glenn Ligon; Courtesy of the artist, Hauser & Wirth, New York, Regen Projects, Los Angeles, Thomas Dane Gallery, London and Chantal Crousel, Paris.: 32–33. Courtesy Alison de

Lima Greene, Estate of Agnes de Lima: 190. Model, Lisette, Addison Gallery of American Art, Phillips Academy, Andover, MA, USA / Museum purchase / Bridgeman Images: 16–17. Photograph Bjorg Magnea: 122–23 (bottom). Photograph Leopold Mannes: 43 (top). Photo by Fred W. McDarrah/Getty Images: 18, 59 (left and right), 79, 94–96. Image courtesy Ryan McGinley: 73 (top right). © 2019 Barbara Moore / Licensed by VAGA at Artists Rights Society (ARS), NY, Courtesy Paula Cooper Gallery, New York: 86 (top), 87 (top left, bottom right), 104, 112–13 (top), 113 (bottom), 115 (bottom), 178–79, 226–27, 227 (top), 272. Photograph Michael Moran: 152–53 (bottom). Photograph Julien Mouffron-Gardner: 27 (bottom). © Siobhan Mullan: 97. Edweard James Muybridge, Science & Society Picture Library / Contributor: 242–43 (background). Image courtesy The New Museum: 52–53 (all images), 54 (left). © The New School: 27 (center), 257. The New York Times/ Redux: 160–61. © The Isamu Noguchi Foundation and Garden Museum, New York / ARS: 104, 112–13 (top), 250. Photograph Phillip Van Nostrand: 42. © Yoko Ono, courtesy Galerie Lelong & Co.: 78. Photograph Yana Paskova/The New York Times/Redux: 38–39. Courtesy Peninsula School: 190. Photograph Spencer Platt/Getty Images: 98. Photo by: Prisma by Dukas/Universal Images Group via Getty Images: 248–49. Photograph courtesy John Reed: 13, 118–19. Photo by George Rinhart/Corbis via Getty Images: 177. Photograph Sarah Rocco: 60 (bottom left). Photograph Virginia Roehl: 54–55. © Copyright Martin Seck: 120–21, 216. Photograph Paul Seligman: 56 (top left), 124–25, 215. Photograph Stanley Seligson: 188 (top right). © Matthew Septimus: 33 (top right), 44–45. Courtesy James Shanks, jamesshanks.com: 123 (top). Photograph Editta Sherman, courtesy Kenneth Sherman: 42–43. Photograph Raymond Shorr: 198, 198–99. Gift of Caitlin Morgan Sireci and Fiore Sireci, The New School Art Collection: 105, 127 (left and right). © Lorna Simpson, courtesy the artist and Hauser & Wirth: 176. Photograph Paul Slade/Paris Match via Getty Images: 85. Photograph courtesy SOM © James Ewing: 217. © Gerardo Somoza: 35. Photograph Vicki J Spitz: 74–75. © Erinn Springer: 57 (top right). Photograph Marc Tatti: 176. Photo by Ted Thai/The LIFE Picture Collection/Getty Images: 174. Photo by Paul Thompson/Topical Press Agency/ Getty Images: 76–77. Photograph Laima Turnley: 109 (overlay). Photograph

Eugene Paul Ullman: 34 (bottom right). Department of Special Collections and University Archives, W.E.B. Du Bois Library, University of Massachusetts Amherst: 86 (bottom). Photograph courtesy Joseph Urban Collection, Rare Book & Manuscript Library, Columbia University: 102–03. Photograph Zach Van Hoozer/Honeyland Films: 32–33, 70–71, 128, 135, 136–37, 149, 164, 253. Artwork © Kara Walker: 212. Photo by Ben Watts/The LIFE Premium Collection via Getty Images/Getty Images: 74 (bottom). Werner Wolff/BlackStar: 82–83. © Edward J. Wormley: 150–151. Photograph Kumiko Yoshioka: 78.

ACKNOWLEDGMENTS

For the things we have to learn before we can do them, we learn by doing them.
—Hannah Arendt

In 2018, New School Provost Tim Marshall proposed that we write, for the first time, the history of The New School in a narrative that would integrate all the stories which, over time, came together to form The New School as we know it today. The result is this big beautiful book that is a document and a portrait of the university. In its realization, the vision of the project was expansive, the timeline was challenging, and it could not have happened without generous contributions from dozens of people.

The restless narrative of *A Drama in Time* was conceptualized and miraculously authored by New School Creative Writing faculty member John Reed. His unique and impactful narrative is a weave of the many extraordinary lives and histories that have made for The New School century. Julia Foulkes, Mark Larrimore, and Gina Walker, along with their long-standing work toward understanding the history of The New School, provided foundational research that made this innovative approach possible.

A core team has been tirelessly dedicated to the multifaceted, often delicate process of a project of this scope, which required the collaboration of individuals and departments far-flung in the cartography of the school. Ashley Bruni has been a passionate and resourceful leader from the very beginning; she has contributed to every aspect of every page now before you.

It is thanks to the dedicated research, organizational leadership, and aesthetic sensibility of Catherine Thomas that the 400-plus images of *A Drama in Time* so beautifully attend the people and stories.

S. N. Kirby took on the gargantuan task of researcher; she also worked on the writing of many of the 'events' as well as the quote attributions and fact-checking. Throughout, she has been instrumental in shaping this history, and her discoveries have made this work more exciting, more intelligent, and more correct.

Praise is due to Justine Bannwart for her cutting-edge, high-concept book design, worthy and reflective of Parsons, the world's premier institution of higher education in design. Caroline Clark has been instrumental in the giant task of conveying the disobedient New School spirit through design.

The majority of the photography and images were sourced from The New School Archives, and their use and attributions are thanks to Wendy Scheir and the work of her team, Katherine Martinez, Anna Robinson-Sweet, and Jenny Swadosh as well as student archive contributors Ella Coon, Harshal Alurkar, Priscilla Gaona, and Agnes Szanyi.

The New School is forever grateful to the generous donors and friends who have made this legacy possible, and to those who continue to support a future shaped by the core values that have defined our past: academic freedom, tolerance, and experimentation.

Thanks are also due to:
—The Executive Leadership of The New School, particularly Chief Marketing Officer Anne Adriance for her invaluable guidance and insight throughout this process
—Deans Mary Watson, Richard Kessler, Joel Towers, Will Milberg, and Stephanie Browner for their support and input
—Andrew Franklin and Peter Jones of Profile Books and Alexis Hurley of Inkwell Management, for getting this project off the ground and shepherding it to print
—Diana Broccardo, Neil Burkey, Graeme Hall, Jason Mitchell, Simon Shelmerdine, and everyone at Profile Books for their commitment
—Silvia Rocciolo, Curator of The New School Art Collection, for her generous help and attention to detail despite the harried turnaround
—Alexandra Lederman for navigating The New School's existing photography collections and tracking down images ASAP
—Naomi Falk for graciously joining at a late date to help in obtaining photo permissions and credits
—The many individuals who granted permission for the use of reproduced materials, with a special callout to Caitlin Morgan and Barbara Moore
—The writerly contributions of Ricky Tucker, Laura Cronk, Robert Polito, Honor Moore, Luis Jaramillo, Helen Schulman, Lori Lynn Turner, Nicole Drayton, Ben Fama, David Lehman, and Cassandra Neyenesch
—Hanna Lauer, Frances Pharr, John Lepak, Maria-Elena Grant, Leslie Galman, Heather O'Brien, Deborah Bogosian, Justin Sherwood, Thelma Armstrong, and everyone else at The New School who gave their time, expertise, enthusiasm and perseverance to this project
—Those who generously made themselves available for research interviews, with special callouts to New School President David E. Van Zandt, Gina Walker, Miles Kohrman, Carol Kim, Mike Fu, Arthur Ou, Andrew Meier, Lillian Wu, and Tara Mastrelli

Whatever we had missed, we possessed together the precious, the incommunicable past.
—Willa Cather

Opposite:

New York School of Fine and Applied Art Students, 1925–7

Following page:

Peggy Ostlund arriving for class at The New School. Peter Morre, 1972